415-883-7903

BEYOND
WORKPLACE
2·0·0·0

Bares

BEYOND
WORKPLACE
2·0·0·0

ESSENTIAL STRATEGIES FOR THE
NEW AMERICAN CORPORATION

JOSEPH H. BOYETT
WITH JIMMIE T. BOYETT

A DUTTON BOOK

DUTTON
Published by the Penguin Group
Penguin Books USA Inc., 375 Hudson Street,
New York, New York 10014, U.S.A.
Penguin Books Ltd, 27 Wrights Lane,
London W8 5TZ, England
Penguin Books Australia Ltd, Ringwood,
Victoria, Australia
Penguin Books Canada Ltd, 10 Alcorn Avenue,
Toronto, Ontario, Canada M4V 3B2
Penguin Books (N.Z.) Ltd, 182–190 Wairau Road,
Auckland 10, New Zealand

Penguin Books Ltd, Registered Offices:
Harmondsworth, Middlesex, England

First published by Dutton, an imprint of Dutton Signet,
a division of Penguin Books USA Inc.
Distributed in Canada by McClelland & Stewart Inc.

First Printing, April, 1995
10 9 8 7 6 5 4 3 2 1

 REGISTERED TRADEMARK—MARCA REGISTRADA

LIBRARY OF CONGRESS CATALOGING IN PUBLICATION DATA:

Boyett, Joseph H.
  Beyond workplace 2000 : essential strategies of the new American
corporation / Joseph H. Boyett with Jimmie T. Boyett.
     p.   cm.
  Continues and updates: Workplace 2000.
  Includes bibliographical references.
  ISBN 0-525-93782-X
  1. Personnel management—United States—Forecasting.   2. Corporate culture—
United States—Forecasting.   3. Industrial relations—United States—Forecasting.
4. Industrial policy—United States—Forecasting.   5. Economic forecasting—
United States.   6. United States—Economic policy—1993–   I. Boyett, Jimmie T.
II. Boyett, Joseph H. Workplace 2000.
HF5549.2.U5B692   1995
658.3'00973'0112—dc20   94-37757
                                                                              CIP
Printed in the United States of America
Set in Century Book
Designed by Leonard Telesca

This book is printed on acid-free paper. ∞

TO OUR DAUGHTERS

LISA BOYETT LUONGO
AND
CHRISTA BOYETT REEVES

Acknowledgments

In conducting the research for *Beyond Workplace 2000*, we relied upon the popular press, academic research, case studies of best practices, and the advice and assistance of numerous individuals in various national research institutes and management associations. We are particularly grateful to the following organizations and associations for information we received from them:

American Management Association Catalyst

American Productivity and Quality Center

American Society for Quality Control

Council on Competitiveness

Council for Continuous Improvement

Economic Policy Institute

Institute for the Learning Sciences

Institute for Research on Learning

National Alliance of Business

Organizational Learning Center at the Massachusetts Institute of Technology

Quality and Productivity Management Association

We also express our sincere appreciation to the staffs of the following libraries for the assistance they provided us during our many months of research:

Atlanta-Fulton Public Library, Alpharetta Branch

Atlanta-Fulton Public Library, Central Library

Atlanta-Fulton Public Library, Sandy Springs Regional Library

Dekalb County, Georgia, Public Library

Emory University Library

The hardy souls who keep these institutions running in spite of funding cutbacks deserve more credit than they will ever receive.

Finally, we would like to thank our agent, Maria Carvainis, and our editor, Hilary Ross, for their continuing interest in and support for this book.

All of the above deserve credit for what is right about this book. Any errors or omissions are ours alone.

Joseph H. Boyett
Jimmie T. Boyett
May 1994

Contents

PART V: LEARNING AND THE NEW WORKPLACE

PART VI: AMERICAN EDUCATION: AN UPDATE

PART VII: THE NEW LEADERSHIP

Introduction

In the last five years, almost everything about working in America has changed. The places Americans work, the way they work, the relationship they have with their boss and peers, the security of their jobs—all of these things and many, many more have changed. We have experienced a workplace revolution. The revolution brought with it heartache, pain, disappointment, and betrayal, but it also brought *hope for a better, if radically different, future* for most of us. The life of practically every American has been directly affected by these changes. Those Americans who haven't had their lives torn apart and rearranged by the forces of this economic upheaval certainly know friends, neighbors, or relatives who have. Today, most Americans see themselves as survivors of a revolution they hope is surely coming to an end. *But it isn't.* America's workplace revolution isn't over. It has only just begun.

Going Beyond Workplace 2000

In *Workplace 2000*, a book published in 1991, we predicted that American business would be forced by demands for significant improvements in quality, customer service, and cost containment to undergo a significant restructuring. America, we suggested, would be forced to reinvent the workplace in dramatic ways. We called this new workplace Workplace 2000 (hence the book's title) and suggested what it would be like. We said:

- American companies would be flatter, leaner, and more aggressive in pursuing customer demands.
- The downsizing and restructuring of American corporations would continue and would result in the elimination of whole layers of middle managers, supervisors, and corporate support personnel.
- Newer, more sophisticated and "intelligent" software would make it possible to move decision making and problem solving to lower levels of the organization and eliminate the jobs of Americans who processed data, analyzed information, and made routine decisions.
- Opportunities for advancement in most companies would all but disappear, as would job security.
- All Americans, whether they worked in a large company or small one, would find themselves working in a small-business atmosphere, with all of the pressure and insecurity that such an environment entails.
- Instability in the workplace and enormous competitive demands on businesses, large and small, would result in extraordinary pressure for maximum performance—a "cult of excellence" would engulf most businesses and demands for performance would increase a hundredfold.
- Flexibility and creativity would count more in the new organization than seniority or who you knew; the most valuable employees would be those who had a solid education, broad knowledge and experience in performing a wide variety of tasks.
- Most Americans' pay would become variable and would be tied to their knowledge and skill and to the performance of their company or unit, rather than to their position or length of tenure with the company.
- The whole workplace would become more participative and egalitarian; prerogatives of status such as executive dining rooms and reserved parking spaces would begin to disappear.
- Regardless of whether they worked in manufacturing or service businesses, Americans would work in teams and be empowered to take action to solve problems—traditional managers and supervisors would all but disappear to be replaced by facilitators and coaches.

Those were the changes we predicted for Workplace 2000. That was the revolution in the workplace that we felt would surely occur, and it has. Now American business is beginning to move beyond Workplace 2000. In the next five years, Americans will experience even more radical changes in their working lives.

Beyond Workplace 2000

Here are just a few of the extraordinary changes Americans are likely to see in the workplace over the next few years:

- Most American companies will find that they no longer can gain a competitive advantage from further improvements in quality, service, cost, or speed, since the gap between rivals on these traditional measures of performance will all but close. As a result, practically every American company will be forced into a constant search for the new, different, and better value-adding product or service, particularly the product or service that creates genuine excitement on the part of customers. Research and development will come out of the lab and permeate the entire company. Every employee will be called upon—in effect, *required*—to engage in a constant and never-ending pursuit of product, service, and process changes and enhancements. Employees and employee teams, who for the past decade have focused their problem-solving and process-reengineering efforts on quality, service, speed, and cost containment, will find their efforts redirected to the constant pursuit of innovation.
- Every American business and every employee who works for an American business will be forced to become agile, flexible, and highly adaptive, since the product or service they will provide and the business processes they will employ will be in a constant state of change. Americans will have to adjust to living with chaos, uncertainty, and unpredictability as a normal part of the work experience. In fact, leaders of the new organization will promote a certain level of chaos as a desirable state necessary for innovation to flourish.
- Every American company will be forced to develop a much better understanding of what it does truly well and will in-

vest its limited resources in developing and sustaining superiority in that unique knowledge, skill, or capability. Employees who succeed in the world of tomorrow will be those who develop a clear sense of their own unique skills and capabilities, continually enhance these, and find ways to match their skills and capabilities to those of the businesses that employ them.

- Organizational structures will become extremely fluid. Structures that were flattened during the 1980s and early 1990s will now be broken into pieces. No longer will there be departments, units, divisions, or functional groups in most American businesses. There will only be multidisciplinary and multiskilled teams, and every team will be temporary. Most Americans won't have permanent job assignments. They will just float from team to team, wherever their unique skills and capabilities are required.

- Finally, there will be a meltdown of the barrier between leader and follower, manager and worker. Bosses, in the traditional sense, will all but disappear. While there will be a few permanent leaders external to work and project teams, these people will act more as coordinators of team activities than as traditional leaders. Leadership will, for the most part, be exercised within the teams, and most people will be required to take on leadership responsibilities at least some of the time. In effect, leadership responsibility will be dispersed throughout the team, and the distinction between leader and follower, at least in terms of permanent positions that people occupy, will all but disappear.

These are some of the dramatic changes we will see over the next few years. They will have to occur because the American economy needs to be sustained and the standard of living of American workers needs to rise.

A Scenario For America's Future

There is an ironclad law of economics that applies to everyone. Ultimately, we can be paid only according to our productivity. To be paid more, we must produce more and better goods and services. It's that simple. We may, of course, choose to ignore this law for a time, but when we do, we borrow from our future and the future of our children. If we ignore it too long, we will bankrupt the future for everyone. In the 1980s, we borrowed heavily from the future, and in spite of all of the heartbreak and headache of the early 1990s, we haven't done enough to get back into compliance with the ironclad law.

Consider the wage gap we have with other countries. In the early 1990s, the average hourly wage in the United States, including benefits, was approximately

- $10 for American textile workers,
- $14 for electrical-equipment manufacturers,
- $16 for industrial- and office-equipment manufacturers,
- $22 for autoworkers, and
- $24 for iron and steel workers.

Contrast that to an average hourly wage of about

- $2 in Mexico,
- $3.50 in Hong Kong, and
- $4 in Korea and Singapore.

The gap between American wages and those of their competitors in a global marketplace ranges from $8 to as much as $20 per hour.

If we can only be paid for what we produce, the question becomes how we run fast enough or work hard enough to make up for that $8- to $20-per-hour differential. The answer, of course, is that we can't. Instead, we have to drive labor costs out of the productivity equation by developing highly skilled employees and designing jobs and work processes in such a way that American workers can leverage their skills to create high-value products and services that justify the wage differential. In short, the only way we can sustain and enhance our standard of living is through consistent and constant innovation. That is what *Beyond Workplace 2000* is all about.

The future scenario for American business and its workers is simple. American companies will employ highly skilled workers who will work in new, high-performance workplaces to create high-value-adding products and services at extremely low costs. These innovative products will command premium prices in a global marketplace and thereby create wealth that can be shared with workers, thus allowing them to enhance their standard of living and become voracious consumers of the innovative products and services they themselves create.

Of course, there are some problems with this scenario. First, we don't have enough high-skilled workers to create such an economy. Second, even if we did find a way instantly to produce a critical mass of high-skilled workers, we don't have enough high-performance workplaces to employ them. Finally, even if we created a nation of highly skilled workers and high-performance workplaces, the world doesn't yet have enough affluent, sophisticated customers to buy the premium-priced, innovative products we would produce. It is really the economic and social dilemma of the rest of this century.

To make the whole scenario work, we have to do three virtually impossible things at the same time:

- drastically upgrade worker skills;
- further revolutionize the workplace in dramatic ways; and
- create a global economy filled with well-educated, technologically sophisticated, relatively affluent buyers for all the new and innovative products and services we will produce.

If we can accomplish all three things, then the scenario works. If we fail at any of the three, there may be no way to stop the slide down the economic ladder for most Americans.

Of course there is a doom-and-gloom cadre out there that looks at the stagnant incomes of the last decade, the layoffs, the education impasse, the crime and violence in the streets, the cynicism of the baby-boomer generation and the skepticism of their boom-buster kids and groan—actually, it's more of a whine. They see us stumbling down the economic mountain. Soon—very soon, they say—we are going to hit bottom, and it's going to hurt like hell. Bloodied and broken, we will pick ourselves up and stumble off to economic and societal oblivion. We say, NO WAY!

America has been in challenging economic situations before and has come back. For example, at the end of World War II, the doom-and-gloom crowd said we would never be able to convert from a wartime to a peacetime economy fast enough to avoid the return of the depression. They were wrong. America rose to the challenge and created a period of economic prosperity that lasted for over twenty-five years. In the 1980s, we heard that America's industrial base had been so eroded, due to the poor quality of our products, that we would never regain the market share we had lost to the Japanese and others in key industries such as automobiles, semiconductors, and computers. But Americans and American business responded with the Workplace 2000 revolution and stopped the decline. By 1994, we were regaining market share and, in some cases, recapturing the lead in key industries.

The future scenario for America is going to work. We are going beyond Workplace 2000—far beyond. We have already started doing what has to be done. The workplace revolution is continuing.

PART

I

THE PURSUIT OF INNOVATION

As we march inexorably beyond Workplace 2000, one thing is becoming increasingly clear. Most companies no longer can expect to achieve even moderately sustainable competitive advantage from further improvements in quality, cost, or speed. The reasons are simple. In most industries today, the gap between rivals or potential rivals in quality, cost, and speed either has already closed or is rapidly closing. For the consumer, the remaining distances between companies in quality, cost, and speed are so narrow they are virtually imperceptible. Having one-millionth fewer defects, being one nanosecond faster in delivery time, or offering products one fraction of a penny cheaper is not enough even to retain existing customers, much less to attract new ones.

The organization of the future must turn to the only remaining source of differentiation, innovation—producing and continuing to produce, through product and process changes, the sensory, emotional, in-the-head-but-mostly-in-the-heart, gee-whiz-look-at-this, Ahhh-factor experience that captures the customer's attention and wins his loyalty. Being constantly and consistently innovative is what it is all about and will continue to be about in the coming decades, and that presents a problem for American business, because their track record for innovation hasn't been very good.

America's Legacy Of Spectacular Failures

There is a significant difference between the process of "invention" and the process of "innovation," and it is important not to confuse the two. Invention is the process of creating the idea for a product and/or its underlying manufacturing processes or technology. Innovation goes beyond the process of invention to the actual production and marketing of a product that consumers will buy.

Americans are pretty good at invention. After all, America has 5.5 million scientists and engineers—double the number in Japan—supporting 15 million companies. Americans have won more Nobel prizes than the rest of the world combined. We invented the phonograph, color television, audio and video tape recording, the telephone, integrated circuits, and thousands of other products. We're known for our creativity in developing product ideas and for inventing some of the best gee-whiz, whiz-bang, techno-stuff in the world. We're just not very good at turning our creative ideas and technological wizardry into products people buy. In fact, we're pretty lousy at it.

It is the *innovation* piece that trips us up. Too often, our product ideas and whiz-bang technological creations in the lab never find their way to the market, or, if they do, they land with a resounding thud. Our world-class flops are truly legendary:

- Ford produced the Edsel. It was loaded with innovations, yet it was also loaded with quality problems. The Edsel produced losses for Ford to the tune of more than $250 million.
- Du Pont created a synthetic leather called Corfam that was suppose to be better than leather. It wasn't, and the flop cost Du Pont $80 to $100 million.
- Polaroid created an instant movie camera called Polarvision.

There was just one problem. Customers preferred video technology to film. Polaroid racked up big losses.

- RCA created a Videodisc that would play back movies but wouldn't record. Consumers preferred their VCRs that would let them not only play movies, but also record their favorite shows. RCA's loss was approximately $500 million.
- IBM produced the PCjr for the home computer market. The PCjr was slow and had a horrible Chicklet keyboard. IBM's marketing cost alone for this dud amounted to $40 million.
- NutraSweet produced Simplesse, a fat substitute which was marketed as the product that would "change the way we eat." It didn't. Not only were there already too many substitutes on the market, but consumers simply liked fat.
- Steve Jobs spent $200 million of investor funds creating his $10,000-apiece NeXT computer. The machine was slow, too expensive, and contained a host of nifty features like optical drives and hi-fi sound that NeXT designers loved but customers hated or, at best, didn't think were worth the cost. Richard A. Page, co-founder and former hardware vice-president for NeXT, put it succinctly. "The customers know what they want," and what they didn't want was NeXT.

These are spectacular examples of product failures, but they are by no means unique. In fact, the typical American R&D project in the 1980s and early 1990s rarely produced a product that could be launched, and when it did, the new product only had about a 50 percent probability of being successful. Only one in ten R&D projects turned out to be commercially successful, and only 56 percent of the new products that were introduced were still on the market after five years. In a 1993 article, *Business Week* said, "overall the new-product battleground [was] a scene of awful carnage."

Indeed it was carnage, and it was also pretty expensive carnage. Yoram Wind, a professor of marketing at the Wharton School, estimated in the early 1990s that American companies could *double* their bottom-line profits if they could make only modest improvements in their success rates with new products. He declared new-product development "one of the few areas left with the greatest potential for improvement."

Why are American companies performing so poorly on the new-product battleground? What's so wrong with the traditional

American approach to research and development? The answer to the latter—*PLENTY.*

The Traditional American Approach To R&D Doesn't Work Anymore

The traditional approach to R&D in the United States dates from the early 1900s. That is when American companies started setting up R&D laboratories separate from the rest of the organization. General Electric was first.

GE created its General Research Laboratory in 1900, and most of the giants of American industry soon followed GE's lead. By the 1930s, over half of the two hundred largest U.S. companies had centralized their R&D efforts. For the next sixty years, this specialization of R&D led to such extraordinary American inventions as television, nylon, transistors, semiconductors, computers, lasers, plastics, and videocassette recorders. This specialization of R&D also led to America's inability to manufacture and market what it invented.

Why? First of all, the creation of specialized functions shifted the focus from incremental enhancements of existing products and processes to the all-consuming search for breakthroughs, particularly and almost exclusively product breakthroughs. Manufacturing efficiency demanded standardized products, long production runs, and minimum changeovers. If the production lines were going to be shut down for changeovers and retooling, it had better be worth the effort, and that meant a breakthrough, not an incremental improvement.

Second, the creation of specialized R&D laboratories resulted in a formal separation between "thinking" and "doing." Thinking was done in the laboratory by scientists and engineers who were physically, intellectually, and emotionally removed from the task of day-to-day production—the doing. Research developed the *ideas* and passed them along to product development which developed the *products.* Product development then tossed the products over the wall to manufacturing which did the best it could to make the products. Finally, manufacturing threw the product out the door to marketing to sell.

Each specialized group was insulated from the others by high, impenetrable functional walls. No one talked to anyone else. No one wanted to. No one was expected to. No one was *allowed* to.

This lack of communication resulted in misunderstandings, turf battles, perpetual redesigns, blaming, delays, and further blaming, all leading to high cost, long cycles for product development, and a loss of customer focus.

The ultimate result of all of this was, as Joseph Pine said in his book *Mass Customization*, the production of "ideas and inventions that could not readily be commercialized, products that could not economically be manufactured, and goods too few people wanted." That was the experience of most American companies, but it wasn't the experience of *all* American companies, at least not all of the time. Somewhat to our surprise, we had some real success stories. Some American companies actually got it right.

In the process of "getting it right," these companies are creating a model workplace for the future. It is a workplace that is devoted to innovation and delighting the customer. The strategy of such a company is different. Its structure is different. Its social contract with employees and expectations from employees is different. It is a revolutionary departure from the workplace we have known before. Welcome to the new millennium. Welcome to the workplace of the new age.

CHAPTER 1

Learning from Our Successes

As America entered the mid-1990s, many of its companies began examining notable innovation success stories, both foreign and domestic. They were searching for ways to dramatically improve their own new-product success rate. Among the real success stories to which they turned were

- Apple, with its PowerBook computer;
- Gillette, with its Sensor razor;
- Reebok, with its Pump sneaker;
- Motorola, with its MicroTac cellular phone;
- Chrysler, with its LH cars;
- IBM, with its ThinkPad notebook computer;
- Ford, with its Taurus; and

a host of other American companies that seemed to be getting R&D right for a change. In the process, these innovation leaders were teaching American business some important lessons about innovation and about the way the new organization must look and act.

Lesson #1: Design With The Customer In Mind

Forget about what the designers want, or what the engineers want, or what the employees want, or even what the company's top executives want. When it comes to product design, insiders' opinions don't matter anymore. The only opinion that matters is the opinion of the dollar-paying customer—period. That's the number one lesson for the new organization.

When you think about it, it is such a simple lesson. In order to design the products and services that consumers want to buy, companies have to know their customers and design products or services with the customer in mind. Deep insight into the needs, lifestyles, and aspirations of current and potential users of the product or service is invaluable in getting the new product right. It is a lesson American companies have learned the hard way. It is a lesson Apple learned when it tried to develop its first portable computer.

Apple's "Luggable" Laptop

Apple's first portable was a seventeen-pound luggable Mac. It had whiz-bang engineering but was a resounding dud in the marketplace. Consumers hated it.

Apple's problem with its first stab at developing a portable Mac was a common one for American companies. Capability took precedence over usability. In designing the product, Apple engineers just kept adding features without checking to see if the features were things the customers wanted or needed. As a result, the machine got overloaded with capability no one really wanted and "underloaded" with the ease-of-use features that most customers really needed. Apple built the computer equivalent to the 10,000-function VCR that no one could figure out how to program.

Apple's Laptop—the Second Time Around

On its second time around, Apple took a different approach. It put usability first. Apple designers went out not just to talk to customers, but to observe how they actually used portable computers. They saw people in airports trying to find someplace to put their mouse. They saw others using their computer balanced on their knees or on the drop-down meal tray on airplanes. Responding to what they observed, Apple designers built in features such as the PowerBook's TrackBall pointing device and palm-rest keyboard. Then they went further.

Apple used a methodology called "product mapping" to compare its PowerBook prototypes to eight other notebook computers on 450 tests of usability covering 159 user-computer interactions. The result? Apple was able to determine which features people used, which features set the PowerBook apart from its competition, and most importantly, which features to leave out because the user didn't need them or want them.

The features Apple left in, like its TrackBall pointing device, its palm-rest keyboard, and others, weren't engineering feats of daring. They just made the PowerBook distinctive and easy to use. Customers seemed to like that. In fact they liked it a lot. To them, it was almost as if Apple had built the PowerBook with them in mind—which, of course, is exactly what Apple had done.

Those Products That Make Customers Say "Ahhh . . ."

In the process of designing a customer-oriented product, Apple had accomplished something more. Not only did Apple produce a product that was distinctive and customer friendly, but it also created a gee-whiz-look-at-this, Ahhh-factor experience for the customer. Here was a product that was *delightful*. It was the kind of product that generates genuine affection for a company and creates loyal customers because it goes beyond satisfaction to delight, to a kind of emotional bond that inevitably translates into future sales.

Other American companies have had the same kind of success when they started getting really close to their customers. Ford, for example, got an Ahhh from car buyers when it put mesh netting in the trunk of its Taurus line of cars to keep grocery bags from tipping over. Motorola surprised customers when they saw that the MicroTac pocket cellular phone not only could survive being dropped to the floor, but could do so without even so much as its plastic casing getting scratched. Chrysler's cab-forward design for its LH cars provided wider doors, easier entry, better front-seat visibility, and such Ahhh-inspiring back-seat leg room that passengers often tapped the driver on the shoulder to express their pleasure and surprise. Of course, these features often weren't even things the customers realized they wanted.

To reach an Ahhh, the customer frequently had to be led to a new product concept. It wasn't enough just to listen to what the customer *said* he or she wanted. Those companies that just listened never came up with the really Ahhh-inspiring products. After all, customers probably would not have suggested microwave ovens, cellular telephones, compact discs, home fax machines, or hundreds of other products.

Even the initial reaction of consumers to a new product wasn't always a reliable guide to the product's likely future success. On first exposure, most people thought hair styling mousse was "goopy and gunky," and they didn't like the way it made their hair feel. Most people considered the earlier answering machines to be rude and disrespectful to callers and definitely not "the answer" to missed calls. And the computer mouse? Many early users considered it awkward to use and simply unnecessary. "No thanks," computer users said. "We'll just type in the commands like we always have."

No, listening to customers and even formal market research wasn't the answer to uncovering those Ahhh-inspiring products. Companies that wanted to gain competitive advantage from innovation had to do much more than just listen. They had to get really close to their customer. They had to be small enough and focused enough and intense enough to get into their customer's head and understand his or her needs, desires, wishes, hopes, and dreams even before the customer did. These companies had to do something else as well. They had to design, develop, and bring products to market faster than ever before, because in advance of getting it out to the marketplace, no one could predict which product might be the next big success. And that's the second lesson American business learned.

Lesson #2: Ready, Fire, Aim

It has been termed "expeditionary marketing." It's a series of low-cost and fast-paced market incursions, and it's something every American company will be doing in the new business world.[1] Its purpose is to learn by doing—a kind of ready-fire-aim approach to product development.

Instead of waiting for the market to reveal itself or for the laboratory to perfect the product, an early version of a product is brought to an undeveloped and ill-defined market. Based upon experience from this early foray, a judgment is made as to whether and how to proceed. The product might be scrapped entirely. More likely, the product will be reconfigured and sent out for another foray. This process is repeated over and over. Each experience, whether positive or negative, brings new insight into the particular combination of features, price, and performance that will yield an Ahhh-inspiring product. In short, the company keeps shooting at a moving target, keeps adjusting its sights, and with experience gets closer and closer to hitting the bull's-eye. Take Sony and Seiko as examples.

Sony builds its Walkman on one basic but flexible core technology. From that core model it can build a wide range of models. It monitors sales closely and adjusts production accordingly. If pink models are selling, more pink models are produced. If children's models are selling, more children's models are produced, and the line is expanded. Sony uses its speed and flexibility to react quickly to customer buying patterns.

Similarly, Seiko releases hundreds of models of watches to find those few it will retain. Again, it is the speed, flexibility, and low cost of design and manufacturing, the "design for response," that makes such real-time product testing possible. There is an added benefit of such rapid incursions into the market. Not only does the company learn about individual market targets, but it accumulates a wealth of knowledge about customer needs, aspirations, and perceptions that can help it with other product launches. It is the kind of fast turnaround in R&D that we haven't had before but that all companies will strive to imitate in the new millennium. The key of course is reducing development cycle times, and that's the next lesson.

Lesson #3: Being Fast Isn't Enough—You Have To Be *Much, Much* Faster Just To Compete

Rapid research and development will be a race in which every company will participate as we move into the next century. How far can we go in reducing development cycle times? We can and will go to or near zero cycle time. Instantaneous or nearly instantaneous development and delivery of new products and services is becoming the norm. Regardless of product or service we are moving in that direction. Just look at the following examples:

- The Limited can already create new styles and get them into stores in forty-two days.
- Swatch can create a new line of watches and get them into stores in thirty days.

- Peerless Saw can design and deliver a unique industrial saw in fifteen days.
- Bally Engineered Structures can create a new refrigerated warehouse in ten days.
- Toyota can deliver a customized car in some markets in five days.
- Nissan expects to be able soon to deliver a customer-designed car in three days.
- Lutron Electronics can develop and deliver one-of-a-kind lighting controls in one day.
- Motorola can create a unique pager in an hour and a half.
- CNN Headline News can produce a new news show every thirty minutes.
- Create-A-Book can compose a unique children's book in fifteen minutes.
- TWA can create a personalized, customer-designed travel package in just six minutes.

What used to take months is now done in weeks; what took weeks is now accomplished in days; what took days now takes hours; what took hours now takes minutes. Faster, faster, faster—that's the new rule. Of course, getting to zero or near zero requires a total rethinking of how research and development is accomplished and *who* is involved in the development effort. That's another lesson.

Lesson #4: Consult Many Different—*Really Different*—Minds

Regardless of what it is called—*simultaneous engineering, concurrent engineering, design for manufacturing, parallel release*—it all means the same thing, and most American companies are doing it or trying to do it. Under this new approach to R&D, employees from different disciplines work interactively to simultaneously conceive, develop, and implement new products or services *and* the processes by which the products are manufactured or the services are delivered. With this new approach, a design team might consist of design engineers, technical writers, customer support people, marketing representatives, lawyers, purchasing agents, human-factors analysts, representatives from manufacturing and quality, and even customers themselves. And it works.

Using this technique, Xerox slashed product development time from five years to less than two years, and Ford built its highly successful Taurus line of cars. Then there was Chrysler.

In 1989, Chrysler president Robert A. Lutz convinced top executives at the company to allow him to experiment with this new approach to product development. Lutz, with the help of Francois J. Castaing, Chrysler's engineering chief, threw out Chrysler's old, sequential, compartmentalized approach to product development and replaced it with a cross-functional team approach. Teams of engineers, marketers, stylists, and manufacturing engineers worked together to design the new models. Not only did they reduce development time by 40 percent, but they produced Chrysler's highly successful LH line of cars.

Marco Iansiti, an assistant professor at Harvard Business School, illustrated the difference between American business's traditional approach to research and development and this new approach in a 1992 *Harvard Business Review* article.[2] Iansiti reported on the results of a study of R&D organizations in twelve mainframe computer companies—AT&T, Bull, Digital Equipment, Fujitsu, Hitachi, IBM, ICL, Mitsubishi Electric, NEC, Siemens, Toshiba, and Unisys. Each of these R&D organizations had been involved in the development of technology for a particular product, the multichip module which houses and connects mainframe computers' most critical integrated circuits, affecting the entire system's speed and reliability. Drawing upon the experiences these twelve companies had in conducting research and development efforts for the multichip module, Iansiti constructed two contrasting case histories for a Traditional Company A and for what Iansiti called a Systems-Focused Company B.

Traditional Company A

Traditional Company A's research group began their R&D effort by experimenting with a new ceramic material composition they had discovered could conduct great quantities of heat. They fabricated small quantities of the material using scaled-down equipment in the lab. They surveyed the literature, talked to scientists at universities, and conducted a number of small-scale experiments aimed at giving them a better understanding of the material's properties. Their research led them to conclude that this new ceramic material could increase the speed and reliability of their company's multichip module.

Excited about the material's potential, the researchers aggressively promoted its use with senior management. Eventually they won top management's approval to fabricate a small number of prototype modules in the lab using the new ceramic material. They succeeded in producing several partially functional modules which, they argued, demonstrated that it should be possible to build a real module based on the new material. At that point, following the traditional approach to R&D, the activities of the research group came to an end and the project was turned over to development.

The development team began the process of implementing the new ceramic material for the multichip module. Almost immediately, they experienced difficulty in trying to increase production yields and in trying to make the product reliable. It was particularly troublesome that the ceramic material would buckle. The buckling was a problem the research group had identified earlier and had supposedly fixed. They had changed the composition of the ceramic and had adjusted the firing process, and thereby had succeeded in eliminating the problem in the lab. But it was occurring again.

The number of people and the amount of money devoted to the project increased dramatically, and the development engineers spent months making changes in the ceramic material and production process in order to fix the problem. Finally, they succeeded and turned the new product over to manufacturing only to have the buckling problem recur. Additional months were spent reengineering the product and eliminating the problem for good. Finally, the product went into full production. It took Traditional Company A six and a half years of development time and eight hundred person-years of engineering and scientific activity to complete the development stage.

Systems-Focused Company B

In contrast, Systems-Focused Company B began the R&D effort by creating a multidisciplinary integration team to oversee research and development and to investigate the impact of technical decisions on the design of the product and its manufacturability.

The team's objective was to balance new research from the lab with the manufacturing system's existing capabilities and to adapt the new technology to what the company knew how to do and what customers wanted.

Company B's integration team monitored basic research performed by the research group, plus research contracted out to outside ceramics-materials suppliers. As results from the initial research came in, the integration team identified the most promising new techniques. Several possible technical concepts were investigated in parallel, including the use of combinations of materials such as aluminum and glass ceramics. As the integration team learned more, it began weeding out various alternatives, always focusing on three criteria: manufacturability, yield, and reliability.

As in the case of Company A, Company B researchers encountered the buckling problem. Instead of defining the problem as "how to get rid of the buckling," the way Company A scientists did, Company B scientists defined the problem as "how can we get the whole system to function effectively?"

At an early stage in the project, the integration team built a prototype of the product *and* manufacturing process using a pilot production line and equipment representative of actual high-volume manufacturing conditions. As a result of asking a broader question and relying on a broader knowledge base, from research scientists to development and manufacturing engineers, the Company B team quickly identified a solution to the buckling problem that worked. They coated the ceramic substrate with a polymer to smooth the surface and control the buckling, and when the project moved from research to development and later to production, the buckling did not recur.

Unlike Traditional Company A, which practiced the old, sequential, throw-it-over-the-wall-and-see-if-they-can-make-it approach, Systems-Focused Company B got lots of minds involved from the first day. What difference did that make? A lot. Whereas it took Company A six and a half years to complete the development phase, it took Company B only four and a half years. That is 30 percent faster for Company B. Company A expended eight hundred person-years to complete the development phase, compared to three hundred person-years for Company B. Company B could then take its 62 percent savings in resources and explore new market segments or even tiny market fragments, which is, of course, the next lesson.

Lesson #5: There Aren't Any Market Segments: All That's Left Are Tiny Market Fragments

American business used to talk about market segments. No longer. Most markets have splintered into hundreds of tiny market fragments, each wanting something different or special. No longer is it good enough for a company to have just one or even a few versions of a new product. Today, customers want it their way, and they go elsewhere if they don't get just what they want.

In response, American business is creating a wider variety of products than ever before. Take 3M for example. Within twenty months of coming out with its first Post-it note, the company developed over a hundred different varieties. Or take Castrol, Inc., the oil lubricant specialist. Castrol makes more than three thousand different formulas for lubricants. Each one is tailored to a specific customer application. Or take the Illinois-based Sanford Company, which niches the pen, pencil, and marker business to death with hundreds of versions. In markers alone, it makes versions for hundreds of specific applications, from marking clothes in Laundromats to non-smearing markers for use on waxed paper, and watercolor markers for toddlers. Product variety and catering to smaller and smaller fragmented markets is what business is now all about.

Lesson #6: Get All The Way Down To The Ultimate Have-It-Your-Way: Let Them Design It Themselves

There is, of course, an ultimate have-it-your-way: the customers design the product themselves. Sound far-fetched? Not at all. That's what NEC almost achieved with its UltraLite Versa notebook computer.

NEC's UltraLite Versa notebook computer had some novel technical design features. For example, the screen could be lifted up and turned around so others could see what was being displayed. It had fingertip grips on the exterior so it could be carried easily in one hand. It had a rounded and smooth design that gave it the look and feel of a consumer appliance, not an office product. And there was one other thing. Every major component of the machine—the display screen, disk drives, power supply, memory, and so on—just snapped in and out. Users themselves could easily reconfigure the machine to their liking. Need a pen-PC screen? Just pop it on. Need a different type of battery or a different disk drive? Just pop out the old one and pop in one more to your liking. It was a kind of design-it-your-way product. And a lot of buyers liked the idea.

NEC, a company that had pretty much bombed in the U.S. PC market, even though it had been a huge success in Japan, released the UltraLite Versa in April 1993. By July of that year, NEC had doubled its share of the computer notebook market and, based upon projected sales, expected to double its share of the market again by year-end 1993.

NEC's competitors were paying attention. IBM, for example, indicated it would be incorporating modularity—have-it-your-way design—into its ThinkPad 750, and other companies were moving in the same direction. It was a new way of thinking about innovation. No longer was innovation the exclusive purview of isolated labs or a know-it-all R&D department. Now innovation was an active, fluid engagement of the customer in creating value, and American business was finding that there were lots of ways to innovate.

Lesson #7: There Is More Than One Way To Skin The Innovation Cat

As we approached the end of the twentieth century, American business was asking questions about innovation and how it should and could be done. Perhaps the most important question was, "What does it really mean to innovate?" Is a company innovative only if it is making breakthrough scientific discoveries and converting those into radically new products? As it turned out, the answer was "not at all." That was another of the key lessons we have learned. Product development through breakthrough research is certainly one form of innovation. But there are many other ways to get the job done. Here are just a few examples:

1. **Innovation from core technology**—Companies like Canon, NEC, Casio, Honda, 3M, and Sony have found that they can innovate by exploiting their expertise in a few core technologies to create a vast array of new products. Honda, for example, produces autos, motorcycles, small generators, lawn mowers, snow blowers, chain saws, and a host of other products from its knowledge and expertise in small-engine production and design.

2. **Innovation by remixing common elements**—Companies like The Gap, The Limited, Nordstrom, The Body Shop, Toys "R" Us, Home Depot, and American Express have discovered they can innovate by remixing common elements in a unique and, for the customer, value-adding way. Home Depot, for example, takes the common offerings of lumber and other do-it-yourself items and mixes in knowledgeable in-store staff, many of whom are former plumbers, electricians, carpenters, and so on, who can provide customers with the extra service dimension of expert advice on do-it-yourself projects.

3. **Innovation from filling unmet needs**—Companies like Procter and Gamble, Black and Decker, Nike, Rubbermaid, Levi Strauss, Pacific Bank, and the Ritz-Carlton Hotel have found they can innovate by identifying and filling previously unrecognized customer needs or by enhancing the benefit/value customers receive from existing products and services. The Ritz-Carlton in Boston, for example, offers custom-designed children's rooms that adjoin parents' rooms. The children's rooms feature such amenities as childproof electrical outlets, stereos and VCRs, toys, and even art supplies.

4. **Innovation from business-process reengineering**—Companies like Milliken, Dell Computers, Wrigley Gum, Frito-Lay, and McDonald's innovate by enhancing or totally reengineering business processes to the benefit of customers. Milliken, for example, turned its own trucks into storage warehouses for Levi-Strauss, loading the Milliken goods on the trucks in the order in which Levi-Strauss needed them to make its just-in-time manufacturing system work.

5. **Innovation from technology fusion**—Other companies, particularly Japanese companies such as Nissan, NEC, and Sharp, have pursued innovation through what is called

"technology fusion." Fumio Kodama, a professor at Saitana University's Graduate School of Policy Science in Japan and author of *Analyzing Japanese High Technologies: The Techno-Paradigm Shift*, has described the "technology fusion" approach to innovation this way:

> Technology fusion ... blends incremental technical improvements from several previously separate fields of technology to create products that revolutionize markets. For example, marrying optics and electronics created optoelectronics, which gave birth to fiber-optics communications systems; fusing mechanical and electronics technologies produced the mechatronics revolution, which has transformed the machine tool industry.[3]

In short, technology fusion involves the marriage of one technology to another to create a new and unique product that could not have been produced from a single technology alone. As Kodama puts it, with technology fusion, the solution is greater than the sum of its parts. In effect, one plus one equals three.

Finally, some companies have discovered that they can innovate in a variety of ways simultaneously. Consider the multiple ways 3M pursues innovation by finding unmet needs and engineering products to fill them. For example, 3M put nighttime reflective materials on bicycle tires in Europe using a product originally designed for road signs. The company also invests extensively in basic science to create new technologies, such as its micro-woven-fiber technology used for Thinsulate-brand insulations and Scotchbrite-brand floor-cleaning pads. It also combines technologies like adhesives and abrasives to create sticky-backed sanding disks for body shops and industry, and it pursues low-cost strategies for the production of videotapes, packaging tape, and other key 3M lines.

The Ultimate Lesson

By the mid-1990s, we had learned numerous lessons about innovation. But what did it all mean? As it turned out, those innovation lessons were significant—quite significant. They led us to a new way of thinking, not just about new-product design and development, but about the way businesses should be run. They even led us to rethink what a business is and what it could be. The ultimate lesson was that American businesses had to be totally reinvented. We needed a new type of enterprise.

CHAPTER 2

Creating the Customer-Sensitive, Knowledge-Creating, Agile Enterprise

Ultimately, innovation, regardless of how it's pursued, is the constant search for the new, the different, the better value-adding product or service that creates the Ahhh-factor, whiz-bang, gee-whiz, how-about-that, would-you-believe, I-love-it, what-will-they-think-of-next delight for the customer.

For companies that embrace innovation as a primary, or in many cases *the* primary basis for achieving sustainable competitive advantage, as all companies must, the pursuit of innovation becomes an ongoing quest for knowledge and for mechanisms to translate knowledge into customer value and delight.

When the organization latches on to that kind of quest as its raison d'être, something changes within it. Old mechanistic ways of thinking about the organization have to give way to newer concepts of the organization as a living, learning, growing entity that processes knowledge and interacts continuously with its environment and its customers.

Such an organization is different from any we have known before. It is customer-sensitive, knowledge-creating, and totally agile. It is flexible and adaptive, more like a living organism than a machine. It is an organization that can thrive on chaos, uncertainty, unpredictability, and continuous change. It is lean in the use of resources. It serves small, niche markets, sometimes as small as a single customer. Most importantly, it produces highly customized products and delivers highly customized services on the spur of the moment. Is such an enterprise possible? Yes it is.

And that is precisely the kind of organization we are creating as we move toward the workplace of the new millennium.

As we entered the mid-1990s, the details and possibilities of such an organization were being sketched out by a number of researchers and thought leaders and were being tried by a few pioneering companies. This new type of business enterprise has been given a number of different names—the *learning organization*, the *virtual corporation*, the *agile enterprise*, the *intelligent enterprise*, and so on. Regardless of what this new organization is called, it has certain characteristics that make it inimitably innovative. For example:

- Its production and service delivery processes are designed in such a way that they can be reconfigured on a moment's notice to produce new and more sophisticated products or services or to respond to changes in levels of demand for products and services. The organization is totally flexible, and process innovation—the creative reinvention of how work is performed—becomes as important as, if not more important than, product innovation.
- Its products and services are designed in such a way that they can be configured to a specific user's requirements at the time of sale or order. Customers are given a virtually unlimited range of choices, allowing them to create a unique product or service, should they choose to do so. The customer/user actually becomes involved in the process of creating the product or service as well as the value that flows from the product or service. The user/customer is no longer just a consumer of value, but becomes an active participant in creating value.
- Its products are designed for upgradability so customers can just replace component parts instead of buying a new version of the product and throwing away the old one. In effect, the old product can be remanufactured simply by switching out modular components.
- It places increased emphasis on attracting, developing, and retaining knowledgeable, empowered workers who can use their individual talents and their access to a wide range of information to significantly increase the organization's flexibility, responsiveness, and level of innovation. In the new organization, workers rather than equipment are treated as

the company's primary assets, because it is the workers who possess the knowledge, the collective learning of the organization, that sets the organization apart and makes it unique.

- It is more apt to offer both products and services rather than strictly one or the other. Physical products essentially become a platform for providing an ever-evolving set of value-adding services to the customer/user.
- It doesn't attempt to do everything by itself. Instead it establishes a network of relationships with other organizations, in some cases even competing organizations, so that it can rapidly tap the specialized know-how of best practice units, wherever they might be, in order to whisk high-quality, low-cost, new products and services to customers on demand.

These are just a few of the characteristics of the emerging intelligent, agile, virtual, learning organization, call it what you will. To create this organization, American business is totally rethinking the way it develops business strategy, the way it is organized, the way it attracts, retains, manages, and motivates its workforce, and the way it selects its leaders.

As the 1980s ended and the 1990s began, we launched a revolution to reinvent the workplace. We began to create Workplace 2000. Now as the twentieth century comes to an end, we are going beyond Workplace 2000 to reinvent the nature and purpose of business itself. The workplace revolution doesn't just continue. Now it drives down to the core of the business. It starts, as we might imagine, with a complete reexamination of strategy, of the actual theory of business itself.

PART II

THE NEW STRATEGY

Traditionally, American companies have built long-term strategies (when they built them at all) on the basis of prior projects, programs, products, and services. This what-we-have-done-in-the-past, historical base was taken as a given and served as the launching pad for the future. The Western/American strategic model posited that businesses excelled by

- correctly allocating resources among competing investment opportunities;
- achieving and maintaining strategic "fit" between the company's resources and opportunities;
- deciding to be low-cost, differentiated, or focused, but not all three at the same time; and/or
- positioning themselves on the value chain so they were in the right business with the right

products and market segments and performing the right value-adding activities.

Such approaches to strategy are no longer enough and, perhaps, no longer even valid. In the world beyond Workplace 2000, organizations that seek a fit between their resources and opportunities will likely find themselves trimming their ambitions as resources become more scarce rather than more abundant. Organizations that seek to be low-cost, differentiated, or focused will find themselves confronted by maverick competitors that are low-cost *and* differentiated or low-cost *and* focused. Organizations that try to position themselves on the value chain will find that, with certain types of products and services, the value chain isn't a chain at all and that there is no longer such a thing as a position. The world beyond Workplace 2000 will be quite different from what we have experienced before, and in such a world, the notion of strategy itself has to change.

Strategy for the new organization is less about fit, positioning, and value chains than it is about the ability to innovate and co-produce value with the customer. Success involves initially linking the company's unique competencies and capabilities—the knowledge that is resident in a company—its business systems, and its processes to the needs of target customers and then maintaining that link over time. When such a link is defined, the company has a strategic focus and it excels. When no such link exists, there is no strategic focus and the company fails or barely survives. Certainly, it fails to achieve its full potential. Such are the concepts and ideas for the new strategy. They are much different from what we have known before. They are certainly much different from what we knew about strategy in the simpler world of the 1960s, 1970s, and 1980s.

CHAPTER 3

Strategies of the Past

What leads to success? Is business success a function of how well businesses are operated, or is success more a function of positioning, of, so to speak, being at the right place at the right time? Before the 1970s, the prevailing view among academics and the business community was that both were important. The strength of the company, how well it was managed, counted as much as its market attractiveness or how much a given market was growing. In the 1970s, however, that all changed.

Strategies Of The 1970s

In the 1970s, American business became preoccupied with growth. Corporate strategies shifted from developing company strengths to expansion. It was the age of the conglomerate. Corporations became collections of what were often unrelated businesses or product lines. The value of the corporation was increased through acquisition, not through the development of the business internally. In such an environment, the corporation owned a wide variety of businesses and produced a wide variety of products. The chief strategic issue was how to allocate financial resources between the businesses and product lines—in other words, which businesses or products would receive an influx of cash and which businesses would be starved for funds? But how could a business answer these questions? To the rescue came the consultants with their "portfolio analysis."

Strategic portfolio models became extremely popular in the late 1960s and remained so through the 1970s. By the late 1970s, there was a wide variety of portfolio models and approaches, each competing for attention. They carried such esoteric names as Business Assessment Array, Business Profile Matrix, Directional Policy Matrix, Product Performance Matrix, Conjoint Analysis-based Approach, Analytic Hierarchy Process, Risk/Return Model, and especially the ever-popular Growth/Share Matrix.[1]

The Growth/Share Matrix was developed during the 1960s by the Boston Consulting Group (BCG). It was simple, elegant, and quantitative, and it used colorful labels, such as "stars," "problem children," "cash cows," and "dogs," to describe the relative value of business units or product lines. Consequently, it became extremely popular.

To use the Growth/Share Matrix, a corporation simply plotted its business units according to two dimensions: market growth rate and competitive position, or market share.

FIGURE 3.1
THE BCG GROWTH/SHARE MATRIX

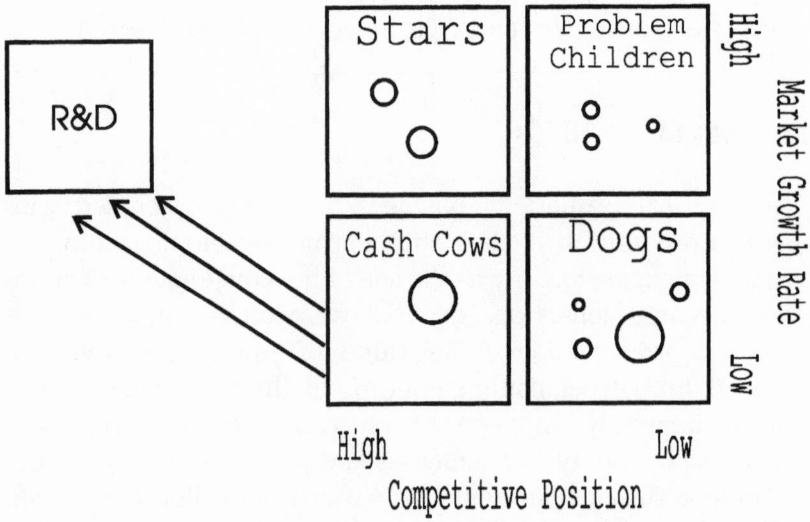

Once the business units were plotted in the matrix, with circles representing their position and the size of the circle representing each business unit's sales volume, then decisions could easily be made about how to allocate scarce funds.

Business units falling within the upper-left quadrant of the matrix were "stars." They enjoyed high market share in high-growth markets. They would require cash to support their growth, but since they were in a strong competitive position, they presumably would have high profit margins and would generate plenty of cash. Generally, stars could be expected to be self-supporting with respect to their cash needs. But if they needed cash, it should be provided, since the return from the investment would be good. Regardless, any temptation to siphon off cash from these units should be resisted, since the unit's position would be hurt.

"Cash cows" were to be found in the lower-left quadrant. These units held highly competitive positions (had high market share) in low-growth markets. Cash cows could be expected to generate large amounts of cash but required little themselves. They could be milked for dollars that could be used to help the "problem children" or to fund research and development.

Problem children, those units found in the upper-right quadrant of the matrix, were true question marks. They needed lots of cash, since they had to fund growth, but they were unlikely to generate a lot of cash, since they were striving to gain market share and weren't yet benefiting from the economies in producing the product that could be expected to come from experience—the so-called learning curve. The problem child was a question mark because it could either become a star at some time in the future or become just another cash-hungry "dog" as the market matured. Generally, the model suggested that promising problem children should be given a short-term influx of cash to see if they could be turned into stars. But problem children should be watched closely lest they become dogs.

Dogs were cash losers and even cash traps. They were businesses with low market share in low-growth markets. Their profits could be expected to be weak or nonexistent. There wasn't much one could do for dogs. It was possible, but not likely, that a dog could be refocused on a smaller market niche and somehow become a star or cash cow in the redefined market. In general, such turnaround efforts had only a low probability of succeeding and should not be attempted. Most often, the model suggested, funds should be withheld from dogs and they should be allowed to die, or better still, they should be sold off or liquidated.

Such was the analysis and recommendations. It was all simple, neat, easy, and logical. Once you knew whether you had a star, a cash cow, a problem child, or a dog on your hands, you knew exactly what action to take. You knew which units should get funds, which should be milked for funds, and which should be abandoned. There was just one problem. It didn't work.

Dogs would sometimes unexpectedly rise from the dead. Stars would fall from the heavens for unexplainable reasons. Cash cows would occasionally just dry up. The growth/share matrix was simple—too simple. As the 1970s came to an end, strategy makers started looking for something else. Was there another simple, elegant model for strategy that might work better? There was, and its name was "generic."

The Generic Strategies Of The 1980s

The 1980s marked a shift in focus from the almost exclusively financial perspective of the portfolio approaches to a more balanced concern for both market attractiveness and company strength. The standard for this new approach to strategic thinking was set by Harvard Business School professor Michael Porter, with publication of his book *Competitive Strategy* in 1980.

Porter's terminology was similar to that of the early portfolio advocates, but his views about strategy and how companies gained competitive advantage were quite different.[2] A key difference was how Porter defined "market or industry attractiveness." In the BCG portfolio model, "market attractiveness" was defined as market growth. If the market for a line of products was growing, that market was, by definition, "attractive." Not necessarily so, said Porter. It was a little more complicated. In fact, market attractiveness was a function not just of one thing, but of five things:

- the ease of entry of new competitors;
- the threat of substitutes;
- the bargaining power of buyers;
- the bargaining power of suppliers; and
- the intensity of rivalry among the existing competitors.

The collective strength of these five forces determined how attractive a market was and how profitable an industry was, since they influenced the key elements of return on investment—prices, costs, and required investment.

Of course, said Porter, the strength of these five forces was not the same in every industry. In some industries, like pharmaceuticals, soft drinks, and so on, many competitors could succeed and earn substantial returns. In other industries, such as rubber, steel, and video games, one or more of the five forces was intense, and only a few companies, regardless of how well they were managed, could earn attractive returns. Each industry was unique, and that uniqueness and how those five competitive forces interacted determined industry profitability. How an individual company fared within that industry was determined by something else—its position.

Positioning determined whether a company's profitability was above or below the industry average. And in the long run, positioning involved pursuing one of three generic strategies: cost leadership, differentiation, or focus. Within the latter, a company could pursue two variants: cost focus or differentiation focus. (See Figure 3.2)

FIGURE 3.2
THREE COMPETITIVE STRATEGIES

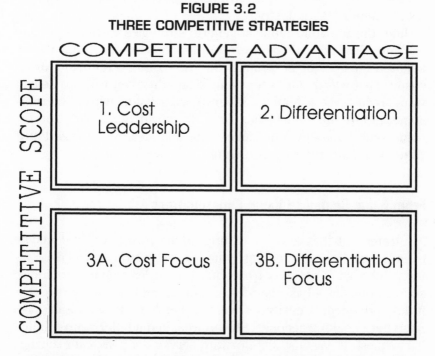

If a company chose to pursue cost leadership, it set out to be *the* low-cost producer in its industry by exploiting some cost advantage such as economies of scale, access to cheap raw materials or labor, control of proprietary technology, low overhead, and so on. Normally, the product of the low-cost producer would be a standard, no-frills product that still met the basic needs of buyers.

A company choosing a differentiation strategy sought to be unique in respect to one or more attributes that buyers deemed important, such as quality or service, and then sought to charge a premium price sufficient to compensate for the additional cost of the uniqueness. Within an industry, there might be several differentiators, as opposed to only one true cost leader. The key was for each differentiator to find some way to define itself in a way that made it truly *different* from any of its rivals.

Finally, a company could pursue a focused strategy and target a small segment of the industry, rather than the industry as a whole. The company could pursue a cost focus or a differentiation focus. As the terms imply, a cost focus meant a firm sought to be the low-cost producer in its target segment of the industry. A differentiation focus meant the firm tried to justify premium prices by demonstrating some unique attributes desired by buyers in the target segment of the industry.

Like the portfolio models, generic strategies were simple and elegant. Basically, there were three choices—or four, if you counted the two focus variants. Be low-cost, differentiated, or focused. That was it. Just a few simple and different ways to deliver value to customers. It all made sense in a sensible world. But then, sometime in the 1980s, that sensible world fell apart. Nothing made sense anymore, particularly not this ideal of value and how value was delivered to the customer.

From Value Chains To Value Constellations

Strategy, if it is about anything, is about the art, and maybe even the science, of creating value for the customer. Once, creating value was, if not easy to accomplish, at least simple to understand. Consider a basic service and how, until relatively recently, it was provided. A customer went to her bank to withdraw cash from her checking account. She approached a teller, who fulfilled her request. It was a straightforward service—a personal exchange between the banking customer and the teller.

Now consider how this same transaction can be accomplished

today. The customer does not have to go to a teller during specified hours of the day, but can go to an ATM. The customer takes
over part of the tasks associated with making the transaction happen in return for the greater convenience of being able to complete the transaction at any time of the day or night. The role of the
bank has shifted from waiting on the customer to a concern for
the design, building, acquisition, maintenance, and support of the
ATMs, as well as the networks and information systems supporting the machines. The bank itself might not actually perform any
of these tasks, but might enter into alliances to have the task performed by other specialized organizations.

The simple act of cash withdrawal has changed in fundamental
ways. It is not just a change in technology, although that is part of it.
It is a change in how value for the customer is created, in what role
the customer and other entities play in creating that value, and in
how much information, knowledge, and other resources are available to all of the participants in the little drama of value creation.

Once it made sense to think of the process of value creation as
a chain of activities leading from the moment of identification of a
customer need, to the design, development, and manufacture of
a product, to the delivery of the product to a customer, fulfilling
the unmet need. That was the value chain.[3]

A company might perform all activities in the chain or just
some of them, but the art of strategy was one of positioning the
company in the value chain with the right products serving the
right markets and performing the right value-adding activities.
Such explanations of value creation are too simplistic today. Take,
for example, the added complexity of value creation as practiced
by the Swedish furniture retailer IKEA.

IKEA is the world's largest retailer of home furnishings. It operates one hundred stores that generated $4.3 billion in revenues in
1992 and yielded profit margins of 8 to 10 percent. IKEA sells low-
cost, high-quality knockdown furniture. Customers do their own delivery and assemble the furniture themselves. On the surface, IKEA's
business seems like a straightforward retail transaction. It isn't.

IKEA doesn't just sell furniture. It mobilizes customers and suppliers in a collaborative effort to create value. IKEA, customers,
and suppliers all have roles to play, and IKEA reserves for itself
the role of orchestrating the creation of value by multiple players.
It does so in a number of ways.

IKEA stores are designed to provide a friendly, family atmosphere. Customers have access to free strollers, playgrounds for children, supervised child care, wheelchairs for the elderly and disabled, and even restaurants. A visit to IKEA is not just a utilitarian undertaking. It is designed to be entertainment. It is designed to be an event that is enjoyable.

Customers are provided with pen, paper, catalogs, tape measures, and everything else they need to make their own selections without sales assistance. They are encouraged to do a little creating on their own—to do a little interior decorating. To help them visualize what life could be like, furniture samples are arranged in the store in groupings to suggest interesting interior designs.

The arrangement, layout, amenities, and overall customer experience in stores is carefully orchestrated to make it easy for the customer to play an active role. The customer doesn't just consume value. The IKEA customer participates actively in *creating* value.

For its 1,800 suppliers in fifty countries, IKEA provides similar value-mobilizing assistance, including such things as

- product design,
- engineering assistance,
- assistance in improving quality,
- assistance in locating raw materials,
- assistance in developing and creating business partnership arrangements, and
- warehousing and logistical assistance to reduce inventories.

Richard Normann and Rafael Ramirez described the IKEA strategy in a 1993 *Harvard Business Review* article as follows:

> The image of a value chain fails to capture the complexity of roles and relationships in the IKEA business system. IKEA did *not* position itself to add value at any one point in a predetermined sequence of activities. Rather, IKEA set out systematically to reinvent value and the business system that delivers it for an entire cast of economic actors. The work-sharing, coproductive arrangements the company offers to customers and suppliers alike force both to think about value in a new way—one in which customers are suppliers (of time, labor, information, and transportation), suppliers are also customers (of IKEA's business and technical services), and IKEA itself is

not so much a retailer as the central star in a constellation of services, goods, design, management, support, and even entertainment. . . . IKEA's extraordinary business innovation is made possible by a fundamental transformation in the way value is created.[4]

Indeed it is a new way of thinking about the process of value creation, and it has important implications.

1. In this new more complex business world, the clear distinction between products and services disappears. Is the ATM transaction a product, service, or both? What about IKEA? Does IKEA provide products, services, or both? Increasingly, the answer is *both*.
2. Value is created not as a result of some predefined, discrete, sequential chain of activities, but as a result of the complex economic exchanges and interactions involving suppliers, customers, business partners, employees, technical teams, and others.
3. The goal of business becomes less about making and doing things for customers than about entering into complex relationships to create value in innovative ways.
4. The key strategic issue becomes one of reconceiving the business and the role the business can and should play in these complex value constellations, rather than one of positioning or managing financial resources.

The strategic challenge becomes one of linking the things at which a company is good—its core competencies—to the wants and needs of customers. The goal isn't just to be a little bit better in quality or cost or speed. The goal is to find innovative ways to engage in strategic alliances and relationships with suppliers, business partners, and others, including customers themselves, to co-produce a gee-whiz, Ahhh-factor experience for the customer.

CHAPTER 4

In Search of Core Competencies

So, how does a company go about the task of defining what it is good at and what it can exploit to create that gee-whiz, Ahhh-factor value for its customers? Increasingly, American companies are finding that it is not enough just to look backward to what they have done in the past—to the products and services they have traditionally offered. Instead, American businesses are finding that they must look inward to discover what they can do really well. This kind of inward-looking search for the future and for future strategy is leading us to a new language of strategy itself, a language filled with terms like "resources," "competencies," and "core competencies." It is a strategic language spoken today in only a few organizations, but it is the language all organizations will use in the future.

What are these "resources" and "competencies" and "core competencies"? In the new language of strategy, a company's resources include such tangible and intangible things as the following:

- the company's physical technology, plants, and equipment, its geographic location, and its access to raw materials
- the training, education, experience, and creativity of the organization's managers and employees
- the company's procedures, systems, and processes
- patents owned by the company
- brand names

In other words, resources are the assets the business owns, controls, or has access to that it can use to generate value for its customers. By themselves, however, resources typically have little if any strategic value to the company. It is only when bundles of resources are put together and used to the benefit of customers that they gain value.

To be put to productive use, resources must be coordinated, combined, and deployed to the benefit of customers. The company must establish a regular, predictable, and productive pattern of activity in which people work together and use a bundle of resources to create value for customers. When that happens, the company demonstrates a competency, and it is competencies, not resources per se, that ultimately determine whether a company develops a sustainable competitive advantage.

The Case Of Wal-Mart

Wal-Mart provides a good example of the differences between resources and competencies. It is also a good example of how a company successfully competes based upon its competencies. Among other things, Wal-Mart owns warehouses, employs workers with knowledge in logistics, has a satellite communications system that sends point-of-sale data directly to vendors, and operates a fleet of trucks that can rapidly move goods from warehouses to stores.

The warehouses, the employee knowledge of logistics, the satellite communications system, and the fleet of trucks all represent resources that Wal-Mart possesses and can employ to the benefit of customers. Each of these resources has obvious monetary value, but individually these resources have no real strategic value. By themselves, they don't help Wal-Mart deliver greater value to its customers, who care nothing about the warehouses, the trucks, or the communication system. By themselves, these resources don't help the customer meet a need or solve a problem. But consider what happens when Wal-Mart combines its warehouses, its knowledge of logistics, its communication system, and its fleet of trucks in an effective and efficient way to ensure that the inventories in its stores are tracked closely and replenished rapidly so that customers never encounter out-of-stock items.

When Wal-Mart deploys its resources in such a way, the resources begin to gain true strategic value, and Wal-Mart demonstrates a competency in inventory replenishment. If Wal-Mart is better at inventory replenishment than any of its rivals or potential rivals, as it happens to be, then inventory replenishment is more than just a competency for Wal-Mart. It becomes a core competency—one it can and does use to gain a real strategic advantage over its rivals. (See Figure 4.1)

FIGURE 4.1
WAL-MART'S CORE COMPETENCY
Inventory Replenishment

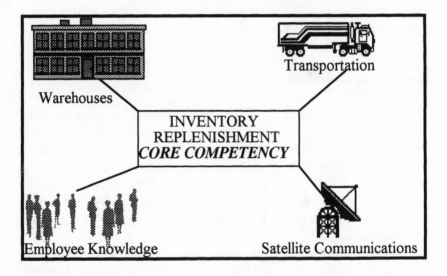

The Core Competencies

All competencies are not equal. Competencies to the firm are like skills to an individual, and like skills, some are more valuable than others. The most valuable competencies, the *core* competencies, have certain characteristics in common.

1. **Core competencies are derived from experience.** A long learning curve makes a core competency difficult to acquire, but it also makes it difficult to imitate, since a competitor would have to go through the same tortuous, time-consuming learning process. Competencies derived from

a company's historical experience become unique to that firm, and as hard as a competitor might try, it can never fully duplicate another firm's unique history.

2. **Core competencies are often based upon a one-of-a-kind resource or resources that are likely to endure for a long time.** Resources vary greatly in how long they can offer a competitive advantage. Technologies, processes, training programs, marketing schemes, and similar resources are notoriously short-lived, some offering true competitive advantage for only a year or two at most before they become obsolete. As unique as they might be, such resources begin losing their value almost as soon as they are put to use. After a few years or months, new and better technologies, processes, training programs, and so on come along, and the older resource will become outdated and diminish in value. Other resources, such as patents, geography, complex buyer-supplier relationships, and highly durable brand names (such as Ivory soap, Heinz sauces, Kellogg's cereals, and Campbell's soup), can offer a competitive advantage for decades.

Some firms are lucky enough to have one or more resources that are not only enduring, but unique. Consider, for example, the world-class restaurant Tours d'Argent in Paris. The restaurant's location provides a magnificent view of the Notre Dame cathedral. The view of the cathedral is deemed so important by restaurant management that it even pays for nighttime lighting of the cathedral so that the view will be retained and even enhanced into the evening. The view of the cathedral is a resource that is highly durable because it is the kind of resource that is unlikely to diminish over time. As long as the view exists, it will continue to offer the restaurant a competitive advantage.

3. **Core competencies are non-transferable.** To imitate a successful strategy, a rival firm must be able to acquire the same or equivalent resources and competencies. The easiest way to acquire the resources is to purchase them on the open market. Yet not all resources are equally available, and even if they are available, they are not easily transferred from one company to another. Resources such as financing and information may be readily available and transferable. Resources such as brand names, employee loyalty, and company reputation may not be so easy to acquire and, if acquired, may not

be transferable or may lose some value if transferred from one company to another. Mergers and acquisitions often result in poorly transferred resources or resources that, once transferred, decline in value.

4. **Core competencies are hard to copy.** One way for a rival firm to acquire strategically critical resources is to purchase them on the open market, as we discussed in the previous section. Another acquisition method is to replicate the resources in-house. The rival firm simply observes what the competitor is doing and copies it. In retail, for example, it is relatively easy for competing firms to copy point-of-sale systems, store layouts, and operating hours. In manufacturing, physical technology, including often highly complex and sophisticated robots and machine tools, can be replicated relatively easily, though perhaps not inexpensively. Such resources and competencies are highly replicable.

Other competencies are less replicable, particularly those that involve complex social phenomena. How does a rival firm replicate the strong interpersonal relations between key managers or the reputations and relationships with customers and suppliers that have been forged over extended periods of time? In such cases, competitive advantages flow to these firms as a result of their possessing strong and complex cultures that are difficult to understand, much less to replicate. Of course, rival firms can attempt to replicate the culture of their leading competitor through some form of social engineering, but such efforts are usually less than fully successful.

5. **Core competencies are those which are fully owned and controlled by the firm.** The value of resources and competencies depends upon the firm's ability to control them fully and to exploit them for competitive advantage. Physical and financial assets of a firm are usually highly controllable and exploitable. There is clear ownership and often little question about how the asset can be used and who will receive benefits that flow from the use of the resource.

Other resources and competencies are less controllable and exploitable, and it may be unclear who receives benefits from the resource when it is used. For example, when a firm's core competencies depend upon the skills of a few, highly trained individuals, the firm's ability to exploit their capability fully may be limited. Such individuals are usually highly mobile. They volunteer their skills to the firm. The skills cannot be coerced from them, and in the process of using their skills, such individuals not only become more valuable to the firm, but frequently more valuable to the wider professional community of which they are a part. As a result, they become even more mobile. In such a situation, the firm may have little if any direct control over the strategic asset. The relationship is one of relative bargaining power. The more valuable the individual, the greater bargaining power he or she has to exercise control over where and how his or her skills are employed and to demand a higher salary and bonus in exchange for his or her efforts.

Even A Single Core Competency May Be Enough

Ultimately, a firm's ability to compete and find the best role to play in the value-creating drama depends upon its ability to identify and exploit resources and competencies that

- are derived from experience;
- are highly durable;
- are difficult for rivals to understand, acquire, or replicate; and
- are highly controllable by the firm.

Needless to say, companies rarely have more than a few competencies that match all or even most of these desirable criteria. Yet even a single "Crown Jewel" competency or resource can offer a strategic advantage if it is recognized and exploited. Consider Harley-Davidson, for example.

Harley-Davidson achieved a remarkable turnaround between 1984 and 1988, but as Robert Grant has noted, Harley really had only one "Crown Jewel" with which to accomplish that turnaround. According to Grant, Harley's "sole durable, non-transferable, irreplicable asset was the Harley-Davidson image and the loyalty that accompanied that image."[1] Harley could not compete with its Japanese rivals in almost every other area of competitive performance, including cost, quality, technology, and global market scope. The only way it could survive was to take strategic advantage of the Harley image, while minimizing its disadvantages in other competencies. The new Harley models introduced during this period of time were based on the traditional design features that kept the company's traditional customers happy, but its marketing strategy centered around the expansion of the appeal of the Harley image of individuality and toughness in an effort to attract more affluent professional customers.

Harley placed tougher controls over its dealers in order to protect its valuable name. It simultaneously widened the exploitation of that name through extensive licensing. Even though improvements in manufacturing efficiency and quality were important to the company's success, it was, according to Grant, the enhancing and broadening of Harley's market appeal that was primarily responsible for its leap from 27 to 44 percent of the U.S. heavyweight motorcycle market between 1984 and 1988. And that increase in market share was accompanied by an equally impressive increase in net income, from $6.5 million to $29.8 million.

Harley exploited a strategically important, highly durable, nontransferable, irreplicable resource to accomplish a turnaround and gain a sustainable competitive advantage. Other American companies must do the same.

CHAPTER 5

Competing on Core Competencies

In 1968, *Forbes* magazine called New York–based Corning Glass Works "one of the strongest companies in American industrial history." That might be considered excessive praise, except for the fact that it was deserved. Corning's history had been one of rapid growth accomplished primarily as a result of a few major technological innovations, a short list of big hits that included Pyrex. These innovations exploited Corning's core competencies in glass and glass-ceramics technologies and, by the mid-1960s, enabled the company to successfully manufacture and sell a diverse group of products, including cookware, light bulbs, picture tubes, and scientific glassware.

Corning also participated in equity ventures that further expanded and enhanced its competencies. For example, it produced agricultural glass with Pittsburgh Corning, silicones with Dow Corning, and fiberglass with Owens Corning.

As the *Forbes* article went to press, Corning was coming off a period of excellent results. Its sales and income had doubled in the previous five years, its return on equity had reached exceptional heights, and its stock was selling at forty times earnings versus seventeen times earnings for comparable companies. Then shortly after the *Forbes* article appeared, Corning started facing a series of crises, the most serious of which was undoubtedly the demise of its television business.

By 1966, as a result of a string of technical innovations, Corning held the dominant position in the U.S. market for television picture tubes, and the television business provided nearly three-fourths of Corning's earnings. Yet by 1975, in less than a decade, the television business was almost all gone. Corning no longer made black-and-white tubes, and its color tube business was losing money. What happened? The Japanese. In the late 1960s they had started entering the U.S. market for televisions, first for black-and-white and then for color sets. Gradually they began running American manufacturers like Corning's customers out of the market. By the mid-1970s, imported televisions accounted for over 60 percent of the market for black-and-white sets and over 40 percent of the market for color sets. Corning's base of customers for its tubes had shrunk from twenty-eight manufacturers to only five.

With the decline of its television business and setbacks in other areas, Corning set out in the late 1960s and early 1970s to do what it had always done: it launched a wide-ranging search for new products, hoping to accomplish the next big breakthrough. During this period, Corning pursued development of such diverse products as safety windshields, glass-based lasers, ceramic roofing shingles, ceramic heat exchangers for turbine engines, optical fibers, medical instruments, optical waveguides for telecommunication, glass razor blades, integrated circuits, and even computer terminals. Many of these development efforts, such as the safety windshields, ceramic components for glass turbines, and glass lasers, built upon Corning's historical core competency in glass-ceramics technology. Others, such as efforts to establish a position in medical equipment, integrated circuits, and biotechnology, did not.

There was a marked difference in Corning's success with these different types of ventures. When Corning pursued ventures that were consistent with its core competencies, it was usually successful. When it ranged far afield and abandoned its expertise, it wasn't. David Dukes, Corning's vice-chairman, has said:

> We have concluded that it's going to be very difficult for us [Corning] to compete in the long term, with sustainable competitive advantage, in things that are out of our main area of expertise. When I look at it [Corning's expertise], I look at materials in general: glass, ceramics, glass-ceramics, and the interfaces between these and polymers, metals, and so forth. But to compete in medical, medical diagnostics, biotechnology—it requires an enormous amount of R&D and technology, and we just couldn't compete. So we said: let's try to refocus. . . . Each

time we got too far from our home base, we didn't know enough about the technology or the markets and therefore we had to find partners or sell off technology. We have been able to get into new areas like optical fiber, where we took our knowledge of glass and leveraged that to get ahead into more of the telecommunications business. So we've built an expertise in optics and optoelectronics, and we feel we can compete pretty well with anybody in that. But that's again core stuff for Corning as opposed to medicine or biotechnology.[1]

Corning had learned an important lesson. It was more successful when it did what it did best and only what it did best. Additionally, by sticking close to its core competencies it actually got even better at what it did best over time and gained an even stronger competitive advantage.

Joseph Morone explained in his book *Winning in High-Tech Markets:*

When it has pursued opportunities that grow out of its core technologies, Corning has built on an ever-expanding base of experiences and competencies. Each attempt to develop a new application for its core technology—whether ultimately successful or not—required another round of R&D that not only drove the company toward new products and markets but also enhanced its core capabilities. . . .

Rather than independent forays into new markets, each new attempt to grow a glass [-based] or glass-ceramic–based business is thus part of a stream of efforts, each drawing from and in turn contributing to a growing base of experience. Over time, this base of experience develops into a formidable source of competitive advantage—but only if Corning remains true to its focus.[2]

Being Broad And Narrow At The Same Time

The lesson is a simple one that applies not just to Corning, but to every company. When a company competes on the basis of its unique core competencies, it usually wins. When it extends itself beyond its core competencies, it usually loses. Yet competing on competencies doesn't mean that a company has to narrow its strategic focus to just a few product lines and risk being at the mercy of the upturns and downturns of a narrow segment of a highly volatile market. A company that competes on its core competencies can and does have the best of both worlds. It can produce a wide range of products and compete in highly diverse markets, yet still have a strategic focus and continuity of product and process innovation that it needs to increase its likelihood of success with new endeavors. This approach to strategy has worked well for a number of companies. For example:

- Procter & Gamble has become a $15 billion corporation largely on the basis of its ability to exploit core R&D competencies in five technologies (fats/oils, skin chemistry, surfactants, emulsifiers, and flavorings) and strong core competencies in marketing and distribution. P&G successfully develops, produces, and markets a wide range of products, including bar soap, cleaners, laundry detergent, shampoos, toothpaste, fabric softeners, mouthwash, deodorants, skin-care products, acne drugs, and even bone-disease drugs.
- 3M has exploited internally developed core competencies in abrasives, adhesives, and coating-bonding and has externally acquired core competencies in imaging and instrumentation to successfully develop and market products as diverse as sandpaper, automotive adhesives, pressure sensitive tape, roofing granules, synthetic resins, magnetic recording tape, highway blacktop, overhead projectors, microfilm printing equipment, surgical tapes and gowns, polishing and grinding wheels, fabric protectors, photo equipment, plain paper copiers, floor surfaces, and hearing devices.

And we could add to this list companies like Sony, Canon, JVC, Casio, Black & Decker, Philips, Wachovia Bank, and Banc One. Like Corning, Procter & Gamble, and 3M, these companies also understand their core competencies and exploit what they do best for competitive advantage. (See Figure 5.1) Then, of course, there is Honda.

FIGURE 5.1
Competing on Core Competencies
Some Examples

COMPANY	CORE COMPETENCIES
Sony	electronics miniaturization
Canon	optics, imaging, and microprocessor controls
JVC	videotape technology
Casio	miniaturization, microprocessor design, and ultrathin precision casting
Black & Decker	small electrical motors
Philips	optical media
Wachovia Bank	personal banking and personalized service
Banc One	community-responsive banking

The Case Of Honda

Honda advertises that a home owner can fit six Hondas in a two-car garage. Far-fetched? No. In addition to a car and a motorcycle, the six Hondas may include a lawnmower, a snowblower, an outboard motor, a generator, and even a pump. That's really seven widely diverse products, and Honda makes them all. Yet Honda remains strategically focused on a limited set of activities in which it strives for and usually succeeds in attaining and maintaining a leadership position. It is strategically focused while simultaneously pursuing diverse markets. The historical and strategic focus for Honda is its core competencies in small, high-quality, efficient engines, in assembly operations, and in marketing and distribution.

James Brian Quinn outlines the evolution of Honda's competencies-based strategy in his book *Intelligent Enterprises*. Quinn attributes the creation of "the world's finest team" for designing small, efficient engines, for bicycles, for motorcycles, and for automobiles, to Soichiro Honda's own personal commitment and engineering skills. Honda, he explained, concentrated its development and production resources on engines and created a very small, efficient assembly operation. Within its manufacturing operations, Honda developed extremely low cost capital-intensive facilities focused on those key components necessary to the uniqueness and quality of its motors. Elsewhere it developed the skills needed to manage its supplier networks, while achieving the most efficient small-scale assembly operations in its industry. Simultaneously, Honda used some very innovative financing to build Japan's strongest distribution network for small motorcycles and to bypass its major competitors in reaching the marketplace. Quinn adds that once Honda succeeded with small motorcycles in its home market, the company parlayed its specialized competencies into a steadily broader line of more efficient, well-designed, and higher-powered motorcycles sold through similar unique distribution arrangements in other countries.

Finally, Honda was able to introduce other product diversity by using its core engine-performance, assembly-quality, and marketing-distribution skills. Increasingly, Honda's management recognized that any product which keyed on Honda's small, efficient engines, extensive fabrication logistics system, small-scale assembly operations, and creatively managed distribution networks could be a further natural line extension.

Like Corning, Honda's strategic focus evolved gradually over time. Its core competencies are grounded firmly in its history. The experience of Corning and Honda is typical of most companies that arrive at a competencies-based strategy. Companies usually arrive at an understanding of their competencies through a long stream of experimentation rather than through a conscious, deliberate search. It is only gradually that managers come to realize that "this is what we are good at and where we need to focus." However, there have been some exceptions. Take the case of NEC versus GTE. Unlike Corning and Honda, NEC consciously set out to acquire core competencies it didn't have so that it could compete in an emerging market. By doing so NEC beat out a better-situated rival.

The Case Of NEC Versus GTE

In the early 1980s, GTE was a $9.8 billion company with a variety of businesses spanning telephones, switching and transmission systems, semiconductors, color TVs, and satellites. GTE was perfectly positioned to become a major player in the emerging information technology industry of the time. NEC, on the other hand, was about one-third GTE's size, and although it had a technological base similar to GTE's, it had no experience in telecommunications. Yet by the late 1980s, NEC had passed GTE in total sales ($21 billion versus $16 billion in 1988) and had become a world leader in semiconductors, telecommunications products, and computers. GTE had essentially become a telephone company with some defense and lighting products. What was the difference? Why did the smaller NEC succeed while the well-positioned and much larger GTE never become a major player in information technology?

In the early 1970s NEC's management adopted a strategic focus to exploit computing and communications (the C&C strategy) and to build the skills and process competencies to do so. C. K. Prahalad and Gary Hamel explained in a 1990 *Harvard Business Review* article that

> NEC carefully identified three interrelated streams of technological and market evolution. Top management determined that computing would evolve from large mainframes to distributed processing, components from simple ICs to VLSI, and communications from mechanical cross-bar exchange to complex digital systems. . . . As things evolved further, NEC reasoned, the computing, communications, and components businesses would so overlap that it would be very hard to distinguish among them, and that there would be enormous opportunities for any company that had built the competencies needed to serve all three markets.[3]

Recognizing that NEC didn't have the competencies to compete in all three markets, NEC top management began establishing alliances with business partners to acquire the competencies. Between the early 1970s and late 1980s, NEC entered into over one hundred strategic alliances to obtain access to the technological competencies it knew it needed, particularly in the semiconductor component field. Since NEC's top management had made the C&C strategy clear to everyone, operating managers knew the purpose of these alliances was to gain quick and cheap access to foreign technology and then to internalize the partner's skills. As a result of its strategic focus, NEC emerged as a leader across a wide range of computer and telecommunications products from mobile telephones to facsimile machines and to laptop computers, and by the late 1980s was one of the top five revenue-producing companies in telecommunications, semiconductors and mainframe computers. GTE, which had been in an equal if not better position to pursue such markets, hadn't. The difference was strategic focus and competing on competencies. In NEC's case, the competencies were defined in advance by management and deliberately sought through acquisitions.

NEC, Harley-Davidson, Wal-Mart, Corning, Honda, Procter & Gamble, 3M, Sony, Canon, JVC, Casio, Black & Decker, Philips, Wachovia Bank, and Banc One are just some of the hundreds of companies which have learned that they do best when they understand and exploit their core competencies—in effect, when they discover what makes them unique and do a whole lot more of what they do so well.

The Implications Of The New Strategy

In the past, most companies that competed on their competencies stumbled into an understanding of what they did best through a process of trial and error much like Corning did. As we move beyond Workplace 2000, that is changing. More and more companies are beginning to build their business strategies consciously around the concept of core competencies. Increasingly, American business leaders are recognizing that a sustainable competitive advantage and profitable market position are possible in this new world of business only when a company gains and keeps an advantageous position in core competencies and underlying critical resources. The task of strategic management is becoming one of understanding, adjusting, maintaining, renewing, and enhancing these unique resources and competencies over time. It is a new way of thinking about strategy. And it is a new way of thinking about the business itself. No longer is a business defined by the products it manufactures or the services it offers. It is defined by the competencies it possesses.

What are the implications of this new way of thinking about the business? There are several, and they are all important.

Implication #1: American Business Will Invest In Maintaining, Enhancing, And/Or Exploiting Core Competencies And Little Else

The financial resources of the business will flow to those areas of the business—the projects, programs, units, and divisions—that make a significant contribution to the core competencies of the business. Other projects, programs, divisions, and so on, including those which considered in a different light would be highly valued, will receive little or no support. The limited resources of the company will be invested where they matter the most—in the core competencies.

Implication #2: The "Make-Or-Buy Decision" Will Be Governed By Core Competency Concerns

Core competencies will be protected and kept closely in-house. Other activities will be outsourced. Will a company manufacture its own products or outsource manufacturing to other businesses? Look to the defined core competencies of the firm and you will find the answer. Companies that fail to identify and guard their core competencies will keep inside the wrong things and outsource those things that make them unique and vital. By doing so they will condemn themselves to becoming hollow, unnecessary, untenable shells. They will quickly disappear as they expend all their energies on things they do poorly and neglect or abandon that which they do well. On the other hand, companies that recognize and treasure what they do best will prosper and be unbeatable.

Implication #3: It All Comes Down To Knowledge And Focus

Competency is knowledge and skill made explicit—nothing else. The competency-based firm is a learning organization. It aggressively seeks to enhance its knowledge in its area of expertise—its core competency—and it rewards those whose personal knowledge and skills match the core competency of the business. How will a person find fame, fortune, or the little job security that will be left in this new world of business? How else but by matching one's personal competency to the core competency of the business. Just as the success of the business depends upon the ability of the business to identify, nurture, and enhance a core competency and to match that core competency to the needs, expectations, and aspirations of a target group of customers, so personal success will flow to those individuals who can identify, nurture, and enhance their own competency and match that competency to the needs, expectations, and aspirations of a business. For people and businesses in this new world, it all comes down to what you know and how you are able to create value for others by using what you know. Knowledge is the new basis for personal and business competition and success.

Implication #4: Americans Will Work In Small, Knowledge-Intensive Units

A new strategy—a new definition of the business itself—leads us to new structure. Structure follows strategy, and in the new world of business, we will see structures like none we have seen before. How different will they be? We are moving from organizational structures that have pre-defined channels for the flow of authority and information to organizations that are much more fluid and free-form. In the past we could depict the organization with lines and boxes on a chart. No more. Now, we will be forced to display the organization as an ever-changing pattern of waves on a computer screen. Instead of permanent, pre-defined, and rigid relationships, we are moving toward a style of organizing in which individuals with differing knowledge bases (differing core competencies) come together for varying lengths of time to address customer needs and/or to engage in searches for radical innovation and the much sought-after Ahhh-factor. It is, as we said, a totally new and totally revolutionary concept of the business.

PART III

III

THE NEW STRUCTURES

The business headlines of the late 1980s became so repetitive that they *almost* became boring. They would have been boring, that is, except that the headlines reflected what was happening to so many Americans, their relatives, and their neighbors. Repeatedly in the late 1980s and early 1990s, Americans picked up their morning newspaper to read headlines like

IBM TO SHED ANOTHER 40,000 WORKERS

JOHNSON & JOHNSON TO CUT 3,000 JOBS

GM RETRENCHMENT TO CUT 70,000 JOBS; 21 PLANTS TO SHUT

SUN MICROSYSTEMS INC.'S RESTRUCTURING PLAN MAY COST 1,000 JOBS

TEXAS INSTRUMENTS TO ELIMINATE 6,000 JOBS

SEARS CUTS 6,900 ADDITIONAL JOBS

BOEING TO CUT 27,000 JOBS

AETNA LIFE AND CASUALTY CO. PLANS TO CUT WORK FORCE BY 4,800

SEAGATE TECHNOLOGY INC. GEARS UP FOR BIG LAYOFF

NEW ENGLAND BANK TO CUT 5,600 JOBS THIS YEAR

DIGITAL EQUIPMENT TO CUT 18,000 JOBS AND VACATE 165 FACILITIES

EASTMAN KODAK WILL CUT 10,000 JOBS

Business Week reported on the status of American high-tech businesses in a 1992 article as follows:

> "Think," an industry byword in IBM's heyday, is giving way to "Shrink." It's not just computers that are getting smaller, it's most of the companies that make them too. They're deconstructing—shutting factories, cutting jobs, spinning off subsidiaries, farming out work, and slashing management.[1]

And so they were. But it wasn't just the high-tech businesses that couldn't seem to get enough of getting rid of people. Everyone was doing it. Between 1988 and 1993, 87 percent of U.S. companies undertook some form of downsizing or cost-cutting initiative. Across the board, industry by industry, jobs were disappearing. American business was, as *Business Week* reported in 1993, on a "weight-loss binge. . . . It comes down to this. Top-heavy organizations are out. Slender, nimble ones are in."[2] Jack Welch, General Electric's chairman, put it this way to his stockholders: "We need to cultivate a visceral hatred of bureaucracy."[3]

A "visceral hatred"—pretty strong words, but by the early 1990s, bureaucracy *had* become anathema. Lean management, eliminating unnecessary work and the people who did it, was in. It was all supposed to lead to reduced costs, improved productivity, and greater competitiveness for American industry, but it didn't. The ultimate realization that downsizing isn't enough is leading us to a new organizational architecture and a new set of assumptions about how American business can and must be structured for the year 2000 and beyond.

CHAPTER 6

Downsizing Isn't Enough

Surprise, surprise. American business downsized, and guess what? As wrenching as it all was, it still wasn't enough. Eastman Kodak was all too typical. It restructured five times between 1985 and 1992, absorbing restructuring costs of $2.1 billion and eliminating 12,000 jobs. Still, its stock price languished, its profit margins were halved, and its bottom line remained flat, with virtually no improvement for a decade. And Kodak wasn't alone.

In a survey of 547 companies that had downsized, the American Management Association (AMA) found that operating profits had improved for fewer than half, while 77 percent experienced a decline in employee morale after downsizing. The consulting firm Kepner-Tregoe reported in a November 1992 study that half of the companies that downsized experienced a neutral or negative effect on quality and two-thirds experienced a negative or neutral effect on internal systems such as finance.[1] A leading actuarial firm reported on an even larger study. It examined the results achieved by a thousand firms that had undertaken downsizing in the 1980s and early 1990s. Robert Tomasko, author of *Downsizing*, reported the results of this study in a 1992 *Management Review* article as follows:

- Almost 90 percent of the surveyed companies wanted to reduce expenses, but less than half actually did.

- About three-fourths hoped for productivity improvements, but only 22 percent achieved them.
- More than half wanted to improve cash flow or increase shareholder's return on investment, but less than 25 percent were able to accomplish either.
- More than half expected to reduce bureaucracy or speed decision making, but only 15 percent did.
- Many of these downsizers sought improvements in customer satisfaction and product quality from their reorganizations; others expected to become more innovative or better able to utilize new technologies; but fewer than 10 percent felt they had met their goals in these key areas.

Between 1987 and 1992, over 3.5 million American workers lost their jobs due to the country's downsizing binge, yet profits for too many of the biggest downsizing bingers remained anemic. Worse, for many companies and their management, downsizing—the cure-all drug of the 1980s and early 1990s—almost became addictive. The AMA reported that 63 percent of companies that downsized in any one year would just come back for another round of downsizing the next year. It was the corporate version of crash dieting. Sure, during the diet the weight came off, but as soon as the dieting ended, the fat returned, often with a vengeance. And the repeated corporate dieting-bingeing was wreaking havoc with the workforce and with its trust of and loyalty to employers.

All Stressed-Up And Burned-Out With No Place To Go

In a 1991 survey, the Northwestern National Life Insurance Company found that one in three Americans had seriously thought about quitting his or her job in 1990 because of job stress and that one in three expected to "burn out" at some time in the not-too-distant future if his or her work life didn't change. Physicians were tracing accidents, ulcers, colitis, migraines, heart disease, and a host of other health problems to increased job stress. Additionally, the cost of dealing with these stress-induced problems and the absenteeism and turnover that accompanied them was estimated to be $73,270 per year *per case.*[2]

Even the senior managers who were ordering the repeated downsizings could see the damage it inflicted. Seventy-four percent of the senior managers of companies that had downsized reported their workers had low morale, feared future cutbacks, and distrusted management, according to one early-1990s poll.[3] A *Time*-CNN poll showed that 63 percent of workers felt less loyal to their employers, 57 percent felt their companies were less loyal to them, and 50 percent expected to change jobs within the next five years. Other research showed that one-fourth of the workforce didn't believe what they were told by their managers, two-thirds felt their managers were untrustworthy, and 30 percent were dissatisfied with their workplace.

As their institutions abandoned them, many in the Ozzie-and-Harriet generation, particularly white-collar middle managers who thought they had some kind of social contract guaranteeing them job security, were finding they didn't and were becoming fearful, anxious cynics. Commenting on what he saw happening, Peter Drucker wrote, "The cynicism out there is frightening. Middle managers have become insecure, and they feel unbelievably hurt. They feel like slaves on an auction block."[4] A Georgia-Pacific headquarters manager reportedly moaned, "I'm obsolete. I'm at a dead end. There's no way up. No way down. And no way out."[5] He was undoubtedly wrong about the latter. There were many ways out. Americans could be thrown out, pushed out, sold out, and bought out. They could find themselves "out" in any number of ways and for any number of reasons. The only thing Americans couldn't seem to get out of in the early 1990s was the constant dread that their job might be the next to go.

Organization Assumptions Of Questionable Soundness

Why did American business persist with these repeated downsizing binges, in spite of the evidence that there was much more to getting lean and mean than just hacking off the most visible fat? Robert Tomasko suggested in a 1992 *Management Review* article that behind all of the statistics and stories were several assumptions of questionable soundness about strategy and organization that, at least implicitly, guided most companies' efforts at reorganization and downsizing. Among the assumptions were:

Assumption #1: The Best Way To Deal With Unnecessary Necessary Overhead Is By Frontal Assault

One questionable assumption held by American managers, says Tomasko, is that when times turn tough, as they eventually always do, the best approach to the situation is through head-on overhead reduction. First, each component of overhead is assigned some kind of "value." Then, you start whittling away at the low-value stuff. The only problem is that whittling away just doesn't work. As Tomasko notes, "Overhead frequently behaves like the many-headed hydra—you can cut off one portion, only to find it quickly grows back."

Assumption #2: Clever, Quick Fixes Will Solve Most Problems

Overhead reduction, early retirement programs, two-tier pay systems, pay concessions—these are often nothing more than just clever, quick fixes. They are supposed to make everything better, but they usually end up doing no good at all and not infrequently end up causing damage:

- Companies adopt early retirement programs only to discover that it's their most valuable people who retire early, not the ones the company wishes would go.
- Two-tier pay systems cut the payroll. That's true. What else is true is that they often cut productivity as well. Lower-paid newcomers quickly decide that if they aren't going to be paid as much as their upper-tier peers, then maybe they shouldn't work as hard either.
- Demands for pay concessions often produce only limited concessions but generate tons of employee ill will, work slowdowns, and occasionally outright work stoppages or strikes.

Assumptions to the contrary, quick fixes just don't work.

Assumption #3: Start With Headcount Elimination

Finally, says Tomasko, we have the ultimate boneheaded assumption: "The place to start is with reducing headcount." Wrong, wrong, wrong, says Tomasko. It isn't headcount that must be reduced, it's cost. Unfortunately, heads are visible and therefore vulnerable, but those heads may not even be where the cost really is. Instead of eliminating jobs, we should be eliminating *work*. Instead of outsourcing people, we should be outsourcing *activities*. Instead of cutting the workforce, we should be cutting out the *work*. What's needed is not slash-and-burn downsizing that leaves the work in place and the company vulnerable to a resurgence of hiring as soon as things improve, but a rethinking of the business itself. It's a task, says Tomasko, for an "organizational architect."

Organizational Architecture

What is an organizational architect? It's someone who doesn't just tinker around the edges with an existing organization but steps back and takes a fresh, new look at what the organization does and why. It is someone who asks questions like, "What work really needs to be done here? How? Where? By Whom? If we weren't doing this already, would we start doing it?" Robert Tomasko provides the analogy to architects designing a building:

> At times during the design process, architects will stand back from their detailed drawings and look at the structure they are planning as a whole, as might a pedestrian walking by. They focus on it in relation to its site; how well does it fit, should more earth be moved to make way for the building, or should the building's design be modified to accommodate some unique feature of the terrain?
>
> They will, at other points in their planning, try to understand what they are doing from the inside out. How will the space be perceived by those using it? Will the floor plan of the new office building help or hinder the work done by those who will occupy it? Without the benefit of this shift in perspective, the architect might design a functionless beauty or an efficient eyesore.[6]

Like the architect of buildings, the organizational architect has this dual perspective in planning the restructuring of the corporation. It is a combination big-picture–microscopic view of the business. And it is a challenging balancing act, as Tomasko explains:

> [Organizational architects] balance competing requirements, and they must marry the company's mission with the principles of human behavior. They must plan structures that can distribute a variety of "loads": employee needs, executive's wishes, market demands, competitor's attacks. They must minimize dead weight (bureaucracy and internally directed activities) and maximize the corporation's ability to handle live loads: customer requests and resources needed to meet them. Organizational architects must create organizations that withstand dynamic factors such as fast and aggressive competitors, as well as to be alert to slower-moving dangers such as technological advances and global economic shifts.[7]

Organizational architecture is an approach to organizational design that is quite different from what we have known. It isn't just a process of moving boxes around on a chart, offering some early retirements, or divesting the corporation of a few worn-out businesses. This is something quite different, as Paul Allaire, chairman and CEO of Xerox Corporation and an early organizational architect, explained in a 1992 *Harvard Business Review* interview:

> When most companies reorganize, usually they focus on the formal structure of the organization—the boxes on the organization chart. Typically, top management just moves people around or tries to shake up the company by breaking up entrenched power bases. Rarely do senior executives contemplate changing the basic processes and behaviors by which a company operates.
>
> Until recently, Xerox was no different. In the 1980s, we went through a number of reorganizations. But none of them got at the fundamental questions of how we run the company.
>
> The change we are making now is more profound than anything we've done before. We have embarked on a process to change completely the way we manage the company. Changing

the structure of the organization is only a part of that. We are also changing the processes by which we manage, the reward systems and other mechanisms that shape those processes, and the kind of people we place in key managerial positions. Finally, we are trying to change our informal culture—the way we do things, the behaviors that drive the business.

In fact, the term "reorganization" doesn't really capture what we are trying to do at Xerox. We are redesigning the "organizational architecture" of the entire company.[8]

Allaire was indeed redesigning the organization, and so were numerous other CEOs. In fact, as we entered the mid-1990s, being the organizational architect was becoming one of the key roles for senior managers. Ray Stata from Analog Devices describes this new responsibility for the top dog this way:

> Historically, leaders were referred to as "captains of the ship" to denote their role in operating the vessel entrusted to their care. But future leaders must be both designers and operators. Their principal contribution will be to shape the design of the organization. . . . Expertise in organizational design will be a critical skill—a skill that will require a considerable technical knowledge about how to analyze, modify and stimulate the behavior of complex human systems.[9]

Strategy, Structure, And Behavior

Allaire, Stata, and many of the remaining American business leaders had come back to a basic principle of management that somehow had gotten lost in the heydays of the 1960s, 1970s, and early 1980s—structure and strategy are intertwined. If a new strategy was called for in a new and more competitive and chaotic business world, then a new structure would be necessary also. Why? Because people had to behave in new, more flexible, more entrepreneurial ways. Not only was such behavior unlikely within existing steep, multilayered, solid, hierarchical structures, it probably wasn't even possible. So if the strategy was to change—and it had to change—then the structure had to change as well. Part of the necessary change in structure was to get flatter and weed out the middle level, but that was only part of the change. Downsizing was a necessary beginning, though certainly not enough on its own. That's where the organizational architect came in. A new way of thinking about the form and shape of the business was needed. What might that new form look like? There was no shortage of ideas.

CHAPTER 7 The New Organization

It has no boundaries. It has been compared to a solar system, a symphony orchestra, a spider's web, a cluster, a network, a star burst, a movie set, and a shamrock. It is open, adaptive and infinitely flat. It is both centralized and decentralized, and perhaps most importantly, it is virtual. What is it? It's the new organization the organizational architects are creating. It is fluid and free-form. It is hard to depict with lines on a chart. It requires motion and movement, because it is constantly changing and reforming itself like patterns of waves on a computer screen. It takes a million different forms, so there is no single "it" to describe. But there are a few emerging principles—some architectural guidelines or themes that the organizational architects are following.

Design Principle #1: The Strongest Structure Is One Built Without Walls

That's right. The organizational architects took a close look and what they saw were too many walls—walls between people, walls between businesses, and walls between businesses and their customers. So they set out to change that. General Electric's CEO, Jack Welch, probably said it best in GE's 1990 annual report. He wrote, "Our dream for the 1990s is a boundaryless company . . . where we knock down the walls that separate us from each other on the inside and from our key constituencies on the outside." In

Welch's vision, such a company would remove barriers among traditional functions, recognize no distinctions between domestic and foreign operations, and ignore or erase group labels such as management, salaried, or hourly, which get in the way of people working together.

Design Principle #2: A Lot Of Little Structures Surrounding A Central Core Structure Is A Stronger Setup Than One Big Structure

Call it the Big-Is-Out-and-Small-Is-In principle. The idea is to have a small, central core and then surround it with a number of firms, specialty units, or individuals with special expertise that actually perform the work. Dartmouth professor James Brian Quinn likens this new structure to a spider's web in his 1992 book *Intelligent Enterprise*.

In this new type of organization, numerous independent units or individuals interact with each other regularly for information and support but have limited or no formal, order-giving hierarchy. University faculty members already operate in such organizations, as do consultants in many consulting firms. The individuals or operating nodes in these and other such organizations would be entirely independent if it weren't for the need for the various units or operating nodes to share information or gain benefit in some way from association with a larger entity. Spider's-web organizations differ from traditional organizations in a number of ways:

1. All of the individuals or operating nodes are in touch directly with each other either by electronic or other means, rather than being in touch just with the central authority. There is also relatively frequent exchange of information between the various operating nodes.
2. The individuals or operating nodes function as independent units with few rules, restraints, or restrictions placed upon them by the center or coordinating group. They may even serve customers who are direct competitors of other operating nodes.
3. Relations between the operating nodes tend to be governed by common goals, performance agreements, or operating contracts related to specific joint projects.

4. The center or coordinating group serves as a clearinghouse, collecting and transferring information from and to the various nodes, and provides overall direction, but it has little formal authority to dictate to the nodes.
5. Within the nodes, hierarchies are limited. The nodes, if they have any formal authority structure at all, have an extremely flat one.

Quinn notes that a major driving force for this new type of organization is customers who demand increasing flexibility and responsiveness in the supply of ever more complex products and services. With spider's-web structures, companies are able to assemble best-in-the-world sources of expertise to meet the needs of this more demanding customer. In short, organizational architects are driven to create spider's-web-type structures because these are the structures most likely to produce the gee-whiz Ahhh-factor experiences for customers.

Design Principle #3: The Organizational Architect's Main Challenge Is To Balance The Tensions Inherent In A Spider's-Web Structure

By their very nature, spider's-web structures present a set of contradictions and tensions that the organizational architect must resolve. Homa Bahrami, University of California, Berkeley, professor, examined some of them in a 1992 *California Management Review* article in which he reported on the results of his study of thirty-seven high-tech firms in California's Silicon Valley, all of which were organized in the spider's-web style. Bahrami wrote:

> [These] firms face significant organizational tensions in spite of their relative youth. Irrespective of their size or stage of development, they need to remain disciplined, lean, and focused, requiring minimal duplication of effort, stringent accountability, and effective control and coordination. However, a loose, hands-off management style is needed to manage expectant professionals, maintain a conducive environment for creative thinking, and provide the capability for rapid response to competitive and market developments. . . . They need flexible organizational systems which can balance dialectical

forces—facilitating creativity, innovation, and speed, while instilling co-ordination, focus and control and the staying power to withstand periods of adversity.[1]

Bahrami quotes an internal memorandum from the executive vice-president of a $700 million high-technology firm on the firm's business philosophy that vividly conveys these tensions:

> "We want an environment that enhances individual creativity, but we do not want chaos. . . . We want people involved in decisions that affect their work and we want teamwork, yet we want our employees to have a bias toward action. . . . We want small groups of dedicated workers (decentralization) but such groups may feel aimless or may be charging in the wrong direction with hidden agendas. . . . We want people to stretch to reach tough goals, so our real emphasis is on easily-measured short-term growth and profits—but we should also have time to develop our employees for the longer haul, to promote from within, to monitor the atmosphere for creativity."[2]

How does the organizational architect deal with these kinds of tensions? The Silicon Valley high-tech firms did several things. First, Bahrami notes that, to tackle critical assignments, these firms frequently used temporary project teams whose members were drawn from many different functional units. These highly focused teams were pulled together at short notice to work on strategically significant projects identified by corporate leaders. The teams disbanded once their tasks were accomplished. Additionally, these firms increased their flexibility by relying more heavily than more traditional firms on temporary workers, specialist vendors, consultants, and contractors.

A second tension-reducing tactic of these firms was to seek a balance between centralization and decentralization. These firms had highly visible and involved, often charismatic, leaders and top management teams that set the strategic direction and defined the boundaries within which line operations and the project teams would operate. The front-line operations and teams were then given wide discretion to function however they wanted within the broad but well-defined strategic and cultural guidelines established by the core leadership team. According to Bahrami:

The critical catalyst in creating this alignment is reliance on formal and informal . . . communications channels . . . [including] electronic-based communication, planning sessions and review meetings, informal opportunities for interaction, educational forums, and open access protocols [to ensure] that impending changes in market realities and strategic priorities can be quickly discussed, evaluated, and implemented.[3]

Finally, these firms intentionally sought to be very cosmopolitan. The top management team was often drawn from a number of different nationalities. These firms sought to recruit a highly diverse workforce, and regardless of size, the firms sought to become global very early in their development. Firms that were barely ten years old already had manufacturing, research, and distribution facilities in the United States, Europe, Japan, and the Pacific Rim. Many generated half or more of their sales from foreign markets and had a large population of non-American employees.

Design Principle #4: Nodes Of The Spider's-Web Structure Should Be Spun Off Periodically To Create New Spider's-Web Structures

This principle calls for the continual regeneration of the corporation through the creation of whole new companies. The new companies are created from nodes in the spider's web that may be sold off or partially owned by the parent company, in the latter case being nevertheless free to operate as entrepreneurial ventures. Hewlett-Packard, 3M, MCI, Cypress Semiconductor, Raychem, and Thermo Electron have all operated in this mode. In such organizations, the primary functions of the corporate center is to raise resources, seed the core competency, manage the culture, and set priorities by selecting people and letting them bid for resources. California-based Teknekron Corporation is a good example.

Founded in Berkeley, California, in 1968, Teknekron Corporation specializes in fostering the creation of new, entrepreneurial ventures in information technology. Between 1968 and 1991, Teknekron created eleven affiliated start-up ventures, four of which were spun off for private or public sale. Another dozen or so start-up, entrepreneurial units never made it to affiliate status. That gives Teknekron a success rate in forming new companies of about 50 percent, which is four or five times the normal success rate of high-tech ventures. Harvey Wagner, one of Teknekron's founders, described Teknekron's concept—what he calls an "open corporation"—this way in a 1991 *California Management Review* article:

> The open corporation [is really] a school for entrepreneurs. New matriculates become employees of the corporation with a single charter: to develop a line of business that rapidly becomes profitable and then grows to the stability required for a separate corporate entity. While "in school," they learn both from a formal corporate training program and—perhaps more importantly—from peers who are or have recently been at the same stage of development.
>
> At Teknekron, a start-up usually comprises two entrepreneurs. They are typically quite young (perhaps a year or two from their most recent degree), have a strong grounding in leading-edge technology, and have already shown signs of being winners. While both are technologically based, the pair is optimally a balance between an "outside," sales-oriented person and an "inside," projects-oriented complement. Because of their youth, they are often quite naive about the elements of business. From their backgrounds, they may already have knowledge of salable technologies and at least vague ideas about where the market for these technologies may lie.[4]
>
> When the new entrepreneurs are hired, their first indoctrination is in the elements of marketing and sales. A target market segment related to the entrepreneurs' background and interest is selected, and members of the corporate staff help establish a market focus and accompany the entrepreneurs on a number of initial sales trips. This "learning by doing" is supplemented by tutored viewings of video tapes prepared by corporate staff and by entrepreneurs who have successfully graduated from the Teknekron "school."
>
> Other elements of the training program involve tutelage on such things as negotiating contracts; assuring completion of projects to the client's satisfaction and at a profit; hiring talented personnel and motivating them; and working with a controller. . . . By the time the initial entrepreneurs have graduated from "school," they have grown their unit to 20–25 people and are ready to spin out to affiliate status.

Wagner continued:

> When the entrepreneurs and their now-many colleagues
> have graduated from the school for entrepreneurs, they are
> ready for the corporate stage. An affiliate of the parent open
> corporation is formed. . . . The new company begins a path in-
> volving more and more separation and eventual spin-off from
> its sister affiliates and the parent company.
>
> Spin-out by private or public sale is the event that trans-
> forms "sweat equity" [of the entrepreneurs] into liquid assets.
> It is the major entrepreneurial reward.

Design Principle #5: In Many Cases The Best Structure Is A Temporary One

Whatever form they take, spider's-web structures are frequently temporary. They may stay together as part of the web for
hours, days, weeks, months, maybe even years, but no member expects to remain part of the same spider's web forever. Even if they
are not spun out to form a new web (see Design Principle #4), they
will eventually move on to another team. Whether they are individuals, teams, or businesses, the individual nodes of the spider's web
bring a particular knowledge, skill, or expertise to solve a particular problem or perform a particular task. It is their individual expertise that is important plus their ability to merge their talents
rapidly with those of others in the group. Peter Drucker likens this
new way of working to the way members of a jazz combo or symphony orchestra work. He writes:

> The prototype of the modern organization is the symphony
> orchestra. Each of the two hundred fifty musicians in the or-
> chestra is a specialist, and a high-grade one. Yet by itself the
> tuba doesn't make music; only the orchestra can do that. The
> orchestra performs only because all two hundred fifty musi-
> cians have the same score. They all subordinate their specialty
> to a common task. And they all play only one piece of music at
> any given time.
>
> In the symphony orchestra, several hundred highly skilled
> musicians play together; but there is only one "executive," the
> conductor, with no intermediate layers between him (or her)

and the orchestra members. This will be the organization model for the new information-based organization. . . . Organizations will have very few such command positions. We will increasingly see organizations operating like the jazz combo, in which leadership within the team shifts with the specific assignment and is independent of the "rank" of each member. In fact, the word "rank" should disappear totally from the vocabulary of knowledge work and knowledge worker. It should be replaced by "assignment."[5]

In a similar vein Tom Peters, in his book *Liberation Management*, likens the new, temporary, spider's-web organization to a crew coming together for a video shoot. Such a crew exhibits many characteristics that will be common in the new spider's-web organizations:

1. Each team member is highly autonomous and must work effectively as part of the whole "orchestra." There are no backups, so each person is accountable for getting it right the first time.
2. While some jobs may be more important than others at particular moments, there are no minor jobs. Everyone has to do his job.
3. Since every job is important, people pitch in to help each other out—to support and cover for each other.
4. The whole system is "brittle." There is no second chance. Everything has to go right, and since each member's professional reputation, which is critical to getting future assignments, is on the line, everyone seeks to do their job in a first-class fashion. As Peters described it, "The quality of the bread on tomorrow's table would be determined by maintenance, enhancement, or degradation of the reputation of people whose economic life depends exclusively upon word of mouth."
5. Everyone seeks to learn and pick up tips from others on the team on how to do the job just a little bit better next time.

The new organization the organizational architects are now creating would be impossible without the advances in computers and communication that have been achieved over the last ten years. Information technology is the revolutionary new structural material that makes these new organizational forms possible. Information technology, or the lack thereof, is the reason why spider's-web–type structures would have been prohibitively expensive if not technically impossible just ten years ago but are very possible and even required now.

Technology And The New Organization

In their book *Paradigm Shift*, consultants Don Tapscott and Art Caston outline several critical technological shifts that make the new organization possible:

1. **The microprocessor has brought information processing costs down substantially.** The advent of the microprocessor, which is essentially a computer on a chip, has meant that information processing costs that used to be measured in tens of thousands of dollars are now measured in hundreds of dollars. This reduced cost has meant that instead of processing information on massive mainframes behind locked doors in corporate computer centers, much processing can now be performed at the point of sale, on the service call, in the R&D lab, or in the marketing department. The intelligence of the organization now can be distributed throughout the organization and even beyond, rather than being confined to one or a few specific sites and accessible to only a few chosen people.

2. **We can now join most microcomputers together in networks, moving processing power from the central mainframe to remote microcomputer locations.** That means that users at widely scattered sites not only can share information, but can actually work with and on the same information at the same time. Everyone functions in real time wherever they happen to be. Teams, suppliers, business partners, customers, and even competitors can be electronically linked.

3. **Widespread networking is made possible in part because the entire computer industry is moving from proprietary to open systems.** The industry is consolidating around national and international standards covering everything from communication protocols to database

structures, from user interfaces to operating systems. Such standards make software and information highly portable. Customers, suppliers, teams, and so on can be electronically linked because their individual computer systems share basic protocols that allow them to communicate with each other.

4. **The existence of widely accepted standards means that data, text, voice, and image processing are merging.** In the past, data processing systems handled data, word processing systems handled text, telecommunications systems handled voice data, and photocopiers and microfilm systems handled image data. Now these separate systems are being merged into a single, multimedia system making it possible for individuals and groups to communicate more efficiently, more effectively, and more naturally using the full range of data, text, voice, and image formats.[6]

The Power Of Groupware

These technological shifts are making it possible for people to work together as never before. Let's take a simple example. It has to do with Rick Richardson, a Price Waterhouse executive. On a typical day Richardson arrives at his office, gets a cup of coffee, and instead of going to a meeting, turns on his computer. First, he checks his electronic mail messages, then browses through news articles the computer has selected overnight, following instructions Richardson gave it. Then, it's on to Price Waterhouse's electronic bulletin board covering a thousand different subjects and accessible to Price Waterhouse employees in twenty-two countries. Richardson checks a bulletin board about Price Waterhouse's financial services business, notes an item of interest to him and adds a comment for everyone to see. And so the day goes. Richardson meets and works with Price Waterhouse employees worldwide without ever having to leave his office. In fact, Richardson doesn't really need an office at all. He could have done the same thing from his home.

Richardson has access to worldwide communication because his company has installed a new type of software called "groupware." By 1993, over three hundred software products carried the label "groupware," and many more were under development. Essentially, there are four main types of groupware:

1. messaging-database-network software like that Richardson was using
2. work-flow software designed to help companies streamline business processes and automate the routing of documents and business forms
3. meeting software that allows face-to-face and video-conference participants to "talk" simultaneously by typing their ideas and suggestions into a computer where the ideas are processed and displayed for all to see
4. scheduling software, a kind of electronic date book that allows colleagues on a network to coordinate their meetings[7]

What does groupware allow companies to do that they couldn't do before? How does it change the way companies are structured and the way people work together? Consider the following example of how Price Waterhouse used a form of groupware called Lotus Notes:

> On Thursday a Price Waterhouse executive learned that a major securities firm was about to award a big consulting contract to help develop a complex new trading operation. Price Waterhouse was invited to bid, but there was a hitch: The proposals were due Monday. A Price Waterhouse competitor had been working on its own bid for weeks.
>
> The four Price Waterhouse executives who were needed to write the proposal were in three different states. But they were able to work together using Notes, which allowed them to conduct a four-way dialogue on-screen. They also extracted key components of the proposal from various databases on Notes. From one, they pulled resumes of the Price Waterhouse experts from around the world who could be assigned to the job. From another, they borrowed passages from similar successful proposals.
>
> As the draft evolved each of the four modified it or made comments. Notes kept track of the changes. Other executives looked at the proposal via Notes over the weekend.
>
> The proposal was ready Monday, and Price Waterhouse won the deal. Its competitor didn't even meet the deadline. A

year later the client hired Price Waterhouse to audit the new operation. That contract will probably last for years.[8]

Small Acts Big And Big Acts Small

The power of software such as groupware is that it compels organizations to rethink the way people work. Groupware and the technology that surrounds it literally makes a new kind of organization possible, and it does something more. The new technology lets small companies, even as small as a company of one or only a few, act big, and it lets big companies act small.

In small companies, cheaper desktop computers and advanced software let small companies do sophisticated work like computer-aided design that once only large companies could afford. Electronic networks and communication systems make it possible for small companies to partner easily with other small companies or with large companies to assemble the skills to tackle jobs they couldn't undertake alone. By tapping widely available commercial data bases, small companies can gain access to a depth of business information that once was available only to the largest concerns with the best libraries and research staffs. Finally, the availability of less expensive computer controls and factory automation makes it possible for small manufacturing concerns to match the quality and productivity of the manufacturing giants.

In big companies, more powerful personal computers have freed departments and divisions from reliance upon the central computing center, thus giving them increased power to make their own decisions and exercise greater control over their own information systems. Internal networks and electronic communication systems make it easier for departments and divisions to share information and engage in cross-functional problem-solving efforts. The electronic storage of data on customer purchasing patterns and more sophisticated software for accessing and analyzing this data are making it possible for big companies to develop the kind of intimate knowledge of customer needs, wants, and preferences that only a small mom-and-pop business could acquire in the past. Finally, new manufacturing methods and technology are making it possible for large manufacturing plants to have the kind of flexibility once reserved for small, specialized job shops.[9]

Freedom From Time And Space

Perhaps more importantly, the new technology has done something that was considered impossible in the past. It set information free from time and space. Now, the same information can be distributed instantly to widely different places at precisely the same time. That makes it unnecessary for people who must work together and share information to be physically located in the same place, and it makes it possible for many more people to be involved in working on a project or solving a problem, just as the Price Waterhouse executives did in developing their proposal.

Demands for creativity and innovation are driving American companies to create this new kind of organization. Technology is making this new organization possible. It is also changing the workplace in revolutionary ways. Working will never again be the same. It isn't just a new workplace. It is a new world, where traditional notions of work and leisure and the employee and employer are no longer valid.

PART IV

RESPONDING TO THE NEEDS OF A NEW WORKFORCE

In the 1980s, as American business chased speed and quality, slashed away at corporate staff jobs and middle management positions, and struggled to find new ways to compete, something else was happening throughout the country and in the workplace. American business woke to discover that not only had their competition changed, but that the American workforce itself had changed. American business faced a whole new set of challenges for organizing, managing, and motivating a workforce that was different demographically from any that we had known before. The challenges of responding to the concerns and needs of this new workforce are made even more urgent because of the incontrovertible fact that the success of the small, innovative, knowledge-intensive organizations we are creating depends almost entirely on the dedication, determination, and applied knowledge of the people who work in them. The whole purpose of creating such organizations is to free people to be innovative and creative and to consistently and conscientiously apply their unique skills and talents to generate a continuous string of awe-inspiring experiences for customers. In such organizations, people may not be the only important asset, but they are by far the most critical asset. The cares, concerns, desires, and distractions of the people who work in such businesses take on greater importance for the success of the business. Being a "good place to work" becomes more than just a laudatory goal. It becomes a matter of survival. The reason for that is simple. Those businesses that respond in a meaningful fashion to worker needs and concerns will obtain superior performance from the most capable and talented people in the workforce. Those who ignore legitimate employee concerns and how these concerns are changing as the nature of the workforce changes will attract second-, fifth-, or even tenth-best workers and will get the benefit of their hands but never their minds and hearts.

There was clear evidence dating back to the mid-1960s that major demographic shifts were under way, so we should have been prepared to handle this changing workforce and the concerns the new members of the workforce brought to the workplace. But we weren't prepared then, and as we approach the dawn of the twenty-first century, most American businesses are still struggling to deal with the needs, expectations, and aspirations of the new workforce.

The new workforce is forcing us to rethink many of our most basic assumptions about the nature of work, the meaning of success, and the proper role of business in addressing major societal problems. Perhaps most importantly, the new workforce demands that we rethink the relationship between work and family life and how conflicts between work and family life should and can be resolved. This rethinking begins with a thorough understanding of how the faces in the workplace have changed.

CHAPTER 8

The Changing Faces of
the American Workforce

There is no doubt that the American workforce has changed in dramatic ways. Not so very long ago the American workforce was predominantly white male. Non-Hispanic white males once represented nearly two-thirds of the U.S. workforce. As America approaches the end of the twentieth century, that is no longer the case. (See Table 8.1 and Figure 8.1) Since the 1960s, the proportion of the workforce that is non-Hispanic white male has been declining steadily. If current trends continue, white males will represent less than 40 percent of the workforce by the year 2005, down from 60 percent in 1960.

FIGURE 8.1
U.S. CIVILIAN LABOR FORCE
Percent White Male
1950–2005

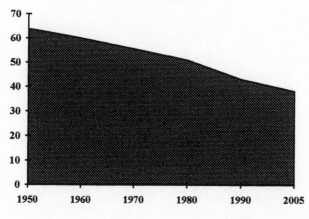

TABLE 8.1
U.S. Civilian Labor Force
Percent White Male
1950–2005

	1950	1960	1970	1980	1990	2005 est.
Percent White Male	63.9	60.0	55.6	50.9	43.1	38.2
Percent Other	36.1	40.0	44.4	49.1	56.9	61.8

SOURCE of data for years 1950 through 1980: Calculated from U.S. Department of Labor, Bureau of Labor Statistics, *Handbook of Labor Statistics,* August 1989, Bulletin 2340, Table 4, "Civilian labor force by sex, race, Hispanic origin, and age, 1948–88."

SOURCE of data for the year 1990 and estimate for year 2005: U.S. Department of Labor, Bureau of Labor Statistics, *Outlook 1990–2005,* "Labor force projections: the baby boom moves on," Table 5, "Civilian labor force, 1990 and projected to 2005, and projected entrants and leavers, 1990–2005," p. 39.

One of the reasons white males no longer dominate the workforce is that women have entered the workforce in record numbers. In 1950, only a little more than one-third of all U.S. adult women over the age of sixteen held a job or were actively looking for work. By 1980, half of them were. (See Table 8.2) The Bureau of Labor Statistics estimates that by the year 2000 over 60 percent of U.S. adult women will be in the workforce. The higher participation rates of women means that by the year 2000, nearly half of the American workforce will be female.

TABLE 8.2
Women in the Workforce
1950–2005

	1950	1960	1970	1980	1990	2005 est.
Number of Women in the Workforce (in thousands)	18,389	23,240	31,543	45,487	58,554	71,394
Percent Female Labor Force Participation Rate	33.9	37.7	43.3	51.5	57.5	63.0
Percent Female Share of the Workforce	29.6	33.4	38.1	42.5	45.3	47.4

SOURCE of data for years 1950 through 1980: Calculated from U.S. Department of Labor, Bureau of Labor Statistics, *Handbook of Labor Statistics,* August 1989, Bulletin 2340, Table 4, "Civilian labor force by sex, race, Hispanic origin, and age, 1948–88."

SOURCES of data for the year 1990 and estimate for year 2005: U.S. Department of Labor, Bureau of Labor Statistics, *Outlook 1990–2005,* "Labor force projections: the baby boom moves on," Table 3, "Civilian labor force and participation rates by sex, age, race, and Hispanic origin, 1975 and 1990, and moderate growth projection to 2005," p. 34, and Table 5, "Civilian labor force, 1990 and projected to 2005, and projected entrants and leavers, 1990–2005," p. 39.

Perhaps more important than the sheer increase in the number of women in the workplace, has been the increase in the number of women who are also *mothers* in the workplace. (See Table 8.3) In 1950, most U.S. women with children under the age of eighteen did not work outside the home. That began to change in the 1960s.

A combination of events and circumstances, including labor requirements, social change, and financial demands, led women into the world of work for pay. By the mid-1970s, over half of women with school-aged children worked and nearly one-third of those with children under two years of age worked. By 1990, three-quarters of women with children in school worked, and over half of all women with children under two years of age worked. Nearly one-quarter of these women were single, widowed, divorced, or separated from their husbands and were the sole support of their families. In the new American workforce, nearly four out of every ten working women had children.

TABLE 8.3
Mothers in the Workforce
Labor Force Participation Rate
by Age of Youngest Child
1975–1990

Percent of Workforce Women with Children	1975	1980	1985	1990
Under 2 Yrs Old	31.8	39.1	48.0	52.0
2 to 3 Yrs Old	41.0	51.0	54.6	61.2
4 to 5 Yrs Old	45.4	54.8	61.7	65.8
6 to 17 Yrs Old	54.7	64.4	69.9	74.7

SOURCE: U.S. Department of Labor, Bureau of Labor Statistics, *Working Woman: A Chartbook,* August 1991, Table A-18, "Civilian labor force and labor force participation rates of mothers by marital status and age of youngest child, March, selected years, 1975–90."

As more women and mothers have entered the workforce, the structure of the American family has changed. (See Table 8.4) Since 1960, the proportion of two-income families has almost doubled, and the proportion of what was considered traditional families—the ones in which the husband was in the labor force and the wife wasn't—has dropped from 61 percent to just 25 percent. Perhaps more importantly, the proportion of children in two-parent families with both parents in the labor force has grown from 36 percent to 61 percent.

The Family Goes To Work

The entry of women, and especially the entry of mothers, into the workforce in record numbers has been characterized as one of the most important developments in the history of the American labor market. Indeed it *is* the most important development, if for only one reason. When women and mothers go to work, family concerns go with them. That hadn't happened before. In the past there was a neat division between work and family. That division no longer exists.

In the old Ozzie-and-Harriet world, Ozzie could go to work for forty, fifty, sixty, or more hours a week and perform his job without worrying about the kids. After all, Harriet was home taking care of them. As far as business was concerned, Ozzie the parent could be treated almost the same as non-parents Joe or Jane. Sure, the business might need to provide optional additional health insurance and other benefits so Ozzie could cover his dependents, but for the most part, family life and parenting placed few additional demands on employees, certainly none that would interfere with their ability to perform on their jobs. In fact, there were actually advantages in Ozzie's being a family man. As the sole breadwinner for his family, Ozzie could be expected to be more loyal and dependable and more willing to do whatever the company asked of him so that his job, paycheck, and future prospects for advancement would be secure.

TABLE 8.4
Family Structure
and Labor Force Status
1960–1990

	1960	1965	1970	1975	1980	1985	1990
Husband in Labor Force, Not the Wife	60.7	55.4	48.9	42.3	35.0	29.3	25.0
Both Husband and Wife in Labor Force	28.4	32.4	38.1	40.8	46.3	49.7	53.5
Wife in Labor Force, Not the Husband	2.1	2.4	2.7	3.7	4.0	4.7	4.7
Neither Husband nor Wife in Labor Force	8.8	9.9	10.3	13.2	14.8	16.4	16.8

SOURCE: U.S. Department of Labor, Bureau of Labor Statistics, *Working Woman: A Chartbook*, August 1991, Table A-17.

When women and mothers went to work in large numbers, that neat division between family and work life changed. With Ozzie and Harriet both at work, there was no one at home with whom family and parenting concerns could be left. Ozzie and Harriet had no choice but to bring their family and parenting concerns with them. That's exactly what they did.

The Not-So-Traditional American Working Family

As America approaches the twenty-first century, it is clear that the traditional demarcation between public economic activity and private domestic activity—between "bread winning" and "care giving"—has all but broken down. So has the allocation of these activities along strict gender lines.

If it is no longer possible for employees to neatly separate work and family, career and the rest of life, then it is equally unrealistic for employers to expect their employees to do so. The family baggage, like it or not, sits right there on the factory floor or in the middle of the office. And there is a lot of baggage, because the American family is in big trouble.

Divorce

In the Ozzie-and-Harriet family, Mom and Dad married for life. They don't any longer. Today, over one-half of all first marriages in the United States end in divorce and nearly 60 percent of all of the people getting divorced have children under the age of eighteen. One million children a year experience the trauma of seeing their parents' marriage dissolve, often in an ugly and protracted dispute in which the kids themselves become barter in the struggle. If current trends continue, fully one-third of all children who were born in the 1980s will see their parents divorce.

Liberal divorce laws in most states make it easy for marriage partners to call it quits. In fact, it is often much easier to go through the simple process of legally ending the marriage than the much more difficult and trying process of figuring out what is wrong and making it better. Exploding drug usage doesn't help. Drugs and alcohol tear families apart. More permissive attitudes toward sex and relationships make marriage seem less the thing to do. In fact, many mothers-to-be, especially teen mothers-to-be, aren't bothering to get married at all.

Unmarried Mothers

Over one-fourth of all children born in the United States today are born to unmarried mothers. Two out of every three black children are born out of wedlock, and one out of every five white children are. Fourteen hundred teenage girls per day become mothers. Two-thirds of these girls are unmarried and only 60 percent will ever receive a high school diploma. Given current trends, by age twenty, 44 percent of all girls in the United States and 63 percent of all black girls will become pregnant at least once. Twenty percent of these teen pregnancies will even be *planned*! The United States has the dubious distinction of having one of the highest birthrates for fifteen- to nineteen-year-olds of all Western industrialized countries.

Single-Parent Households

The high divorce rate and the explosion of out-of-wedlock births means that many American children live in single-parent households. The percentage of white children living with one parent has almost tripled over the last three decades, and the number of black children living in one-parent households has doubled. Now, nearly 20 percent of all white children and over half of all black children live in one-parent families.

Children In Poverty

Frequently, single-parent homes are also poor homes. Almost 45 percent of single-parent households that are headed by a woman—and most are headed by women—fall below the poverty line, compared to only 7.8 percent of two-parent households. Correspondingly, approximately one-half of all children in single-parent families live in poverty, and three-fourths can expect to live in poverty for some period of time, possibly an extended period of time, before they reach eighteen years of age.

Neglect In Effect If Not In Intent

If children in single-parent homes have it bad, children in two-parent households don't find their lives to be that much better. There may be two parents in the family, but they aren't around during most of the day, since both are usually working. Of course there is always "quality time"—those small, precious moments set aside intentionally to make up for long periods of absence. But, for too many families, quality time with the kids really means *little* time with them. As a 1992 *Fortune* article reported, it isn't neglect in *intent*, but it is neglect in *effect*.[1] The sad truth is that many working parents simply do not have time for their kids, and the traditional sources of help for working parents (relatives and neighbors) aren't available. They are working too.

Consequently, many kids end up caring for themselves. By some estimates, nearly 1.4 million kids ages five to fourteen are latchkey kids, left to fend for themselves during much of the day, and as many as 3.4 million kids in roughly the same age group take care of themselves either before or after school for several hours each day. An early 1990s study of 1,650 families with children in Boston public and parochial schools demonstrated just how bad things had gotten. Seventy-five percent of the working parents in that study said they couldn't be home every day after school, and 24 percent said they had to leave for work before their children left for school. Fifty percent of the working mothers said they could not call their children from work or receive calls from their children at work, *even in an emergency*. Yet only 14 percent of these children were in after-school programs.[2] The rest were left on their own, because day care or after-school care either weren't available or, if they were available, were too expensive.

Impact Of Day Care On Kids

Unfortunately for working parents, even day care doesn't appear to be a good solution.

- Some studies indicate that children who receive care from someone other than their mother for more than twenty hours per week during the first year of their life have a

higher risk of later developmental and behavioral problems
than children who receive care from their mothers.[3]
- Day-care infants cry more than other infants when separated
from their mothers and throw more temper tantrums.
- Toddlers who are placed in day care early in their lives display less enthusiasm when confronted with challenging tasks,
are less likely to follow their mother's instructions, and are
less persistent in dealing with difficult problems.[4]
- A Connecticut study of eight- to ten-year-old children found
more misbehavior and greater withdrawal among those children who had been in day care as infants.
- A study of North Carolina kindergarten and first graders found
that children who had early day care are more likely to hit,
kick, threaten, push, curse, and argue with their peers.[5]

Experts agree that quality day care requires well-paid and well-
trained day-care providers, a high staff-to-child ratio in day-care
centers and safe and suitable physical environment for the day-
care site. With such quality day care, the negative effects on children largely disappears. But studies indicate that 60 percent of
pre-school children whose mothers work receive care in private
homes where the quality of the care the children receive is difficult
if not impossible to assess. And licensed day-care centers throughout the United States have their own problems.

Parents can't quite be sure of the quality of care their children
are receiving, even in licensed day-care centers. While the National Association for the Education of Young Children recom-
mends a standard national accreditation procedure for child-care
workers, only a small fraction of child-care workers have any type
of accreditation. In fact, child-care workers, accredited or not, are
hard to find and hard to keep. Nationwide, licensed day-care centers experience an annual turnover rate of more than 40 percent.
In a sense, it isn't surprising that few people want to work in day
care. After all, day-care workers are paid less than most zookeep-
ers, and the job of day-care provider carries less prestige. Parents
can't help but worry about who is caring for their kids.

Then there is the risk to the child's physical well-being. The
Centers for Disease Control found that children who receive care
outside the home are at increased risk of developing minor and
major ailments such as colds, flu, strep throat, infectious hepatitis,
and spinal meningitis.[6] Furthermore, when auditors for the U.S.

Department of Health and Human Services conducted a study of 149 licensed day-care, foster-care, and Head Start programs in 1993, they found a host of problems. Playgrounds were littered with debris. Fire extinguishers in the day-care centers hadn't been filled properly and were, in effect, useless. Toxic chemicals were stored within easy reach of children, and kitchens were filthy and infested with cockroaches.[7]

In some respects it is surprising that the physical dangers aren't worse. The American Academy of Pediatrics and the American Public Health Association reported that half of the states do not even require immunization or hand washing in child-care facilities, and most states, even if they have health requirements, have little staff or funds to conduct inspections and enforce the requirements.

Firearms, Guns, Violence

Then, of course, there is the problem of youth violence. American kids are killing, dying, and bleeding. Homicide by firearms is the third leading cause of death for fifteen- to nineteen-year-old white youths and *the* leading cause of death for fifteen- to nineteen-year-old black youths.[8] The number of children dying from homicide has increased 48 percent since 1984. The number of children arrested for murder each year has jumped 55 percent in the last ten years. More adolescents now die from violence, especially violence involving firearms, than from any other cause, and guns are a factor in 75 percent of all adolescent homicides and over half of all adolescent suicides.[9]

There certainly is no shortage of weapons. There are over 200 million privately owned guns in the United States, and guns can be found in half of all American homes. Every year, 4 million new guns are manufactured in the United States, for civilian use. Over 25 percent of these guns, 1.4 million, are semi-automatic weapons.[10]

Our children are getting these guns, taking them to school, and too frequently using them to kill or maim their classmates and teachers. A national study, conducted by the Centers for Disease Control in the early 1990s, found that 4 percent of high school students had carried a gun to school at least once in the prior month. In a Seattle, Washington, survey, 6 percent of eleventh graders said they had taken a gun to school, and one-third of these gun-toting students said they had actually fired a gun at another person at least once in their life. Some teenagers said "popping" a person was a *noble* act, a matter of pride and honor. Even taken as teen bravado, that is a chilling statement.

For too many American youths, violence is a way of life. The average American child has watched 8,000 murders and 100,000 acts of violence by the time he or she has reached the sixth grade, and not all of this violence is in the movies or on television. Frequently, our children have only to step out their front door to see all the violence they can stand. A ten-year-old who lived in a southside Chicago housing project described his life as follows: "You can't come outside. You got to duck and dive from the bullets. They be shooting most every day."[11]

The Need For Elder Care

As if the lack of quality day care and youth violence aren't enough to make 1990s workers worry, many of them are getting hit from both ends of the age spectrum. One out of four people at work today has some responsibility for the care of an elderly relative. Most of these elder-care caregivers are in their forties, and many of them still have dependent children that add to their burden of responsibilities. These caregivers spend an average of ten hours a week on caregiving, and 25 percent of employees with elder-care responsibilities devote at least some work time to caregiving.

If anything, elder care is even more complex and often more emotionally stressful than child care. To a large extent, child care essentially means arranging for safe and reliable supervision of children during those portions of the day when the parents are working. The level of sophistication of child care diminishes over time as the children become older and more capable of fending for themselves. Elder care, on the other hand, is just the opposite in terms of range of care required and the progression of the care. The National Association of State Units on Aging and the National Council on the Aging, Inc., pointed out the following in an early 1990s report:

- Some aging relatives need only a modest amount of help but on a regular basis; others may need intensive support but for a limited time; and still others need steadily increasing levels of support over a period of years.

- There are more variations in the situation and condition of the elderly (compared to children) by virtue of their age. Older people are adults, ranging approximately from age sixty to one hundred. They have lived for years with responsibility for themselves and often for others. They have the authority for their own decision-making and—unless in a protected status determined by the legal system—have the right to accept or reject help arranged for them.
- Compared to the rest of the population, older people have more health problems. They may or may not be physically able to carry out their personal care and household chores, manage errands, and get themselves to doctors and stores. They may need frequent emotional support, information, and assistance for the activities of daily living, and/or help in obtaining any of these. Aging relatives may live nearby or far away. Even very dependent relatives may not live with a family member who provides most of the care. Responsibility for providing assistance to an older person may be shared among spouses, children, and other family members.[12]

Not only is elder care complicated and stressful, but in most cases, the caregiver has little time to prepare for assuming the caretaker role. Half of the time, the elderly person becomes incapacitated suddenly after a stroke or a fall that results in a broken bone.

Even when the incapacity isn't caused by a sudden illness or accident, it often comes as a shock. Elder-care agencies report a predictable surge in desperate calls for help from middle-aged children right after Christmas. The story is all too common.

A daughter calls to say that she went to her parents' home for the holidays. What she found was troubling and even frightening. Dad had been stopped on the highway for a minor traffic violation, and because he seemed confused and disoriented, the traffic court had taken away his license to drive. Now he can't drive Mom to the grocery store, to the pharmacy, or to her doctor's office. Who's going to drive them where they need to go?

Mom's arthritis had gotten so bad it had become almost impossible for her to dress herself. Unpaid bills were in the trash, including a notice from the utility company threatening to cut off power to their home. There were Social Security checks lying on the kitchen table that had never been deposited, and their checking account hadn't been balanced in months. Mom and Dad, who used to be so capable, were forgetful now, exhibited mood swings, were losing weight, and weren't grooming themselves like they used to. Obviously, something had to be done. But what?

The "what" is care and lots of it. The typical elder-care caregiver looks forward to spending at least five years providing such care. Often, the caregiving has to be performed at a distance, since 30 percent of caregivers live a significant distance from the person for whom they provide care. Eventually, that means hiring someone to perform much of the caregiving, and that becomes very expensive.

In the early 1990s, the cost of nursing-home care averaged more than $30,000 a year—more than $50,000 in larger cities—and many of them cost much more. Since the median net *worth* of the average person over sixty-five was only $73,500 and their average annual income was only $14,000, most seniors faced financial ruin if they required even a modest stay in a nursing home. Medicare, to the surprise of many elder-care providers, doesn't pay for nursing-home care, and Medicaid covers only the very poor. Of course, in many cases, the cost doesn't matter. Quality nursing facilities are in short supply, and the situation isn't getting any better.

The Sandwich Generation

Every day, 5,600 people in this country celebrate their sixty-fifth birthday, and the fastest-growing segment of the U.S. population is the one over eighty-five years of age. Of the latter, only one in four can live alone without difficulty. Families are being forced to choose between paying for a nursing home for an aged parent or paying the college tuition for their son or daughter. It is the "sandwich" generation—squeezed between the demands of the young and the old—and when the baby boomers retire, the demands will only worsen. By 2030 the entire baby boomer generation, a full one-third of today's U.S. population, will be sixty-five or older. Four-generation families—great-grandparents, grandparents, parents, and children—will become the norm, and there will be great-great-grandparents in some families. The "sandwich" is destined to get more layers, and each layer will just add to the demands for care. The "sandwich" generation will be squeezed even harder. Such is the nature of American family life and the family baggage working parents are bringing to the workplace.

CHAPTER 9 Business Impact and Response

How do the worries and concerns that working parents and elder-care providers have about their families affect business? A number of studies in the late 1980s and early 1990s have shown a growing conflict between work and family concerns that impacts employee performance, productivity, and the ability of American businesses to attract and retain workers. For example:

- In some studies, one-half of women and one-third of the men at work said child-care responsibilities interfered with their work. One-sixth of the employed mothers in one national study reported that they had stayed home from work at least one day in the previous month to care for a sick child.[1]
- An AT&T study found that among people with children under eighteen, 73 percent of the men and 77 percent of the women had dealt with family issues while at work. Twenty-five percent of the men and 48 percent of the women said they had spent unproductive time at work because of child-care issues. Dissatisfaction with child-care arrangements was the most reliable predictor of employee absenteeism and unproductive work time.[2]
- U.S. West, a $10.5 billion Englewood, Colorado, telecommunications firm, found that 80 percent of its employees had dealt with family issues during work hours and that one-third had taken off a day or more to deal with family prob-

lems. Seventy percent said balancing work and family demands was causing them job stress.[3]

- In a study conducted by du Pont, 20 percent of employees with elder-care responsibilities said their health suffered as a result of the added stress, and another 25 percent said their marriages suffered.[4]
- In another study, 14 percent of caregivers said they were under such pressure that they eventually switched from full- to part-time work. Twelve percent quit outright, and another 28 percent admitted they had considered quitting.[5]
- In a 1992 survey of working parents, 65 percent of working mothers said they could not continue working without child care. Seventeen percent said they had been forced to quit a job some time in the past due to the lack of availability of child care.[6]
- Twenty-five percent of working parents responding to a 1992 survey said they would change jobs if it resulted in better child care for their children.[7]
- Finally, it has been estimated that five thousand parents reject work offers each day because they cannot find adequate or affordable child care.[8]

The Long-Term Impact

Low productivity, tardiness, absenteeism, turnover, stress, distraction—such is the *short*-term impact of family-work conflicts on business. But there is also a *long*-term impact. The health of the family affects the economic well-being of the nation. Jerry Z. Mueller, associate professor of history at The Catholic University of America and author of the book *Adam Smith in His Time and Ours: Designing the Decent Society*, explained this linkage between family life and the nation's economic growth in a 1992 *Washington Post* article. He wrote:

The long-term economic growth of the nation . . . lies in creating a "high-skill, high-wage economy." But . . . the deterioration of the family is itself a barrier to this favored economic goal. For a high-skilled work force is a highly self-disciplined work force. If the basic institutions that foster self-discipline erode, how will these workers be created?

A highly skilled work force is necessarily a highly educated work force. But how effective can even well-funded schools and highly motivated teachers be if they are confronted with students who have not learned self-discipline at home, whose parents are absent, or unwilling or unable to supervise them? The institutional problems of the family are a cause of economic stagnation, not merely its effect.

The Business Response

In recognition of both the long-term and short-term impact of work-family conflicts on business performance, a number of American businesses have launched initiatives to make themselves "family-friendly." In fact, being family-friendly has become somewhat of a fad. The number of companies offering child-care assistance and other family-friendly programs doubled from 1986 to 1989 and tripled between 1988 and 1993. A host of American companies have hired work-family managers, and the number of candidates for *Working Mother*'s annual "100 Best Companies for Working Mothers" list has increased steadily, surging 30 percent in just one year.

So, what are these companies doing to make themselves more family-friendly? Here are some of the more popular practices.

Resource Referrals

One means of assisting employees is through resource referral. Employees are given lists of approved child-care providers, information packets, and counseling on such things as how to obtain medical care; custodial, housing, legal assistance; additional counseling; and other support for elderly relatives. Resource and referral services have become a popular family-friendly benefit, perhaps because such services are so inexpensive. Child-care resource and referral services cost as little as $10 per employee per year, while elder-care resource and referral services cost from $5 to $15 per employee per year.

Child- and Elder-Care Workshops and Seminars

Other popular options are free lunch-time or after-working-hours workshops and seminars on tips and techniques for meeting and managing child-care and elder-care responsibilities. New England Telephone in Boston, for example, offered employees with latchkey kids an on-site workshop on safe and effective "self-care." The course met for two hours per night, one night per week, for five weeks and covered such topics as how to set up after-school schedules for kids left home alone, how kids should be taught to deal with peer pressure, and home/neighborhood safety.

Child-Care Credit/Dependent-Care Accounts

Many U.S. companies now offer their workers the option of opening a child- or dependent-care account. Employees can place a portion of their paycheck before taxes in these accounts each month. When dependent-care (child-care or elder-care) expenses occur, the employee pays the bill and then is reimbursed from his or her dependent-care account, thus paying for the dependent care with pre-tax dollars.

Direct Financial Assistance

Some companies are now providing subsidies or other financial assistance to help make child care and/or elder care more affordable for their employees. Xerox, for example, established a subsidy that offered each employee up to $10,000 over the course of their career to help pay family-related expenses. Other companies have negotiated with day-care facilities to arrange discounts of 20 percent or more for their employees. Some of these companies go further and subsidize a percentage of the parent's child-care cost through reimbursements or direct payments to the child-care provider to reduce further their employees' out-of-pocket costs.

Long-Term-Care Insurance

To help employees cover the costs of elder care, some companies have begun offering their employees optional health insurance coverage to pay for long-term care for themselves, their dependent children, spouses or parents. Typically this coverage is designed to fill gaps in Medicaid and Medicare coverage.

Emergency Day Care

A number of American companies now offer short-term emergency child-care services their employees can use for a limited period (usually a specified number of consecutive days) when their normal arrangements for child care are disrupted because of the sickness or unavailability of the normal child-care provider. Time Warner, for example, opened an emergency day-care center in the lobby of the Time and Life Building in Manhattan to provide short-term day care for parents whose regular day-care arrangement goes awry for some reason.

Colgate-Palmolive, Consolidated Edison, Time Warner, Ernst and Young, National Westminster Bank, and the law firm of Skadder, Arps, Slate, Meagher and Flom formed a consortium to contract with two child-care providers to provide emergency child care for employees when, for example, a child suddenly became ill or the scheduled day-care provider is not able to perform his or her regular duties. Care is available for up to ten hours a day for up to three consecutive days per employee. Colgate pays the cost of the program for its employees. Other firms have the employee pick up at least a portion of the costs.

On- or Near-Site Adult Day Care

Some American companies actually operate or finance their own day-care centers. For example, SAS Institute, a Cary, North Carolina, software company, provides its employees free on-site child care for children ages six weeks to five years. The center, which was started in 1982, is affiliated with the American Montessori Society, and the majority of the teachers are trained by Montessori. An employee has to work with SAS for one year to become eligible, but once he or she becomes eligible, the only costs to the employee are for the child's lunch and snacks.

Miami-based Bankers Insurance has taken the concept even further. It not only has on-site pre-school day care, but an on-site public school. Established in 1987, the on-site public school was the first publicly supported, corporate-based satellite learning center in the nation. The Dade County school district pays the teachers. Bankers Insurance pays for construction, maintenance, custodial work, utilities, and security, and parents provide transportation.

Stride-Rite, which opened its first child-care center in 1971 in its Roxbury, Massachusetts, facility, has expanded the concept to include elder care. In March 1990, Stride-Rite opened the first intergenerational center in the United States at its corporate headquarters in Cambridge, Massachusetts. The center was designed to accommodate fifty-five children, ages fifteen months to six years, and twenty-four elders sixty and older. Each group has its own wing of the facility, with the wings connected to a common dining area, kitchen, library, and administrative area. The children and elders share reading, story time, and walks. In addition to serving as a child- and elder-care center, the facility also serves as a training and research site for Wheelock College and Somerville-Cambridge Elder Services. The cost of the program for employees is subsidized by Stride-Rite.

Voluntary Reduced Time/Part-Time

Some companies are allowing employees to reduce their work time and pay by 5 percent to 50 percent for a specified period, such as six months or a year, so they can take care of child- or elder-care responsibilities. While on voluntary reduced time, or "v-time," the workers typically retain their health insurance and other benefits, although the amount of the benefit they retain may be prorated based upon the percent reduction in work time they have chosen.

Another example is the company that offers employees what it calls "select time." Under this program, any employee who has worked for the company full time for one year and needs to reduce his or her work hours in order to care for a dependent, such as a child, sick spouse, or elderly parent, can put together a proposal showing how the employee can accomplish his or her job with reduced work hours. If approved, the employee can arrange to work from two to four days per week, instead of the typical five days, while retaining full medical benefits.

Job Sharing

Other companies are offering their employees the option of sharing jobs. With job sharing, two part-time workers share what otherwise would be one full-time job. Steelcase, Inc., of Grand Rapids, Michigan, began a job-sharing program in 1982 and expanded it to hourly workers in 1988. Under the Steelcase program, potential job sharers must be full-time employees who have worked for the company at least one year and can have no supervisory or budgetary responsibilities. The employee has to find a job-sharing partner, and together the partners have to arrange to work a full forty-hour week. The job sharers split benefits fifty-fifty, with the option of buying additional medical coverage.

Compressed Work Schedules

Other companies now allow full-time employees to work a forty-hour workweek in less than five days or an eighty-hour bi-weekly basic work requirement in less than ten work days. For example, an employee might be allowed to work four ten-hour days instead of five eight-hour days, or the employee might be allowed to work five nine-hour days one week and four nine-hour days the second.

Flextime

A popular trend among a number of organizations, including the federal government, is to provide employees with some flexibility in choosing the time they will arrive at work and leave work. Usually, companies define certain hours of the day, such as nine A.M. to three P.M., as "core time," during which all employees must be present each day, and then allow employees to adjust their arrival and departure times around these core hours. Hewlett-Packard, for example, has adopted a flextime program at a number of its locations. Employees may arrive any time between six A.M. and eight-thirty P.M. and leave eight hours later.

Telecommuting/Flexiplace

Finally, some companies have adopted what is considered by many to be the ultimate in flexibility and family-friendliness. These companies allow at least some of their employees to spend all or part of their workweek working from their home. Most companies offering these flexiplace programs require employees to meet performance and other requirements and to obtain their supervisor's approval in order to work at home. Additionally, some companies restrict the telecommuting option to specific types of jobs, such as, at J. C. Penney, telephone catalog sales. Once an employee is approved for at-home work, most companies provide the necessary computers and other equipment. Additionally, some companies, like J. C. Penney and Travelers Insurance, pay for ergonomically appropriate desks, chairs, and lighting. J. C. Penney also requires that the employee's supervisor go to the employee's home prior to the start of the flexiplace work arrangement to ensure that the home has adequate work space.

But Is It Really Family-Friendly?

Referrals, workshops, dependent-care accounts, financial assistance, day-care assistance, flextime, compressed workweeks, flexiplace—American companies are offering an ever-expanding list of family-friendly benefits. But are these so-called family-friendly benefits really family-friendly? Has anything really changed in American business, or is it all just a bunch of hoopla? Some think it's *mostly* hoopla.

CHAPTER 10 Is It Help or Just Hoopla?

Sue Shellenbarger writes the *Wall Street Journal*'s *Work and Family* column. In a 1992 *Human Resource Management* article she summed up what she saw happening as follows:

If the river of press releases crossing journalists' desks in the United States were to be taken at face value, the American workplace is becoming a very family-friendly place indeed.

Companies are rushing to publicize their new child-care referral services, flextime, and other work-family benefits. *Working Mother* magazine and other organizations that rank companies based on their "family-friendliness" are deluged with calls from companies eager to be listed. Judging by appearances, meeting employees' family needs is of great importance to employers today.

But the work-family publicity explosion reflects not so much a solution to an epidemic of work-family conflict, it reflects the basis of the problem. To many companies, fashioning a family-friendly image is nothing more than that—an issue of image, not substance.

Only a few major employers have adopted substantively new policies and programs, and an even smaller number are actually trying to change the deep-rooted American management culture that grew out of the white male workforce of the 1950s. Most work-family policies primarily benefited skilled professionals or a few categories of hourly workers whose skills are in short supply such as nurses. . . . The rank-and-file American worker . . . is mostly untouched by the trend toward family-friendly policies.[1]

We agree with Shellenbarger. While many of these efforts to be family-friendly were grounded in good intentions, the real impact has been minimal. Often, the programs apply only to a small number of a company's employees and fail to provide meaningful assistance to the few working parents or elder-care caregivers the programs do reach. Take resource and referral services as an example. The services are fine as far as they go, but the reality is they don't go very far. Such services help working parents and elder-care caregivers by easing the search for care providers, but they don't help with the much harder task of determining whether that care is *quality* care. Additionally, resource and referral services are of limited value when there is a shortage of affordable and acceptable child- and elder-care providers, as is the case in many U.S. communities. How much help is it for a working parent to have a list of quality care providers that are either fully booked or too expensive?

Employees have similar problems with dependent-care accounts. Such accounts offer workers the advantage of paying for child or elder care with pre-tax dollars, which can be a considerable savings. Yet only about 3 percent of eligible employees participate in such programs. Low-income caregivers in particular find such programs practically useless. As Sue Shellenbarger points out,

> for lower-income employees, the accounts have several major flaws. The paperwork can be daunting, forcing employees to predict their day-care requirements for a full year when they simply may be unable to do so. Second, postponing part of a paycheck, as these spending accounts usually require, can cause cash-flow problems for people on tight budgets. Third, many of the people who most need dependent-care assistance are also most likely to be paying their caregiver off the books, thus being prevented from reporting the caregiver's name and Social Security number to their employer. Finally, the tax breaks afforded by the spending accounts may not be important to them or as attractive as taking a tax credit, making the employer's offer of assistance meaningless.[2]

And what about flextime? It does provide caregivers with some increased control over their work schedule, but the benefits, while generally welcomed by caregivers, are actually limited. In fact, there is some evidence to suggest that flextime benefits those without children more than those with children. That was the surprising finding of two researchers, Halcyone H. Bohen and Anamaria Viveros-Long. Bohen and Viveros-Long studied a variety of flextime programs to determine the effects of flextime on different types of employees. They expected employees with the greatest work-family conflict to benefit the most but found just the opposite. In speculating on why this might be the case, Bohen and Viveros-Long wrote that "parents with young children may be precluded from varying their schedules—even when they have a flextime option—because the logistics of their lives are so fixed. For example, the schedules of the baby-sitter, child-care center, school, or other parent may dictate when they can go to and from work."[3]

Finally, there are the much exalted telecommuting/flexiplace/work-at-home programs. Surely these are true "family-friendly" programs. Not really. While often touted as a solution for workers' child-care problems, flexiplace rarely is such a solution. In one survey, only 8 percent of respondents who chose to work at home said that their primary motivation was to have more time for their family. Over one-quarter of employees working at home cite the "difficulty of separating personal and work life under such a work arrangement" as a major *disadvantage* of working at home, not an advantage.[4] In fact, two-thirds of the professionals and one-third of the clericals who work at home say they still need to use some form of child care while they work, particularly if they have pre-school children.

Interestingly, the primary justification for work-at-home programs may have nothing to do with resolving work-family conflicts. Instead, having employees work at home may provide significant advantages to businesses and society in general by reducing the need for office space and commuting. Flexiplace, if used widely enough, eventually lessens the need for new or expanded facilities and drastically reduces traffic congestion and the related cost of building and maintaining a transportation infrastructure.

Decidedly Family-*Unfriendly*

The truth is that while the highly touted family-friendly initiatives of most American companies sound good, they actually benefit few working parents and elder-care caregivers. While 35 percent of companies say they have work-at-home programs, few have more than a small percentage of employees working at home. Less than 5 percent of eligible workers take part-time offers, and less than 1 percent of those who are eligible try job sharing. The reality is that employee access to progressive programs varies widely, not only between companies, but even within a single company. Employees' options frequently depend upon the job they hold and, more importantly, on their supervisor's willingness to allow them to exercise their options. In reality, many supervisors respond in decidedly family-*unfriendly* ways. Consider the following situations:

- A successful regional sales manager asks her boss if she can take her nanny and nursing infant with her to a national sales meeting. The answer? "No! This is not a vacation. It's a business meeting."
- A public relations writer discloses to a prospective employer that she is trying to have children. The response? The job offer is immediately withdrawn.
- A man admits that he regularly parks his car in the lot furthest from the office complex so he can avoid passing his boss at five-thirty P.M. when he has to leave each day to pick up his children at their child-care center.
- After an experienced office worker changes to a part-time schedule because of child-care problems, she is the first to be released in a layoff because of her "unusual work arrangement."

When Family Leave Became Law

Perhaps nothing illustrates the predisposition toward the family-unfriendliness of American businesses as vividly as the business response to the Family and Medical Leave Act of 1993. The act, which had been vetoed on two previous occasions by a business-friendly Republican administration, was passed by Congress and signed into law by President Clinton on February 5, 1993. The law covers all businesses with fifty or more employees working twenty-five hours or more a week. It requires that employees of such businesses be allowed to take up to twelve weeks of unpaid leave each year to recuperate from a serious illness or to take care of a new child or sick family member. Employers have to continue to provide health care benefits during the leave. Upon return to work, the employee must be given back his or her old job or be placed in an equivalent position. Although the provisions of the act are far less generous than those of similar laws in Japan and Western Europe, which provide longer and paid leave, it was roundly attacked by conservative pundits and defenders of small and large businesses alike.

Many small-business owners and persons claiming to speak on behalf of small-business owners voiced their fear that when the act became effective in August 1993, the personnel costs of small businesses throughout the country would suddenly skyrocket. Masses of employees, they maintained, would take advantage of the new law and go on leave. Small businesses would be forced to hire temporary replacements, while continuing to pay exorbitant benefits to the workers on leave. Operating costs, they added, would shoot up and already slim profit margins would erode further, and eventually, masses of small businesses would be forced into bankruptcy and have to close. Thousands would lose their jobs. That was their dreadful scenario.

Others voiced concern about the impact of the Family Leave Act on employment opportunities for women. *The New York Times* quoted concerns expressed by Tana Starr, president of Artkraft Strauss, a New York City–based manufacturer of neon signs and sports scoreboards, as follows: "If you're an employer, you will look at a young woman and say, 'Can we really entrust her to do crucial responsibilities that no one else can do because she's going to take three months off?' . . . You protect women so they can nurture babies and that's very nice, but you keep them on the lower end of the pay scale."[5]

Still others expressed their fears that the act would take what had always been an informal, loose-knit, unspoken, owner/supervisor discretionary policy and make it a legal right and administrative nightmare. Worse, some suggested, the Family Leave Act would be just the beginning. Soon, the government would be issuing broader mandates, including paid leave, and the law would be extended to cover smaller employers and employees working fewer than twenty-five hours per week.

To protect themselves from what they saw as certain disaster, some business owners and managers took preemptive action. The advocacy group 9 to 5, the National Association of Working Women reported a flurry of complaints in the summer of 1993. Most of these complaints were made by pregnant women who reported that they had been fired just to get them out of the way before the law went into effect. The National Federation of Independent Businesses reported that many of its member small-business owners were saying that they would avoid hiring additional workers or would hire only temporary workers in order to keep their payroll under the law's cutoff of fifty employees. And at least one earlier study reported many small-business owners as saying that, with a Family Leave law in effect, they would think twice about hiring young women who might become pregnant. There was, in short, much growling, snarling, threatening, and chest pounding. But the act took effect anyway, and all of the fears and concerns appear to have come to *nothing whatsoever.*

The law took effect and very little happened—good or bad. Six months later, large and small employers were reporting few ill-effects from the new law. A survey conducted by the Institute of Industrial Relations at the University of California, Berkeley, concluded that small businesses had felt the impact of the law *less* than large companies, not more. In California, for example, the institute found that 90 percent of the employers had experienced insignificant or only minor increases in administrative costs as a result of the law, and the 4 percent of businesses that had incurred major expenses to achieve compliance with the law were all employers of over ten thousand workers.

In reality, the law had little impact on most companies. Few eligible employees actually exercised their rights. The doomsday predictions that employees would take leave in droves for everything from Johnny's sniffles to a worker's sprained ankle were totally unfounded. Maybe it wasn't too surprising. After all, most companies did little more than post a notice about the law and take the few steps necessary to comply minimally with its provisions. Most employees, to the extent they understood their legal rights at all, were reluctant to exercise them, since they understood the unpleasant consequences that might follow. One owner of a small business told *The New York Times,* "I can't imagine anyone here taking 12 weeks—they'd suffer ostracism."[6] Employees understood. The Family and Medical Leave Act had done little to prod employers into implementing new or improved work-family policies. For example, a 1994 survey conducted by the Alexander Consulting Group, a Newbury, Massachusetts, consulting company specializing in human-resource issues, revealed that in spite of the Family Leave Act

- over half (54 percent) of responding companies still had no formal work-family policies beyond those mandated by law;
- 83 percent had no manager or committee to deal with work-family conflict issues; and
- in almost one-third of the companies, senior managers were still saying that work-family programs are not very important or not important at all.

So much for legally mandated family friendliness.

The truth is that corporate brochures may talk about how companies are becoming family friendly, but, as the *Wall Street Journal* reported, the way business is actually conducted is "antithetical to a family-friendly workplace. . . ."[7] Paul Kingson, associate professor of sociology at the University of Virginia, adds that American businesses' response to work-family conflict so far has been, at best, "halting, uneven, and shallow."[8] Of course, some people felt that was the way it should be. In fact, they felt that American business, if anything, had perhaps gone too far to accommodate work-family concerns.

The Case For Doing Nothing Or, At Least, Not Much More

As we entered the mid-nineties, no one seemed totally happy with the response of American business to work-family conflicts. On one side were the advocates of family-friendly policies and practices who were shocked at how superficial the response of American business had been to family needs. On the other side, there were those who were convinced American business had already gone too far. Their argument went something like this:

The business of business, they argued, is creating jobs, and that's what business should stick to. American companies shouldn't open a Pandora's box of raised expectations, employer liability, and possible unfairness toward workers who aren't parents or elder-care caregivers by getting involved in this work-family squabble. The only obligation of business, they said, was to treat employees with dignity and respect. People should be respected as individuals with the intelligence and ability to solve their own problems, including the problem of how to balance work with family demands.

Employees who had problems in balancing work and family life should be treated with compassion, insight, and respect, of course, but employers didn't need to create a whole host of new programs to deal with such concerns. In fact, it would be wrong to do so, they argued. Special programs, particularly those with the word "care" in their name, such as "elder care," "child care," and so on, did more harm than good, since all they did was to make employees dependent. That was the last thing American business needed. Instead of dependent employees, American business needed employees who were productive and *independent*.

The best thing to do about the work-family "care" programs was to get out of them. Anyway, the whole work-family conflict was mostly media hype. Instead of running stories about family-friendly workplaces, the media should be running stories about how many of these supposedly family-friendly companies had laid off workers. What families really needed in this country, they argued, wasn't more family-care programs but secure employment. That's what American business should focus on.

The employer's role was to provide a safe and hopefully secure workplace. If an employee had a family issue to take care of, then he or she should just take time off to deal with it. Time off was the only benefit employers needed to provide. Let the employee go to his or her manager with a request and see whether some time off could be worked out on a paid or unpaid basis. That was the only equitable way to handle work-family conflicts. It had to be done with compassion, but on an individual basis. Elaborate family programs weren't needed.

That didn't mean that some so-called family-friendly programs weren't appropriate in some situations. Flexible work schedules, job-sharing programs, and so on might be worth pursuing. But they should be handled on a case-by-case basis and they shouldn't be limited to workers with family responsibilities. If a single person with no children wanted to work a flexible schedule and could be more productive by doing so, there was no harm in such a work arrangement. But that was something for the individual and his or her boss to decide.

What it came down to, those against broader work-family programs argued, was a matter of choice. Choice on the part of the business and the worker. Businesses had to be free to structure jobs any way they wanted. The only question should be, "How could the job be performed most effectively?" If that meant long hours or frequent relocations or inflexible schedules that might put some workers at a disadvantage because they had family responsibilities, so be it. The business had the right to set the requirements for the job. The worker could choose to meet those requirements or not. If, for whatever reason, the employee was unwilling or unable to make the commitment and meet the requirements, he or she didn't have to work for the company.

Finally, those against work-family programs argued, there is the issue of fairness. After all, there are many people who don't have children or other family responsibilities. When business sets up family-friendly programs, people without family responsibilities are not only excluded but often have to suffer some negative consequences. Family-friendly flexible schedules for those without family responsibilities often just mean that people aren't available when they are needed and that the task of getting the job done just gets that much harder. Childless employees end up filling in for parents who take off to care for their children. Yet when the same childless workers need some time away from work to take care of their own personal matters, they don't get the same support. And it is the childless employees in companies trying to be "family-friendly" that get stuck working weekends and holidays or taking the undesirable business trips. In short, being "family-friendly" often just isn't fair.

So went the arguments of those opposed to what American business had already done to address work-family concerns. The struggle over what to do about work-family conflicts had turned into what the *Wall Street Journal* called a "family feud." There was heated debate over how deeply employers should involve themselves in workers' lives. Were work-family conflicts legitimate business concerns? If so, how could and should American business get beyond the hoopla to provide real help? As we entered the last half of the nineties, there was no consensus on how to answer these questions. But some new approaches for dealing with the issue of work-family conflicts were emerging. They required, of course, addressing the issue in an entirely new way.

CHAPTER 11

Getting Beyond the Hoopla to the Real Issue

So, what is the answer? If referrals and dependent accounts and flextime and work-at-home and all the other work-family initiatives we have been trying are not enough—and may not even be the right thing to do—then what *should* American business be doing? How can we go beyond the halting, uneven, and shallow to begin making real changes? And is the issue really about work-family conflicts and the concerns of the sandwich generation alone, or is it about something more? We think the issue isn't just a work-family issue, but indeed is about something much broader. The real issue extends to new notions about career patterns, definitions of success, and the proper relationship between work and the rest of life. This isn't just about resolving, or at least managing, the conflict between work and family life, although work-family conflict certainly is at the core of the issue. In a broader sense, the issue we are dealing with under the rubric of "work-family conflict" involves resolving the conflict between work and life itself. How can we address this broader issue? Here are some ideas about what we can and should be doing to move beyond the "family feud" and hoopla that amounts to good public relations and not much else. Here are some ideas about what we need to be doing to offer real help not just to workers with family responsibilities, but to all workers in the new workforce.

We Need To Address The Broader Work-Family-Conflict Issue As A Societal Problem Requiring Community-Wide Responses

One of the first things we need to do in our efforts to address the broader issue of work-family conflicts and work-life conflicts in general is to recognize that problems like child care and elder care are not going to be solved or even significantly lessened by companies working alone, solely through internally focused programs. Businesses have a role to play in addressing the problems, but alone businesses can't solve the problems. Concerns like how to provide child care and elder care are community-wide concerns and require community-wide solutions. We will begin making progress only when American companies begin sponsoring programs that help the *communities* in which they operate, not just their own employees. Fortunately, we already have some models of what those community-wide and collaborative efforts might look like.

IBM, NationsBank, Nynex, and a number of other companies have established multimillion-dollar funds to improve and expand child care in cities where they have large numbers of employees. Specific programs funded by these efforts include such things as the recruitment and training of additional day-care workers, the expansion of day-care facilities, the creation of before- and after-school programs where none existed before, the extension of operating hours for child-care facilities to align more closely with parents' work hours, and so on.

Other companies have taken the funding concept even further by entering into collaborative efforts with dozens of other companies. The most notable example of such a collaborative effort and the largest to date is the American Business Collaboration for Quality Dependent Care (ABC) launched in September of 1992 by 109 U.S. companies and 28 public and non-profit organizations. Collectively these organizations have pledged to invest $25.4 million in 44 communities to finance some 300 child- and elder-care projects over a two-year period. While these types of community-focused efforts may not be the total solution, they provide a much-needed boost to the quality and availability of child care and elder care.

We Must Decouple Face Time From Performance Evaluation

"Face time" and performance are still linked in the minds of too many American managers and supervisors. Employees continue to report that their managers and supervisors equate how many hours employees are visibly at work with the level of their contribution. Employees say that working at home or working when your supervisor isn't present—for example, early in the morning under a flextime arrangement—doesn't count. That's one of the reasons so few employees actually take advantage of alternative work arrangements that are available to them.

In a 1992 *Human Resource Management* article, Charles Rodgers, a principal of Work/Family Directions in Boston, told a story that illustrates what happens all too often when employees take advantage of alternative work arrangements. Rodgers's story was about Edward, a young engineer for a major technology company. Edward had worked for the company for over seven years and had developed an excellent reputation. His performance appraisals had always been outstanding. Then Edward decided to arrange his work schedule to arrive at six-thirty A.M. and leave work at five-thirty P.M. so he could spend more time with his school-aged sons and coach their sports teams. Everything seemed to work out fine: Edward was happy with the arrangement and his performance didn't suffer. Then he had his annual performance review. That's when Edward's manager told him that he had serious reservations about recommending Edward for a promotion, since Edward left the office at five-thirty, whereas his peers worked until seven. The supervisor said that that made him wonder whether Edward could be counted on and whether Edward truly had the "right stuff" to move up the ranks.

Such obsessive focus on face time simply has to stop. We must judge people on their performance, not on the hours they are in sight. Decoupling face time from performance evaluation not only will make American companies more family-friendly by enabling employees to experiment with a wider range of alternative work arrangements, but ultimately will make American companies more customer-friendly and stockholder-friendly. Why? Because *what gets measured gets done*, and when we start measuring and evaluating people based on performance—what gets done—rather than on face time, employees will starting performing rather than just putting in time.

We Must Remove The Stigma From Non-Linear Careers

In the American business tradition of the Ozzie-and-Harriet world, careers were supposed to be linear. A person's résumé was expected to show steady, uninterrupted advancement from one level of salary and responsibility to the next higher level. It was assumed that something was wrong if a person had gaps in employment or a record of advancement that wasn't continuous. The person's career was seen as stalled and his or her prospects for future advancement were subject to question.

But, these were assumptions that were applied, almost exclusively, to Ozzie's career. Historically, Harriet's and other women's work experiences have always suffered temporary interruptions and detours that had no relationship to their competency or seriousness about their careers. As we approach the turn of the century, assumptions about the linearity of careers are becoming as invalid for men as they have always been for women.

Men's career patterns and paths are becoming more like the traditional woman's experience and are being determined by many of the same constraints and influences. Like women, men are beginning to experience career interruptions as well as dual-career and parenting demands. Instead of being on the "fast track," men are increasingly finding themselves on a "slow-burn" to success, with careers that are marked by detours into and sojourns in the contingent (part-time, temporary, contract) workforce. As men's work-life experiences become more like those of women, American business must begin to accept the reality of the non-linearity of careers.

We also need to start thinking about career tracks that provide ample recognition of the legitimacy and importance of parenting for both women and men. In a 1989 *Harvard Business Review* article, Felice Schwartz proposed a "mommy track." Schwartz argued that there were two groups of women managers, those who considered their careers to be their chief priority and those who were both career-oriented and family-oriented, and that the two groups should be treated differently. Career-primary women could be expected to work longer hours and could be promoted and relocated like a man. Women oriented to both career and family would accept lower pay and little advancement in return for a flexible schedule. Women's groups vigorously opposed the idea of a "mommy track." These groups and others saw the proposal as just one more way to lock women out of executive positions and further harden the glass ceiling.

Schwartz's idea never really took off, but maybe it is time to revisit it. This time, however, instead of a "mommy track," how about "family track" for both men and women? How about a track that recognizes children and parenting as central to the welfare of society? How about a track which assumes that a career that alternates between work and family is legitimate, worthwhile, and rewarding. After all, today's children are tomorrow's workers and consumers. To ignore the special needs of parents not only results in increased absenteeism and tardiness, lost productivity, and heightened job stress in the short term, but has significant long-term consequences to society and to future economic and business prospects. Why not publicly recognize that *business and society* will suffer in both the short and long term if the work-family conflict is ignored. Such a recognition obviously means that we must engage in some rethinking of how work is performed.

We Must Reengineer Work With The Family In Mind

In the early 1990s, American business finally came to the conclusion that drastic changes in the way businesses were organized and run were needed if we were to get further improvements in product quality, customer satisfaction, cost, and speed. We finally realized that we could no longer just jury-rig new technology and new work methods onto old, outdated work processes. We had to start with a clean slate and totally reengineer the business with the customer in mind. Now we need to do the same thing with respect to work-family issues.

We must challenge the assumptions and rethink the rules governing work arrangements and business careers. We need to design the processes by which work is performed and the policies by which value is measured from a different set of assumptions about the proper relationship between family and work life. We need to adopt new assumptions such as the following:

- Work processes must be designed with the understanding that no employee, whether male or female, is willing or able to make a 100 percent commitment to a career any longer and that even if some people are willing to make such a commitment, they shouldn't be encouraged to do so. Such one-sided commitments are not in the best long-term interest of business or society.
- Work and family are linked, not separate, activities. Each sphere of life impacts on and is impacted by the other. Therefore, in designing work arrangements, we must consider how the work arrangements affect the family and how the family affects the work arrangements.
- Every employee, whether a parent or not, has and should have responsibilities, desires, and interests that extend beyond the workplace. We should make it possible for people to make their life their career, not their career their life.
- Women are needed in responsible positions in the workplace, and men need to participate in the raising of children. Business *and* society benefit when women and men perform both career and nurturing roles.
- Family is as important as work. Therefore, the focus of business policies and practices with respect to the work-family relationship should not be on how to minimize the impact of the family on work (i.e., getting family members taken care of without adversely affecting work), but rather on designing work policies and practices that actively support the family.
- Finally, today's children are tomorrow's workers and consumers, so the long-term economic well-being of the society is dependent upon the quality of care children receive today. Designing work arrangements and work processes with the needs of America's children and America's working parents in mind is good for business.

If these assumptions were followed in reengineering business practices, what kind of organization might we create? Obviously it could take a thousand different forms, but it might incorporate some of the elements found in HCI Consultants, Inc.

HCI is a computer consulting firm, based in Herdon, Virginia, that among other assignments provides computer training courses for federal government employees. Founded in the late 1980s, HCI has some unique features. First, HCI staff members set their own work schedules, putting in two to five days a week. They work as much or as little as they want. Second, all staff members have similar backgrounds and are cross-trained so that if a member of the staff has a family conflict or other problem and can't teach a class, someone else can cover for them. The staff calls this "company share." They share work and swap hours as needed. They even baby-sit for each other in emergencies. When not teaching classes, many HCI staffers work at home writing reports or developing training materials. Staffers stay in touch by fax and phone and hold a regular monthly dinner meeting that covers, in addition to business topics, such family topics as child care and what to do about sibling rivalry. In a July 1993 article, *Working Mother* magazine called HCI "a model of flexibility." Indeed it is. It also may be a model of the kind of small, family-sensitive, and family-supportive entrepreneural business organization of which we will see more in the future.

We Must Rethink The Definition Of Success

Ultimately we need to rethink how we define career and personal success. The traditional national definition of success has been largely a male definition based upon the notion that success is best measured by salary, title, position, and number of levels from one's position to the top of the organizational hierarchy. Such a definition of success doesn't make sense anymore. Salaries have become highly variable. Titles have disappeared or become meaningless. Every position is, at best, insecure, and now everyone is just a few levels from the top. Today, success must have more to do with how one feels about one's career and one's future prospects than about salary, title, position, or the other traditional measures. A true definition of success today must be more holistic and, yes, more subjective—more like the traditional female definition of success.

Women have always incorporated such subjective feelings in measuring their success. The female definition has also typically expanded the concept of "success" beyond the workplace to include satisfaction, not just with work and career, but with relationships and family. It is a more holistic view of life and the role of work in life. It is also a view of life that more and more Americans are adopting.

Not so long ago, the American hero was adrenaline-pumping and career-driven. The prevailing wisdom was that you couldn't work too hard or too long. Sixty-hour workweeks gave you warrior status, and exhaustion for overwork could be worn as a badge of honor. Not anymore. American men, as well as women, have begun reassessing this 1970s and 1980s superdevotion to money and career. A 1993 *Working Woman*/Roper poll reported the following:

- Fifty-three percent of the respondents said their definition of what it took to be successful had changed in the last five years.
- Eighty-six percent said they now would rather make an adequate salary doing a job that makes the world better than earn a lot of money.
- Sixty-three percent said that if they felt their job was secure, they would trade a raise for more free time.
- Fully two-thirds said that making a lot of money wasn't as important to them as it had been five years before.[1]

Two-thirds of the working parents in another national survey conducted at about the same time said they would gladly take a pay cut to have more time with their family. In the same survey, 45 percent of men and 64 percent of women said they would turn down a promotion if by accepting it they would have to give up time with their family.[2]

Respondents to the *Working Woman*/Roper poll said that the most important sign of success was not how much money a person had, but whether the person had a happy family life. Second was having enough time for friends and relatives, and third was being in control of their lives. Those were the signs of success. Asked to choose among a list of things that would make them feel personally successful, the survey respondents listed money, career, and power *dead last*. When asked to elaborate on their own personal definitions of success, the respondents said things like, "I'm not interested in making a lot of money anymore," and "Family and kids are more important . . . more of a success than having a good job."

As we approach the end of this century, the unspeakable is being voiced. Americans are publicly questioning how hard and how much people should work. Even *Fortune* magazine has said, "It is easy to forget that hard work is not inherently good or moral, but only as noble as what you are striving to achieve."[3] Richard Louv, a columnist for the *San Diego Union*, quotes a Wichita working parent who expressed what many Americans are beginning to think: "Maybe we need to start questioning how many things we need, and whether it's really worth it to work this hard and be away from our children so much."[4]

We Must Make The Family Visible

Lotte Bailyn, a professor of management at MIT's Sloan School of Management, summarized the American family-career rules of our recent past. She said, "[F]amily, according to traditional US career rules, needs to be invisible at work, to be dealt with only at the margins."[5]

Americans now recognize that there is a price to pay for dealing with family and life outside the workplace only in the margins and that the price of a career-only focus may be just too high. Americans are beginning to think they can and must do better. That's why they are insisting that the family and non-work concerns become visible again in society. They are looking to American business to respond. The businesses that will be *in business* in the future *will* respond, because they know success in the new world of work depends on one asset more than any other—their employees, with all their knowledge, skill, and creativity. And they know that the best people won't share their knowledge, skill, and creativity without receiving something in return.

PART V

LEARNING AND THE NEW WORKPLACE

In the new world of work that we are creating, businesses will compete on the basis of their competencies, the collective knowledge resident in the corporation, and not on the basis of their product-market positioning alone. In short, they will compete on the basis of their ability to learn. Consequently, a key to global competitiveness will be the pace, efficiency, and extent to which American businesses can acquire new knowledge. The problem we face in creating and sustaining this new "learning organization" is that American businesses haven't been very efficient in or focused on learning in the past. In fact, most American businesses have severe and chronic learning deficiencies.

The Learning-Disabled American Business

In a 1991 article in the *Strategic Management Journal*, Gary Hamel of the London Business School examined the results of a study of nine international business alliances. These alliances were formed during the 1980s between American, European, and Japanese firms. Each alliance offered the companies involved the opportunity to learn from each other.

Hamel was interested in determining what contributed to or detracted from the alliance partners' ability to learn. He found that there were several broad determinants of whether and how much a partner in an alliance learned from the experience. Two of these broad determinants, what Hamel calls "intent" and "receptivity," are important because of what they say about the learning deficiency of American firms. "Intent" is defined as the extent to which one or both firms viewed the collaboration as an opportunity to learn. "Receptivity," on the other hand, involved the capacity of each partner to learn from the alliance. American businesses fared poorly on both determinants compared to the Japanese.

A Lack Of Intent

First, there was the problem of intent. The Japanese firms participating in the alliances Hamel studied had, in most cases, explicit intent to learn from the alliance. American firms just didn't seem to care that much. This "lack of intent" was important because, said Hamel, "in no case did systematic learning take place in the absence of a clearly communicated internalization intent." When there was an explicit intent, the employees involved in the joint project understood the importance of learning and learning occurred. When no such explicit intent was expressed by management, little or no learning occurred. One manager of an alliance partner that *did* learn from the experience explained his company's approach as follows, "We wanted to make learning an automatic discipline. We asked the staff every day, 'What did you learn from [our partner] today?' Learning was carefully monitored and recorded."

Contrast that with the American manager who said, "Our engineers were just as good as [our partner's]. In fact, theirs were narrower technically, but they had a much better understanding of what the company was trying to accomplish. They knew they were there to learn; our people didn't." And that pretty much summed up the American experience. The Japanese came to American-Japanese alliances having the intent to learn and being prepared to learn. Americans didn't have such intent, so American businesses didn't go away from the alliances with new skills or enhanced competencies, as did the Japanese.

Hamel found that American and other Western partners in alliances often ignored prime opportunities for learning. There was almost an American arrogance about learning, particularly if the American partner was large and the Japanese partner was small. Hamel quotes a Japanese executive as saying, "When we saw [our larger Western partner] doing something better, we always wanted to know why. But when they come to look at what we are doing they say, 'Oh, you can do that because you are Japanese,' or they find some other reason. They make an explanation so they don't have to understand [what we are doing differently.]"

A Lack Of Receptivity

Perhaps it shouldn't have been too surprising that the Americans were poor learners. In contrast to the Japanese, most American executives saw no real payoff from learning. To them, running the business wasn't about competencies or skills, but about end-products and markets. The top management in these firms had no appreciation for the need to acquire, maintain, and build corporate-wide skills, so they and their companies made no investment in doing so. As Hamel points out, for many of the American firms, "alliances were viewed as shortcuts to a more competitive product line (by relying on a partner for critical components or perhaps entire products), rather than as shortcuts to the internalization of skills that could be applied across a range of businesses."

In addition to intent, Japanese and American firms differed in how receptive each was to the other. Invariably, the Japanese saw themselves as students of their Western partners, and eager students at that, while the Americans and Europeans most often positioned themselves as teachers. "Humility," said Hamel, "may be the first prerequisite of learning," and the Americans, in particular, were anything but humble.

Finally, American businesses were much more likely than their

Japanese counterparts to suffer from a kind of fragmentation of learning and knowledge that made organization-wide learning difficult. Hamel points out that many of the American businesses lacked "a mechanism for 'summing up' individual learning, i.e. first recording and then integrating the fragmentary knowledge gained by individuals" and for transmitting this newfound knowledge throughout the organization to those who could most benefit from it. Hamel quotes a senior Japanese manager who compared the Japanese and American/Western approach as follows:

> Within [my firm] there is a great deal of mutual responsibility. Responsibility is a very gray area in Japan; many people are involved. There is much more overlap in responsibility than in [our Western partner] where information seems to be compartmentalized. [Our partner] thought we asked too many questions, but in [my company] information is shared with many people even if they are not directly involved. Engineers in [one department] want to know what is happening in design [in another department] even if that is not related to their direct responsibilities.

This Japanese manager's Western counterpart said:

> In joint meetings, staff groups [from our Japanese partner] would almost always be multi-disciplinary, even for technical discussions. [They] clearly wanted to understand the implications of our technology. You had the feeling that most of [their] people who were sitting in the [joint] meetings were there only to learn. We would have never taken anyone into such a meeting without a direct interest in what was discussed.

It was that kind of attitude that caused American businesses to miss totally the learning opportunity in alliance after alliance and encounter after encounter. Worse, in many of these alliances and other contacts with the Japanese, American businesses not only failed to learn new skills, but actually found themselves significantly "deskilled" by their Japanese partners. It wasn't just a matter of an occasional inadvertent leakage of key competencies but the aggressive sucking out of knowledge and skill by our Japanese partners, who had a much greater appreciation for organizational learning than we did. Fortunately, that is now beginning to change.

The Learning Organization

In the late 1980s and early 1990s, a number of American businesses started paying more attention to the issue of organizational learning. Leaders in companies like Home Depot, 3M, Wal-Mart, Heinz, Southwest Airlines, Levi Strauss, and Motorola have come to the conclusion that managing, controlling, directing, and facilitating learning in their organizations is a key role of management and that what, how much, and how fast their organizations learn or fail to learn has important strategic implications. At least three national institutes have been created at major U.S. universities and research sites to study the issue of organizational learning. The research of these institutes and the learning experiments at the core of leading American companies are beginning to pay off. The American "learning organization" is gradually becoming a reality. How is such an organization different from what we have known before? What is it like to work in such an organization? Learning organizations are very different and very demanding. They have to be, because the true "learning organization" has to overcome a lot of obstacles.

CHAPTER 12 How Individuals and Organizations Learn

How do individuals and organizations learn? Most of us, if we think about the process of learning at all, probably think of learning as something that takes place in the classroom, where an individual interacts with an "expert"—someone who knows and, by a variety of means, transfers information to someone who doesn't know. It is analogous to copying data from one floppy disk to another. Learning, we think, is mostly an individual, passive activity that somehow is separate and distinct from work. And we think that the most important kind of learning, at least as far as the workplace is concerned, is the kind in which employees learn the company's explicit skills, rules, procedures, and so on—the stuff taught in the typical corporate training program. We couldn't be more mistaken.

Thanks to some ground-breaking "learning" research, we now know that

- real, effective learning isn't individual, but social;
- true learning is anything *but* a passive activity; and
- the most important stuff for people to learn in organizations isn't the explicit stuff of rules, procedures, and so on, but the messy stuff of tacit learning.

Tacit learning is the stuff of intuition, judgment, expertise, common sense, group core competencies, and texture—the rich, nourishing soup of information that is imbedded in the seeming chaos of the workplace. This most important kind of learning at work takes place, and in fact must take place, as part of the course of work itself. Real learning is not a solitary process by which learners acquire abstract, objective, individual knowledge. Real learning is the acquisition of the skills needed to function in a workplace community where people share ways of doing things— ways of talking, beliefs, values, and practices—as a result of their joint involvement in a work activity. Finally, we now know that these shared assumptions and beliefs, especially when they are deep-rooted and go unchallenged for lengthy periods, can stand in the way of organizational growth and change. We know, in short, that what the organization has learned in the past may inhibit what it can learn in the future.

The Cycle Of Learning

So how do people and organizations learn? What is the link between individual and organizational learning? What stimulates learning, and what causes it to break down? What must be made explicit for the learning organization to exist?[1] To answer these questions we first need a definition for "learning."

The dictionary says learning is the acquisition of knowledge and skill, but knowledge and skill aren't the same thing. *Skill* has to do with the acquisition of know-how—the ability to produce some action. *Knowledge* has to do with the acquisition of know-why—a conceptual understanding. If real learning ultimately means that one's capacity to take effective action is increased, then the acquisition of *know-how* and *know-why* are both important. One isn't truly useful without the other.

Daniel Kim, learning-lab research project director at the MIT Center for Organizational Learning uses the following example to illustrate the importance of having both *know-how* and *know-why* skills:

> [A] carpenter who has mastered the skills of woodworking [the know-how] without understanding the concept of building coherent structures like tables and houses [the know-why] can't utilize those skills effectively. Similarly, a carpenter who possesses vast knowledge about architecture and design but who has no complementary skills to produce designs can't put that know-why to effective use.

How do people acquire know-how and know-why? Or, in other words, how do people learn? Essentially, people learn through a continuing cycle of experience. People have concrete experiences, and they reflect upon those experiences. Based upon those reflections, they form concepts and generalizations. They test these concepts and generalizations in new situations, and that testing leads to new experiences. Then the whole cycle is repeated. (See Figure 12.1)

FIGURE 12.1
THE OBSERVE-ASSESS-DESIGN-IMPLEMENT (OADI)
Cycle of Individual Learning

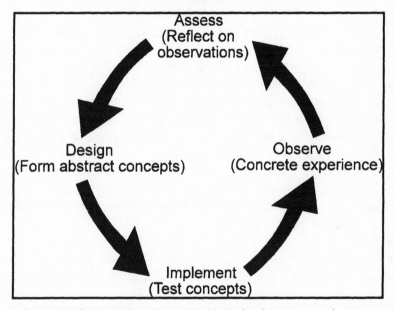

SOURCE: Daniel H. Kim. "The Link Between Individual and Organizational Learning," *Sloan Management Review,* Fall 1993.

Of course, the knowledge and skill (the know-why and know-how) gained from these cycles of learning aren't lost. The learning is stored in memory where it can be retrieved for later use.

Typically, we think of this human memory as just a storage device, analogous perhaps to a hard disk on our computer, but such simple analogies are incorrect. Human memory is used for storage, that's true. However, it is much more sophisticated than just simple storage. Not only does what we learn affect our memory, but, as Kim points out, *"what we already have in our memory affects what we learn"* (emphasis added). Over time, we don't just pile up unrelated bits and pieces of information in our brain cells. No, over time the abstract concepts we have been developing and testing in our learning cycle begin to pile up inside our heads. We develop notions, assumptions, ideas, and theories about the world. We develop "mental models" in our brain of how we think the world works. Our mental models can be simple generalizations such as "people are untrustworthy," or they can be complex theories about business, economics, politics, consumer behavior, and so on. Regardless of whether they are simple or complex, these notions have a powerful impact on individual behavior. In discussing mental models, Kim writes:

> Mental models represent a person's view of the world, including explicit and implicit understandings. Mental models provide the context in which to view and interpret new material, and they determine how stored information is relevant to a given situation. They represent more than a collection of ideas, memories, and experiences—they are like the source code of a computer's operating system, the manager and arbiter of acquiring, retaining, using, and deleting new information. But they are much more than that because they are also like the programmer of that source code with the know-how to design a different source code as well as the know-why to choose one over the other.

Everyone develops mental models. They are a natural part of human existence. Over time people within organizations develop shared mental models—shared assumptions about the world, about the way things get done and the way things should get done based upon their own shared experiences. These shared mental models become the organizational equivalent of the individual mental models that have so much impact on individual learning and behavior.

Some of these organizational mental models become codified and turn up in organizations as the manuals, documents, policies, and procedures that spell out what is done and why. But this codification is always only a small portion of the organization's memory.

Regardless of how bureaucratic an organization happens to be, there is always more information in the heads and hearts of people than what is written on paper or stored in the computer files and cabinets of the organization. Think of mental models as the index to the rest of organizational memory (the paper, computer files, and so on). Without the mental models, the rest of memory becomes essentially unusable, because the interconnections, linkages, and interpretive principles that give meaning to the bits and pieces of data are lost. That's why turnover in businesses is so costly. It is not just that the organization loses "how-to" skills when an employee leaves: the organization loses a piece of its memory. If there is too much turnover, then the organization can't accumulate learning or even retain learning and quickly becomes dysfunctional. As Kim points out, the loss of people and their shared mental models can be much more devastating to a business than any physical disaster.

Imagine an organization in which all the physical records disintegrate overnight. Suddenly, there are no reports, no computer files, no employee record sheets, no operating manuals, no calendars—all that remain are the people, buildings, capital equipment, raw materials and inventory. Now imagine an organization where all the people simply quit showing up for work. New people, who are similar in many ways to the former workers but who have no familiarity with that particular organization, come to work instead. Which of these two organizations will be easier to rebuild to its former status?

Most likely, retaining all the people will make it easier to rebuild than retaining only the systems and records. In the first scenario, the organizational static memory is eliminated, but not the shared mental models of the people. In the second scenario, individual mental models and their linkages to the shared mental models are obliterated. Thus when new individuals come in, they have their own mental models that have no connection to the remaining organizational memory.

Communities Of Practice

How do people share their mental models? According to the Palo Alto–based Institute on Learning, one way is through participation in and becoming part of what the institute calls "communities of practice." The institute defines a "community of practice" as "a natural occurring and evolving collection of people who together engage in particular kinds of activity, and who come to develop and share ways of doing things—ways of talking, beliefs, values, and practices—as a result of their joint involvement in the activity."[2] Communities of practice provide the setting/context for organizational learning. They are significant because they represent the way individual mental models get shared. What exactly is a community of practice? What does it look like? How is it created? Here is an example.

In the 1980s, J. Orr, a doctoral student at Cornell, studied service representatives at a large corporation. Orr was investigating how the service reps *actually* performed their jobs, as opposed to the way the work was described in the corporation's manuals, training courses, and job descriptions. His detailed descriptions of the service reps provide a good example of a community of practice and illustrate how such a community develops.[3]

The service reps Orr studied were responsible for repairing the company's machines. They had been provided training and detailed repair instructions. The intention of the documentation and training—the step-by-step approach to diagnosis and repair—was to simplify the service reps' job. Essentially, all the service rep had to do was to note the error code shown on the machine's display, look up the error code in the repair manual, and follow the detailed repair instructions provided in the manual. In reality, the company-provided repair instructions frequently were inadequate. To perform their jobs, service reps often had to develop sophisticated work practices that went far beyond the diagnostic and repair procedures outlined in the detailed repair manuals and official instructions.

As Orr observed the way in which service reps actually performed their work, as opposed to what their official job description said, he discovered that, for the reps, learning extended far beyond the classroom and that their integration of learning and working was an occupational necessity. When confronted with a problem that fell outside their training and one that didn't fit the predetermined "solutions" outlined in their repair manuals, the service reps had no choice but to resort to their own working-learning approach to problem solving. John Seely Brown and Paul Duguid summarized some of Orr's findings in a 1991 article describing a typical working-learning experience as follows:

On one service call a rep confronted a machine that produced copious raw information in the form of error codes and obligingly crashed when tested. But the error codes and the nature of the crashes did not tally. Such a case immediately fell outside the directive training and documentation provided by the organization, which tie errors to error codes. Unfortunately, the problem also fell outside the rep's accumulated, improvised experience. He summoned his technical specialist. . . . The specialist was equally baffled. . . .

Solving the problem . . . required constructing a coherent account of the malfunction out of the incoherence of the data and documentation. To do this, the rep and the specialist embarked on a long story-telling procedure. The machine, with its erratic behavior, mixed with information from the user and memories from the technicians, provided essential ingredients that the two aimed to account for in a composite story. . . .

Ultimately, these stories generated sufficient interplay among memories, tests, the machine's responses, and the ensuing insights to lead to diagnosis and repair. . . .[4]

What is the significance of the service rep story from the standpoint of organizational learning? Just this. Storytelling is critical to organizational learning and the development of shared mental models. For the service reps, the practice of creating and exchanging stories helped them make sense out of a seemingly random series of events in order to arrive at an understanding of what caused the machine to fail. That is much richer "learning" than the reps received in their formal, company-sponsored training. As Brown and Duguid point out, "Unlike the documentation, which tells reps *what* to do but not *why*, the reps' stories help them develop casual accounts of machines, which are essential when documentation breaks down. . . . What the reps do in their storytelling is develop a causal map out of their experiences to replace the impoverished directive route that they have been furnished by the corporation." And the storytelling not only helped individual reps solve unusual problems, but served as a basis for transmitting knowledge within the organization, therefore helping the entire organization to learn. Brown and Duguid noted that "an important part of the reps' skill, though not recognized by the corporation, comprises the ability to create, trade, and to understand highly elliptical, highly referential, and to the initiated, highly informative war stories. . . . [S]tories . . . act as repositories of accumulated wisdom."

The other characteristic of the service reps' work is that it is communal and collaborative. Reps work with specialists and other reps to trade stories, develop insights, construct new ways of performing their work, and, over time, develop a *shared understanding* or *view of the world*—a kind of rep's view of the machine—that may be totally different from the views of managers, trainers, engineers, and others in the same organizations. Of course, this shared view of the world is highly useful. The reps would, in fact, be much less efficient and effective without such shared understandings. Yet there is a danger here. The mental models that the reps develop and that others in the organization develop can get in the way of further learning.

The Problem Of Mental Models

Mental models, both those of individuals and the shared mental models of communities of practice, are enormously powerful and useful. Our individual mental models help structure our individual actions and help us make sense of the multitude of experiences that bombard our senses daily. Our organization's mental models define those things to which the organization as a whole pays attention, how individuals within the organization respond to problems and opportunities, and how the leaders of the organization interpret its environment and respond. Mental models help people and organizations cope, but these same mental models, both individual and organizational, can also impede learning.

For all of their power, mental models are basically nothing more than classificatory schemes, structures, and ways of organizing what would otherwise be an unmanageable flow of human and organizational life. They are maps of reality and nothing more. The danger is that over time they can *become* something more. As the mental maps we construct work for us and lead us to repeated success, we can forget that the mental models we invented even exist. The models of reality we have constructed can become our reality, and when that happens, learning is slowed or even stops and our responses to the world can become dysfunctional. What used to work under a different set of circumstances doesn't work anymore, but locked in our view of the world, we are unable to understand what isn't working or why. In *The Fifth Discipline: The Art and Practice of The Learning Organization*, Peter Senge, author and director of MIT's Center for Organizational Learning, described just how that happened to the American automotive industry in the 1970s and much of the 1980s. According to Senge,

> for decades, the Big Three of Detroit believed that people bought automobiles on the basis of styling, not for quality or reliability. Judging by the evidence they gathered, the automakers were right. Surveys and buying habits consistently suggested that American consumers cared about styling much more than about quality. . . . These beliefs about styling were part of a pervasive set of assumptions for success at General Motors:
>
> GM is in the business of making money, not cars.
>
> Cars are primarily status symbols. Styling is therefore more important than quality.
>
> The American car market is isolated from the rest of the world.
>
> Workers do not have an important impact on productivity or product quality.
>
> Everyone connected with the system has no need for more than a fragmented, compartmentalized understanding of the business.
>
> . . . These principles had served the industry well for many years. But the auto industry treated these principles as "a magic formula for success for all time, when all it had found was a particular set of conditions . . . that were good for a limited time."

Of course, American automakers clung to these beliefs (these mental models) too long, and German and Japanese automakers, who educated American consumers to the benefits of quality, captured nearly 40 percent of the domestic market by the mid-1980s.

Was the problem that Detroit had a mental model that emphasized styling over quality? Not really. Detroit's problem was that the automakers didn't *recognize* their mental models. The models had ceased being models and had become reality for the automakers. As Peter Senge explained, the Detroit automakers didn't say, "We have a *mental model* that all people care about is styling." They said, "All people care about is styling."

One of the chief ways in which the new learning organization will differ from any we have known before will be in its efforts to bring to the surface and challenge these individual and shared mental models. How will this be done? One way will be through meetings known as "dialogue sessions."

CHAPTER 13 Dealing with Our Mental Models

Imagine a meeting at which there is no agenda, no leader, and no task for the group to perform. Imagine a meeting where the whole purpose isn't solving problems but rather improving conversation. That meeting is a dialogue session, and it is something we will see more of in the organization of the future.

If holding meetings for the sole purpose of promoting and improving conversation seems strange, consider that Alan Webber, former editor of the *Harvard Business Review*, has argued that the most important work in the new economy is promoting conversations and that some writers conceive of organizations as essentially nothing more than networks of conversations. Think of the importance of conversation and storytelling to the work, learning, and effectiveness of the communities of practice we discussed earlier. Think of the importance of conversation as a way of uncovering and challenging the deep-rooted mental models that can inhibit change.

The reason we need dialogue sessions or something like them is because increasingly we are putting together groups of individuals from differing cultures and differing communities of practice in order to generate innovative solutions to problems. Yet these individuals bring to the group conversations their own ways of talking and their own beliefs, values, practices, and meanings, each of which can stand in the way of communication. When complex or volatile issues are being discussed, communication failures can prevent groups from dealing with the issues effectively. Dialogues are special kinds of structured conversations or group meetings that attempt to overcome such communication failings.

Dialogue is different from just good face-to-face communication, like the active listening so many teams were taught in the 1980s, although active listening is practiced in dialogue sessions. Active listening focused on improving communication by having people pay attention not just to the spoken word, but to body language, tone of voice, and so on. People were taught to focus on what the other person was saying rather than on framing a response to what was said. In dialogue, people are taught to focus on their underlying assumptions in order to uncover and make explicit their mental models. Ultimately, the goal of dialogue is for the group as a whole to develop a common language and a common thinking process that will allow the group to generate more creative and innovative solutions to problems.

Dialogue sessions are designed to help members of groups to overcome the tendency, particularly of cross-functional or multicultural groups, to drop into debate before fully exploring all of the ideas potentially available in the group. What happens is all too common. In the course of practically any group meeting or conversation, people start weighing different views as they are expressed. Individuals pay close attention to some things that are said and completely ignore others. Inevitably there comes a point at which one or more parties to the group discussion sense they have been misunderstood or that their ideas are being challenged. When that happens, the natural tendency of the misunderstood party is to offer more explanation, question the challenger, or launch into a debate. People begin defending their point of view while declaring others to be either somewhat or totally wrong. The group quickly becomes polarized as individuals take sides in the argument. Learning stops as people focus on winning the argument rather than on continuing to explore options.

Dialogue sessions are quite different. Normally, at least in the early stages, the sessions have a facilitator, who explains the dialogue concept to the participants, intervenes in the sessions as necessary to help the participants clarify what is happening, and closes the sessions by asking everyone to comment on the process. A typical dialogue session runs about two hours, and sessions are held every two to three weeks.

The ground rules for a dialogue session typically include the following:

1. Participants agree that if they begin to feel that they are misunderstood or are being challenged during the session, they won't immediately act upon their feelings, but will simply let the matter go (i.e., suspend their reaction). In other words, instead of launching into a defensive debate of their views, the participants agree just to let the conversation continue in the hope that as a result of further conversation the misunderstanding will be resolved and/or the issue will be clarified.

2. Participants agree to leave their positions at the door and act as colleagues. They agree that, except for the facilitator, who is there to keep the session on track, there will be no particular hierarchy in the meeting. To emphasize that everyone is equal during the meeting, people sit in a circle.

3. Participants agree to use the meeting to explore the thinking behind their views and to reach a deeper understanding of their beliefs and assumptions and those of the others.

4. Finally, participants agree that the purpose of the dialogue session is to explore the dialogue process itself and for the participants to gain some understanding of it. The meeting is unlike other meetings they may have attended in that the purpose of the dialogue session is not to make a decision or solve an external problem.

Having established the ground rules, a facilitator typically opens the first session by asking everyone to think of an experience of "good communication" and to comment on that experience.[1] With that, the conversation begins. As it progresses members of the group begin weighing different views and ideas that are expressed. They pay attention to some things that are said and ignore others. Eventually, as in all conversations, the point of misunderstanding or disagreement is reached. So far the conversation has proceeded as normal, but now a decision point is reached. People must decide whether to drop into debate or abide by their agreement to suspend their reaction and let the dialogue continue.

People vacillate. They switch back and forth between dialogue and debate. They become frustrated. During the debate extreme views may be stated and defended. The whole room heats up, and people start getting anxious, even angry. Some participants go silent. Others yell. The facilitator helps the participants begin seeing what is happening in the room, perhaps by drawing a map of the ongoing conflict like the one in Figure 13.1. Participants are forced to reflect on the nature of their conversation and what is happening in the room. If they weather the crisis and stick with dialogue, the dynamic changes.

FIGURE 13.1
A CONFLICT MAP

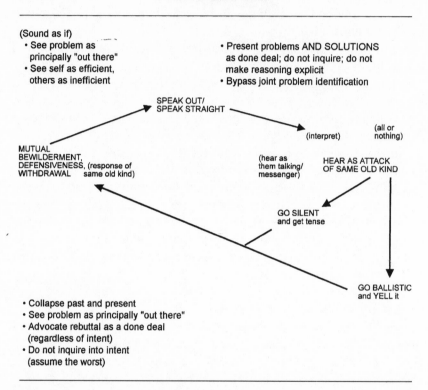

SOURCE: William N. Isaacs. "Taking Flight: Dialogue, Collective Thinking, and Organizational Learning," *Organizational Dynamics*, Autumn 1993.

The participants begin truly suspending reaction. They stop categorizing things. They start listening. They start thinking about how and why they think and react and why they behave the way they do. The whole environment in the room begins to cool down. Participants start observing subtle things like how people in the room differ in the pace and timing of their speaking and thinking. People begin to notice how the flow of the conversation affects everyone in the room, and they begin to realize that there is a deeper meaning behind the ideas that are being expressed.

Eventually, as the dialogue sessions progress, the group begins to understand and discuss the assumptions (the mental models) behind what people are saying. They begin to recognize the fragmentation of their own and others' thinking and the impact that fragmentation has on the group and their organization. Eventually, the group begins to develop a shared set of meanings, or a common language. Individuals in the group still may disagree, but the rhythm and pace of the thinking and conversation is different. The group begins to speak and think together and to explore new, breakthrough ideas derived from the collective thinking of the group itself.

Dialogue sessions can lead to extraordinary changes in communication patterns. Take, for example, what happened at one steel plant. Labor and management in this plant had a history of confrontation. Labor-management meetings frequently ended in shouting and even violence. Both groups were skeptical that there could ever be any reconciliation or trust between them. Yet faced with stiff competition from other mills, they finally agreed to enter into a series of dialogue sessions. William Isaacs described the results of the sessions after one year in his 1993 article in *Organizational Dynamics:*

> They learn[ed] to inquire into the assumptions behind their thinking. This free flowing exchange . . . not only allowed new insight, it . . . altered fundamental assumptions about the union's relationship to the business. The union president, speaking about the progress they had made, put it this way:

> > When we first started [the dialogue sessions] . . . the only thing that we ever talked about was the past: How you've screwed me in the past. How you've lied to me in the past. How you went from 5,000 workers down to 1,000. How you've promised us job security and right on down the line. You know, we don't hear that any more. That went away. That's gone. Now we're looking at the future. . . .

> People report change of this sort across the group. . . .
> . . . For the first time managers and union personnel have been talking together and thinking about the business. . . .
> Over the months, there has been a remarkable change in the pattern of relationship and quality of inquiry among this

group. After one recent session, a union man said, "You know, I can't tell who is on what side anymore." Initially the union men would never disagree with each other publicly, in front of the managers. Their story was singular: all problems in the plant were the managers' faults, and any new program or plan was essentially intended to take advantage of them. Now some months later, they openly disagree and inquire with one another, and they challenge one another to think together, instead of separately.

Perhaps even more important than its effect on helping members of diverse and sometimes warring groups improve their communication, dialogue also appears to help people uncover, challenge, and break free of the kind of deep-seated mental models that have made American industry blind to the need to change and incapable of learning. The reflective thinking which dialogue sessions engender helps individuals and groups come to grips with how they divide the world into categories and make distinctions between categories.

Eventually, people are able to see that while these categories are helpful in reducing the complexity of the world, they can also be harmful if they are taken as representing reality. Fred Kofman of MIT illustrates this point by telling the story of what happened when the platypus was discovered. Scientists didn't know quite what to think of this strange animal, and a great debate ensued as to whether the platypus was *really* a mammal, a bird, or a reptile, since it had at least some characteristics of each. Kofman reminds his listeners that the platypus was *really* a *platypus*. The animal was real, not the categories, and forcing it into any specific category was only a matter of convenience that, in the case of the platypus, probably obscured and inhibited learning rather than advanced it. Dialogue sessions encourage people to confront this non-reality of classificatory schemes and in doing so help people gain new insight and new perspectives on complex issues.

Because of their usefulness in helping diverse groups to improve communication, uncover mental models, and reach higher levels of creativity, we are likely to see dialogue sessions, or something very similar to them, occur with greater frequency in American organizations. American workers will increasingly find themselves in these strange meetings where the objective of the meeting isn't to solve problems, but to enhance conversation. It will be a unique experience for most of us, but then, there will be a lot of strange and unique experiences for us in the new learning organization.

Scenario Analysis

Dialogue sessions represent one method that will be used with increasing frequency to help people uncover and challenge their mental models. Another technique we will see some companies using to accomplish the same results is known as scenario analysis. Scenario analysis takes a number of different forms and is perhaps best associated with the planning process, but its real value lies in forcing people to re-think their basic assumptions.

Essentially, a group or team is presented with descriptions of three or more possible and plausible future scenarios for their organization. One of these is designed to match as closely as possible the current prevailing view or shared mental model of the organization. The team is presented with the scenarios and then asked to describe how the business would have to be run differently under each. The purpose of the exercise is to force the participants to question their views of reality.

One of the first companies to use scenarios for this purpose was Royal Dutch–Shell. That company's early experience with scenario analysis vividly illustrates both the power of the tool to reshape mental models and the difficulty in using the tool and getting the scenarios right.[2]

Royal Dutch–Shell began using scenario analysis in the early 1970s. Corporate planners at Royal had become concerned about some trends they saw in oil production and consumption worldwide. Their long-range forecasts predicted among other things, that

1. the oil market would switch from a buyer's to a seller's market;
2. the price of oil would fluctuate wildly; and
3. the Middle East would become the balancing source of oil supply.

These forecasts were disturbing to the planners because, at the time, the long-established and widely held view of Shell managers was that the oil business was stable and predictable and that the demand for oil would expand in an orderly fashion. The prevailing wisdom was that this stable environment would allow Shell to add oil fields, refineries, tankers, and marketing outlets routinely for the foreseeable future. The planners were horrified at this disconnect between what their trend analysis said the future would be like and what the Shell managers were expecting and prepared to handle in the future. The planners were certain that they had to do something to impress on Shell's managers that the world was about to change and that the old assumptions about the stability of the oil businesses were outdated. The question was how to get the message across. The planners chose to use scenarios.

Actually, Shell was already experimenting with scenarios as a planning tool to present information from their forecasts. Now the planners began building some of their gloomy predictions from their trend analysis into the scenarios. They began presenting these revised gloomy scenarios to Shell's managers in September 1972. There were actually six scenarios in all—three in the A Group and three in the B Group. The A Group of scenarios were those the planning group considered to be most probable, that is, that there would be a disruption in the oil supply. The three scenarios in the A Group differed only in the potential solutions to the coming oil shortage: (A1) private enterprise would respond, (A2) governments would intervene, or (A3) nothing would be done and the world would experience an energy crisis.

The planners considered the B Group of scenarios highly unlikely. They were presented only as a contrast to the A Group scenarios and as a way of showing how implausible some of the business-as-usual prevailing views about the stability of the oil supply were. Each of the B Group scenarios offered a way that the impending oil crisis postulated in the A Group scenarios could be avoided, but none of the proffered solutions to the crisis were very likely.

Shell's managers listened to the scenarios, showed their appreciation for the fine work the planners had done, yawned, and did nothing. Obviously something was wrong. While the scenarios had sparked some intellectual interest, the managers hadn't changed their behavior. This lack of reaction by the managers caused the planners to rethink what they were trying to do, as Pierre Wack, Shell's former senior planner, explained in a 1985 *Harvard Business Review* article:

We had first tried to produce scenarios that we would not be ashamed of when we subsequently compared them with reality. After our initiation with these first sets of scenarios, we changed our goal. We now wanted to design scenarios so that managers would question their own model of reality and change it when necessary, so as to come up with strategic insights beyond their minds' previous reach. This change in perspective—from producing a "good" document to changing the image of reality in the heads of critical decision makers—is . . . fundamental. . . .

Shell's planners quickly learned that they weren't producing scenarios that addressed Shell managers' major concerns. The managers simply couldn't relate to the scenarios. Wack explains:

We came to understand that making the scenarios relevant required a keener knowledge of decision makers and their microcosms ["microcosm" is Wack's term for mental model] than we had ever imagined. . . . The reason for [our] failure was . . . we did not design scenarios that responded to managers' deepest concerns.

Shell's planners tried again in 1973. This time they tailored their scenarios to the managers' major concerns and, in Wack's terms, "hit planning pay dirt" with scenarios that forced Shell's managers to identify and reassess their assumptions about the future of the oil business. Working with the more realistic scenarios, the planners helped Shell's managers understand how their assumptions could not possibly hold up in the future that was coming. Then they helped the managers work through the changes they would have to make to succeed in this new world.

Commenting on the results of Shell's efforts with scenario analysis, Peter Senge wrote in 1990:

The net result of Shell's efforts was nothing short of spectacular. In 1970, Shell had been considered the weakest of the seven largest oil companies. *Forbes* called it the "Ugly Sister" of the "Seven Sisters." By 1979 it was perhaps the strongest; certainly it and Exxon were in a class by themselves. By the early 1980s, articulating managers' mental models was an important part of the planning process at Shell.[3]

Dialogue sessions and scenario analysis represent two methods for helping people uncover and challenge their mental models and thereby open themselves to learning. But building a learning organization involves much more than just introducing scenario analysis to the planning process or launching a few dialogue sessions. The architects of the learning organization have much more in mind.

CHAPTER 14

The Architecture of the Learning Organization

The architects of the learning organization are challenging some of the fundamental assumptions of Western management and Western culture—assumptions about such things as how problems get solved, the value of competition, and impetus for change. Consider, for example, the opinions voiced by Fred Kofman and Peter Senge of MIT's Center for Organizational Learning in the Autumn 1993 issue of *Organizational Dynamics*.

In a theoretical paper entitled "Communities of Commitment: The Heart of Learning Organizations," Kofman and Senge outlined what they described as the three main dysfunctions of American institutions—our fragmentary thinking, our insistence on making competition our primary model for change and learning, and our tendency to change only in reaction to outside forces. These dysfunctions, Kofman and Senge argue, stand in the way of the learning organization and must be removed. While other researchers on learning organizations might well question whether these are, in fact, *the* three main dysfunctions or even whether they will or must be removed, the Kofman and Senge article suggests the kind of thinking that is going into the creation of the new learning post–Workplace 2000 organization.

From Fragments To Wholes

The first dysfunctions of the American workplace, say Kofman and Senge, is the fragmentary way Americans approach problem solving. Americans, they argue, fragment complex problems into pieces in order to solve them. Each piece is addressed individually in isolation from all of the others. The whole then is re-created from its parts, all of which have now supposedly been "fixed." That type of analytical approach to problems may have worked reasonably well in a previous, simpler, less chaotic, mechanistic world, but such an approach, say Kofman and Senge, doesn't work anymore. Today the really important problems, such as the runaway costs of the American health-care system and the decline of corporations' vitality and innovativeness, just won't respond to piecemeal solutions.

Given that piecemeal solutions don't work anymore, what should we do? Kofman and Senge argue we have to replace our traditional analytical perspective with a systems perspective. In their words, we have to see the "primacy of the whole." They write:

> The defining characteristic of a system is that it *cannot* be understood as a function of its isolated components. First, the behavior of the system doesn't depend on what each part is doing but on how each part is interacting with the rest. A car's engine may be working just fine, but if the transmission column is detached from it, the car won't move.
>
> Second, to understand a system we need to understand how it fits into the larger system of which it is a part. . . .
>
> Third, and most important, what we call the parts need not be taken as primary. In fact, how we define the parts is fundamentally a matter of perspective and purpose, not intrinsic in the nature of the "real thing" we are looking at. . . . [Note: Recall the platypus issue.]
>
> Rather than being objective, what we call the parts is highly subjective. No set of categories is natural or inherent to a system. There is no intrinsic right or wrong. . . .
>
> Rather than thinking of a world of "parts" that form "wholes," we start by recognizing that we live in a world of wholes within wholes. Rather than trying to "put the pieces together" to make the whole, we recognize that the world is already whole. . . .
>
> . . . To reestablish fluidity, the capacity for learning and change, we must . . . once again confront the whole.[1]

"Confronting the whole" means that people in the new learning organizations will have to become comfortable with the complexities of the world and with the fact that everything is interconnected. "In learning organizations, people are always inquiring into the systemic consequences of their actions, rather than just focusing on local consequences. . . . They are patient in seeking deeper understanding rather than striking out to 'fix' problem symptoms—because they know that most fixes are temporary at best, and often result in more severe problems in the future."[2]

How will people learn to think in these systemic terms? In an earlier work, Senge discussed exposing people to "systems archetypes,"—a limited number of generic structures or principles that help people in organizations begin to recognize when they are failing to think in systems terms.[3] Among the systems archetypes described by Senge were:

1. **The Escalation Archetype** in which two people or organizations each see their welfare as depending on a relative advantage over the other. Whenever one side gets ahead, the other is threatened, leading it to act more aggressively to reestablish its advantage, which threatens the first, increasing its aggressiveness, and so on. A good business example is a price war between two companies. One reduces its prices; the second feels threatened. A decline in sales leads the second company to reduce its price, which leads to lower market share for the first company. The first company responds by reducing its prices even more. And so on. Think of the airfare wars.

   The key management principle to be learned, of course, is that such escalation can end up damaging both parties and that something must be done to end the spiral. Sometimes that means that one party must take overtly aggressive but intrinsically peaceful action in order to reduce the threat to the other party and thereby bring the escalation to an end.

2. **The Tragedy of the Commons Archetype** in which individuals or organizations use a commonly available but limited resource solely to their own benefit without regard to the common good. People fail to "manage the commons," and soon the valuable resource is depleted. Many environmental problems result from the tragedy of the commons. For example, in the Sahel region of sub-Saharan Africa,

overgrazing by herdsmen turned fertile pastureland into a barren desert.

3. **The Shifting of the Burden Archetype** in which a short-term solution is used to correct a problem. Since it seems to work and to produce some quick results, the short-term solution is used more and more while the fundamental problem is never addressed. The person who uses drugs or alcohol as a short-term solution to stress is "shifting the burden."

4. **The Balancing Process with Delay Archetype** in which a person, group, or an organization responds to feedback by making an adjustment but overshoots the mark. The person, group, or organization fails to recognize that there is a delay between its action and the feedback it receives about the effect of its action. A good example is the manufacturing company that steps up production to fill a shortage, only to find that by the time the product is ready to ship there is already a glut in the market. The managers then cut production, but because of the delay between their action and the results of their action, they only end up creating a shortage.

These are four common system archetypes. Senge lists another six, and a dozen or so in total have been identified by various researchers. The usefulness of the archetype is that it forces people to begin thinking in systems terms. Each archetype, after all, contains all of the elements of systems—reinforcing processes, balancing processes, delays, feedback, interrelationships, and so on. Senge explained, "The purpose of the systems archetypes is to recondition our perceptions, so as to be more able to see structures at play, and to see the leverage in those structures."

They do, and if Kofman and Senge have their way, people in American business will spend a lot more time talking about archetypes and a lot less time talking about specific, isolated problems. In fact, Kofman and Senge think we should probably stop spending so much time on problem solving anyway. They see our obsession with problem solving as symptomatic of our second major learning dysfunction—our reactiveness.

From Reactive To Creative

Kofman and Senge bemoan our tendency as a society to change only in reaction to outside forces. Real learning and growth, they argue, come from aspiration, imagination, and experimentation, not from just waiting for problems to occur and fixing them by changing something. Instead of problem solving, Kofman and Senge would like to see us focus on creating. They write:

> The persuasiveness of a reactive stance in management is evident in the fixation on problem solving. Many managers think that management *is* problem solving. But problem solving is fundamentally different from creating. The problem solver tries to make something go away. A creator tries to bring something new into being. The impetus for change in problem solving lies outside ourselves—in some undesired external condition we seek to eliminate. The impetus for change in the creating mode comes from within. Only the creating mode leads to a genuine sense of individual and collective power, because only in the creating mode do people orient themselves to their intrinsic desires.

Of course, moving to this type of creating mode won't be easy. We will have to give up another of our treasured beliefs—our belief in the power of competition.

From Competition To Cooperation

Kofman and Senge maintain that we have become overly dependent on competition as our only model for change and learning. They explain that

> in the United States, we tend to see competition among individuals as the ultimate mechanism for change and improvement in human affairs. We continually think in terms of war and sports analogies when we interpret management challenges. . . . We rarely think about how the process of developing leaders may be more like parenting than competing, or about how developing a new culture may be more like gardening than a military campaign.

Kofman and Senge further maintain that much is wrong with our fixation on competition, or at least our failure to balance competition with cooperation. First, they argue, our focus on competition means that we often end up competing against the very people with whom we should be trying to cooperate. Managers compete, divisions of companies compete, even teams compete, and the result of all of the competition frequently is that groups don't work together and share knowledge. When that happens, everyone loses.

Second, said Kofman and Senge, our obsession with competition forces too many people into the mode of focusing on *looking good* at the expense of *being good.*

Learning requires that people acknowledge that there is something they don't know and asks them to try doing things they are not very good at. But in most American corporations, such learning isn't possible, since, Kofman and Senge maintain, "ignorance is a sign of weakness; temporary incompetence is a character flaw." The result of this overemphasis on competition is that we focus on the short term and on quick fixes and ignore the systemwide consequences of our actions. We need to restore the competition-cooperation balance so we can learn once again.

Pursuit Of The Learning Organization

Kofman and Senge's vision of the learning organization isn't the only one. There are others, and the reality of the learning organization is that it is more of a vision than a concrete entity. Kofman and Senge note that when they speak of a learning organization, they are not describing a phenomenon or a physical reality, but a vision of a type of organization that can and should exist.

The exact nature of the learning organization isn't yet clear. We don't have an example to which we can point as the model of what such an organization is and does. Some things are becoming clear, however, and we have tried to sketch them in this chapter and elsewhere in this book. They are things like the following:

- the constant pursuit of innovation and creativity in products and processes
- the maintenance and enhancement of core competencies
- focused, network structures

- a concern for people
- communication and cooperation
- systems thinking

Most of all we think the new organization, whether you call it a "learning organization" or something else, above all else will celebrate learning and knowledge as a strategic necessity. It will be an organization for the highly educated and highly skilled. It will be a thinking organization, requiring an enormous number of thinker-doers. Therein lies the problem, because we don't know where we will get enough such people.

PART VI

AMERICAN EDUCATION: AN UPDATE

In *Workplace 2000* we wrote that the new American workplace would require the most educated workforce of any economic system in history. We saw that prospect as frightening for a number of reasons:

- Most young Americans lacked the education to succeed and perhaps even to survive in the workplace we were creating.
- With few exceptions, American educational institutions, from primary schools to colleges and universities, offered young Americans almost no help or hope in bridging their educational gap.
- Poor education characterized not only the generation being educated at the time and entering the workforce in the twenty-first century, but the generation previous to it too, which, if any-

thing, was even more poorly educated and even less prepared for Workplace 2000.

America faced the challenge not only of revolutionizing its educational system top to bottom, but reeducating a substantial portion of the adult workforce. As the decade of the 1980s ended, it was clear that America's educational system was a national disgrace and that efforts to fix the problems were floundering.

Our Education Crisis

The statistics and media reports on our education crisis in the late 1980s were daunting, to say the least.[1]

- Overall, 25 percent of all American high school students dropped out of school before graduation.
- Among the poor, minority, and non-English-speaking students in inner-city schools, the dropout rate was nearly 60 percent.
- Students who stayed in school didn't learn much. For example, less than a third of American high school seniors knew

    in which half-century the Civil War occurred;

    what either the Magna Carta or the Reformation was;

    what the Declaration of Independence was; or

    who wrote the Emancipation Proclamation.

- A third of the seniors didn't know

    who discovered America; or

    what *Brown v. Board of Education* was.

- Fewer than one student in five could match Dostoyevsky, Conrad, James Joyce, Hemingway, or D. H. Lawrence with the books they wrote. When asked to do so, the students actually scored *worse* than would have been expected from random guessing, which *Fortune* noted suggested "an almost militant ignorance."
- Less than one-fifth of eleventh graders could write an intelligible note applying for a summer job at a swimming pool.

- Only 37 percent of twenty-one- to twenty-five-year-olds in one government-sponsored study could comprehend material in a simple *New York Times* article about an airline disaster.
- Only 38 percent of young adults could use a chart to pick the right grade of sandpaper.
- Only 38 percent could figure the amount of change they should receive from $3.00 if they ordered a $.60 cup of soup and $1.95 sandwich.
- Only one in five young adults could read a bus schedule well enough to tell when a particular bus should reach the terminal.
- One third of the entire U.S. adult population was functionally illiterate.

Describing the late 1980s education crisis, *Fortune* reported, "It's like Pearl Harbor. The Japanese have invaded, and the U.S. has been caught short. Not on guns and tanks and battleships—those are yesterday's weapons—but on mental might. In a high tech age where nations increasingly compete on brain power, American schools are producing an army of illiterates." In 1988, then secretary of labor Ann McLaughlin said, "Without immediate action . . . large segments of our community will end up uneducated, untrained and unemployed and, in the workplace of today and tomorrow, perhaps even unemployable."[2]

The Crisis Continues

So, have we gotten any better? Has the education of Americans improved in the half decade since McLaughlin called for "immediate action"? Not by much. Consider the results of a 1993 Department of Education study. The department tested 13,600 adults in 165 tasks in the categories of prose, document, and quantitative literacy. The results weren't at all encouraging. Almost half of the adults could not make sense of a simple magazine article or read a bus schedule. Nearly half scored below the minimum literacy level researchers felt was necessary for training and retraining. These adults couldn't write a letter explaining that an error had been made on a credit card bill. They couldn't use a chart to pick out the proper kind of sandpaper for wood, and they couldn't figure out how many minutes a bus ride would take when given the starting time, the destination, and a bus schedule. Of course, that task required *sophisticated* skills. After all, to complete the task the adults had to be able to read numbers, the word "Saturday," and to tell time. Nearly half of them could not.[3] Of course, these were adults. What about the children? Could America's kids do any better? As it turned out, not much.

In 1992, the Department of Education issued a "reading report card" reflecting the test results for 140,000 American students. The tests showed that two-thirds of America's fourth graders, eighth graders, and twelfth graders were not proficient readers. Another study found that only 91 percent of high school seniors could solve math problems that required more than an educated guess.[4] And the latest reports from the National Assessment of Educational Programs show practically no change in the average reading, writing, mathematics, and science proficiency of American students in twenty years. In short, it is not so much that we have lost ground in educational competency as it is that we have failed to improve. That would matter less if it weren't for the fact that the basic skills and knowledge required of American workers *has* changed. Americans need to know more than ever before in order to be considered functionally illiterate, but they *don't* know more. Consequently, we are seeing a job squeeze in some industries where there should be no job squeeze at all.

American business can't find the skilled workforce it needs, particularly from the vast majority of potential workers who are non-college-bound high school graduates. Fewer than one-third of American employers in a 1993 Harris poll said they thought a typical high school graduate was capable of holding a job.[5] In a National Alliance of Business survey, fewer than 40 percent of principals surveyed said that non-college-bound high school graduates were prepared to hold a job. Seventy-three percent said they didn't think high school graduates could write adequately, and 71 percent said that the graduates' math skills just weren't up to par. And it wasn't just their lack of basic skills that had business leaders worried.

There were other perhaps even more disturbing findings from early-1990s surveys that pointed out something much more basic. It had to do with notions of right and wrong, responsibility and accountability. In one survey of over 100,000 American teenagers,

- 40 percent of the teens said they would keep the extra if a cashier gave them too much change from a purchase;

- 30 percent said they would not ask for more work if they finished their assigned tasks early;
- 25 percent said that if they worked in a store they would give free merchandise to their friends; and
- 30 percent readily admitted that they would cheat on a test.[6]

The Promise Of Tomorrow

Sadly, in spite of the crisis we face in education, we haven't accomplished very much in the last half decade to find a way out of the crisis. We have only barely begun our journey to a new education system. We are still mired in a bewildering array of local experiments, and the national debate about what to do is now well into its second decade without an end in sight. In spite of "Education Presidents" and continuing media attention, we still have no true national consensus, except on the obvious: that what we have been doing to educate our people isn't working. Yet there are some glimmers of hope.

The Goals 2000: Educate America Act

Some say it is as important as the efforts of the last century to open secondary education to everyone, as significant as the Supreme Court's landmark decision in *Brown v. Board of Education* to end legalized segregation in public schooling, and an extraordinarily difficult break with the 150-year-old American tradition of local control of public schools. Others think it is just another example of federal government intrusion into what is rightly and solely the responsibility of local communities. The "it" at the center of this controversy is the Goals 2000: Educate America Act, which was passed by Congress in March 1994. The legislation provides, for the first time in American history, a role for the federal government in deciding what happens in the nation's classrooms. It establishes a National Education Standards and Improvement Council to develop national academic standards in math, science, history, geography, foreign languages, and the arts for fourth, eighth, and eleventh graders. It encourages states to design new ways of measuring student achievement. It also challenges states to lower the dropout rate, improve pre-school programs, and reduce crime in schools. It even includes provisions for job training and adult literacy. Finally, it codifies into law national education goals established by President Bush and the state governors in 1990 and includes such goals as the following:

- The nation's high school graduation rate will be at least 90 percent, and students will be competent in English, history, geography, foreign languages and the arts.
- American students will lead the world in math and science.

Will the act make a difference? Maybe, but then maybe not. After all, the goals laid out by the act are vague, compliance with the national standards was deliberately left voluntary, and measurement was largely left up to the states. Perhaps *The New York Times* put it best in a November 24, 1993, story about the pending legislation. It said, "The problem is, this is all so amorphous and conditional—if Congress passes it; if states vigorously support it; if standards are specific enough but not so specific that they stifle teachers' creativity; if anyone appropriates any money for implementation." While it all sounded good, the *Times* noted, no one could tell whether Goals 2000 "represents a new rigorous future or the latest nuisance from Washington." The greatest fear for teachers, said the *Times*, was, "that Goals 2000 will be another unfinanced revolution accompanied by an explosion of paperwork."

While the *Times*'s skepticism may be understandable, some promising experiments in education are under way, and we are beginning to reach consensus on new ideas about how classrooms and schools should be organized and run. We have taken the first steps toward establishing a meaningful relationship between the world of business and the world of education. Through some innovative work-study programs we are beginning to provide some rational school-to-work transition for young Americans who choose not to go on to college after high school. And, perhaps most importantly, we are beginning to reach consensus on the skills businesses require if students are going to be "ready to work." We haven't by any means solved all of our problems. We haven't even *begun* to solve them. But we just may be beginning to begin. At least that is something. Here then in the next few chapters is a brief update on where we stand as we enter the last few years of the twentieth century.

CHAPTER 15 The Skills Required for the New Workplace

In May 1990, the U.S. Department of Labor created the Secretary's Commission on Achieving Necessary Skills (SCANS) to examine the demands of the new American workplace and to assess whether American youth were capable of meeting those demands. SCANS is just one of a number of commissions and organizations that have attempted to identify skills required for the future over the last few years. Other organizations that have issued policy reports on basic skill requirements for American workers include the American Society for Training and Development, the National Academy of Sciences, and Stanford University. Each of these policy reports differ in their specifics, but there is a considerable degree of overlap. (See Table 15.1)

TABLE 15.1
Workplace Skills and Competencies:
Examples from Selected Reports

Skill Areas	SCANS	American Society for Training and Development	National Academy of Sciences	Stanford Study
Academic	• Basic Skills • Thinking Skills	• Reading, writing • Computation • Learning to learn	• Reading, writing • Computation • Reasoning • Science and technology • Social and economic studies	• Written communication • Numeracy
Social	• Interpersonal skills	• Communication • Interpersonal skills • Teamwork • Negotiation	• Oral communication • Interpersonal relationships	• Oral communication • Cooperation • Working in groups • Peer training • Multicultural skills
Organizational	• Resources • Information • Systems	• Problem solving • Creative thinking • Organizational effectiveness • Leadership	• Problem solving	• Problem solving • Decision making • Evaluation • Planning • Obtaining and using information
Attitudinal	• Personal qualities	• Self-esteem • Goal-setting/motivation • Personal/career development	• Personal work habits and attitudes	• Initiative
Other	• Technology			

SOURCE: U.S. Congress, Office of Technology Assessment, *Adult Literacy and New Technologies: Tools for a Lifetime*, OTA-SET-550 (Washington, D.C.: U.S. Government Printing Office, July 1992) Table 2–1—*Workplace Skills and Competencies: Some Examples from Selected Reports*, page 38.

The SCANS report is one of the latest and in many respects is the most comprehensive policy statement. For that reason, it represents an excellent starting point for understanding the skills required for the workplace beyond Workplace 2000. Such an understanding is critical for Americans who want to secure some semblance of stable employment for themselves and their children. We agree with the Secretary's Commission that

1. American parents must understand the SCANS competencies and skills and insist that their sons and daughters master them;
2. employers must redesign their business policies and practices to ensure that they are hiring and developing this know-how in their employees; and
3. educational institutions must teach the SCANS competencies and skills.

SCANS research identified five competencies and a three-part foundation of skills and personal qualities that all employees in the new workplace will need. These are shown in Figure 15.1. (See Appendix 1 for more detailed information on SCANS skills and competencies.)

FIGURE 15.1

WORKPLACE KNOW-HOW

The know-how identified by SCANS is made up of five competencies and a three-part foundation of skills and personal qualities needed for solid job performance:

1. COMPETENCIES. Effective workers are those who can productively use
   - **resources** (can allocate time, money, materials, space, staff)
   - **interpersonal skills** (can work on teams, teach others, serve customers, lead, negotiate, and work well with people from other cultural backgrounds)
   - **information** (can acquire and evaluate data, organize and maintain files, interpret and communicate information, and use computers to process information)

> - **systems** (can understand social, organizational, and technological systems, monitor and correct performance, and design or improve systems)
> - **technology** (can select equipment and tools, apply technology to specific tasks, and maintain and troubleshoot technologies)
>
> 2. THE FOUNDATION. Competence requires
> - **basic skills** (reading, writing, arithmetic and mathematics, speaking and listening)
> - **thinking skills** (thinking creatively, making decisions, solving problems, seeing things in the mind's eye, knowing how to learn, and reasoning)
> - **personal qualities** (individual responsibility, self-esteem, sociability, self-management, and integrity)

Beyond The Three Rs

It is obvious even from this cursory look at the SCANS skills that they go far beyond the traditional reading, writing, and arithmetic we associate with American schools. The three Rs are still there and are still important, but even they are quite different. As the SCANS commission reported:

[T]omorrow's career ladders require even the basic skills—the old 3Rs—to take on a new meaning. First, all employees will have to *read* well enough to understand and interpret diagrams, directories, correspondence, manuals, records, charts, graphs, tables, and specifications. Without the ability to read a diverse set of materials, workers cannot locate the descriptive and quantitative information needed to make decisions or to recommend courses of action. What do these reading requirements mean on the job? They might involve:

- interpreting blueprints and materials catalogues;
- dealing with letters and written policy on complaints;
- reading patients' medical records and medication instructions; and

- reading the text of technical manuals from equipment vendors.

At the same time, most jobs will call for writing skills to prepare correspondence, instructions, charts, graphs, and proposals, in order to make requests, explain, illustrate, and convince. On the job this might require:

- writing memoranda to justify resources or explain plans;
- preparing instructions for operating simple machines;
- developing a narrative to explain graphs or tables; and
- drafting suggested modifications in company procedures.

Mathematics and computational skills will also be essential. Virtually all employees will be required to maintain records, estimate results, use spreadsheets, or apply statistical process controls as they negotiate, identify trends, or suggest new courses of action. Most of us will not leave our mathematics behind us in school. Instead, we will find ourselves using it on the job, for example, to:

- reconcile differences between inventory and financial records;
- estimate discounts on the spot while negotiating sales;
- use spreadsheet programs to monitor expenditures;
- employ statistical process control procedures to check quality; and
- project resource needs over the next planning period.

Finally, very few of us will work totally by ourselves. More and more, work involves listening carefully to clients and co-workers and clearly articulating one's own point of view. Today's worker has to listen and speak well enough to explain schedules and procedures, communicate with customers, work in teams, understand customer concerns, describe complex systems and procedures, probe for hidden meanings, teach others, and solve problems. On the job, these skills may translate readily into:

- training new workers or explaining new schedules to a work team;
- describing plans to supervisors or clients;

- questioning customers to diagnose malfunctions; and
- answering questions from customers about post-sale service.

The Five Competencies

The three-part foundation of skills and personal qualities provides the basics. No employee of the future will be able to function without a high level of proficiency in these basics, yet they are far from enough. The worker of the future will need much more if he or she is to come to the job ready to work. That "much more," as defined by the SCANS commission, is contained in the Five Competencies (resources, interpersonal skills, information, systems, and technology). The commission noted in its 1991 report *What Work Requires of Schools* that, "these five competencies . . . span the chasm between the worlds of the school and the workplace. They are the basis of the modern workplace dedicated to excellence. They are the hallmark of today's expert worker. And they lie behind every product and service offered on today's market—putting food on tables, travelers in rooms, airplane passengers at their destination, patients in the operating room, and automobiles on the street."[2]

The Five Competencies are summarized in Figure 15.1 and described in more detail in Appendix 1. As the commission points out in its report, the competencies do not represent technical skills or subject-matter knowledge such as engineering, architecture, computer programming, and so on. Instead, the Five Competencies represent skills that are generic and needed across all industries and occupations. "In the broad sense," said the commission, "the competencies represent the attributes employers seek in today's and tomorrow's employee." In short, regardless of job title or position description, employees must be able to demonstrate their skill in managing and using

1. **Resources.** Workers must be able to schedule time, budget funds, arrange space, or assign staff.
2. **Interpersonal Skills.** Competent employees are those who can work well with team members and can teach new workers; can serve clients directly and persuade co-workers either individually or in groups; can negotiate with others to solve problems or reach decisions; can work comfortably with col-

leagues from diverse backgrounds; and can responsibly challenge existing procedures and policies.

3. **Information.** Workers need to be able to identify, assimilate, and integrate information from diverse sources; prepare, maintain, and interpret quantitative and qualitative records; convert information from one form to another and convey information, orally and in writing, as the need arises.

4. **Systems.** Workers must understand their own work in the context of the work of those around them; they must understand how parts of systems are connected, anticipate consequences, and monitor and correct their own performance; they must be able to identify trends and anomalies in system performance, integrate multiple displays of data, and link symbols (e.g., displays on a computer screen) with real phenomena (e.g., machine performance).

5. **Technology.** Workers must demonstrate high levels of competence in selecting and using appropriate technology, visualizing operations, using technology to monitor tasks, and maintaining and troubleshooting complex equipment.

But The Skills Aren't There

Do young Americans possess these skills? Do they have the basic foundation of knowledge and the Five Competencies? Do they know what they need to know to work, contribute to society, and to hold down jobs? Not by a long shot, and sadly, many of the most important of these skills aren't even being taught. The Secretary's Commission reports that "less than half of all young adults have achieved these reading and writing minimums; even fewer can handle the mathematics; and, schools today are only indirectly addressing listening and speaking skills." That has to change, but it won't be easy. We are not just talking about changing the subject matter taught in the nation's classrooms. The creation of a workforce with the necessary skills for the new workplace—the SCANS skills or something very similar to them—will require more than just new subject matter. It will require a whole new way of teaching, a way of teaching students not just facts but how to *think.*

CHAPTER 16

The New Learning Place
for the New Workplace

Teaching thinking is a lot different from teaching facts. It doesn't happen in factory schools where teachers lecture, students memorize, and classes change every fifty minutes. People don't learn to think when their instruction is compartmentalized with history over here, English over there, and a little math and science way out there somewhere. It all has to come together like it does in real life. More importantly, to teach people to think we have to engage more than just their minds. We have to engage their hands and hearts also.

Some Promising Experiments

Many of the lessons about how to teach thinking are being tested and refined in experiments in the new education.

Learning in a Shopping Mall

Kids in Pinellas County, Florida, now go to the mall to learn, as well as to shop. The mall, called Enterprise Village, is an 18,000-square-foot school-business partnership in the form of a minimall. The minimall was created in the late 1980s when eighteen companies, including McDonald's and Florida Power Corporation, agreed to donate $50,000 each to establish Enterprise Village as a hands-on school resource for fifth graders in St. Petersburg and the surrounding area. The mall is open 120 days each year to fifth graders who are completing an eight-week economics unit required by the county. The kids come to the mall to sell, shop, retrieve products from warehouses, prepare advertising, and so forth. In short, they apply what they have learned about economics. The kids actually run the mall for a day. After completing a lengthy curriculum that focuses on career decision-making, how checking and savings accounts work, and the importance of quality, ethics, and teamwork, the fifth graders apply for a position at the mall and are assigned a job in one of the eighteen businesses in Enterprise Village. The job may be as a computer operator, a counter clerk, a bank teller, a bookkeeper, a manager, or even as the mayor or the director of the Chamber of Commerce.

Students begin their day running the mall by obtaining a loan from the bank that allows them to sell products or provide services. Then they retrieve their supplies from the warehouse, establish the prices they will charge, develop advertisements for their business to run on the village radio station or in the village newspaper, and open the mall for business. Their goal is to make enough money from their business during the day to pay back the loan they obtained in the morning and perhaps even make a profit.

Three times during the day, the student employees receive paychecks of $5 or $6 in Enterprise Village currency that they deposit in their checking accounts. They may then visit the village shops to purchase such things as T-shirts, baseball caps, sunglasses, and even food at the village McDonald's with the money they have earned.

At the end of the day, the students total up their profits, if any, and assemble for a speech from their mayor. They end the day by entering voting booths to register their opinions about the overall experience, which is typically a wish for more time and money at Enterprise Village. As a follow-up to their experience running the minimall, the kids take a field trip to St. Petersburg Beach, where they tour the city hall and local businesses to observe the work environment and retail process. They also conduct a kind of parents' night, in which they give presentations on their experience and participate in a panel discussion about what they accomplished and learned at the mall.[1]

Learning from the Fertilizer Problem

In a Fort Worth high school, chemistry students are assigned the problem of determining the best lawn fertilizer for the school to use. Working in groups, the students must investigate the chemical composition and the effects of various fertilizers, decide when they need more information and which experts in industry or academia they should contact, weigh costs and other feasibility factors, and reach consensus on their recommendations. The student teams then prepare their own reports with computer-generated graphs and charts and present their findings and conclusions to school decision makers, who accept or reject their recommendations.

In completing their assignment and developing their report, the students don't work just with their chemistry teacher, but with a variety of teachers from different subject matters (writing, computer graphics, etc.). In one exercise, the students are exposed to all five of the SCANS competencies—resources, information, interpersonal skills, systems, and technology. A 1993 SCANS report evaluated the project as follows:

> Working on such a project, students acquire and practice skills in ways they will actually use them on the job; they use many skills in combination, and all skills are directed towards a purpose.
>
> This project, it should be noted, is not based on a problem neatly defined in advance with an answer that the teacher knows and the students must arrive at. New complexities and side issues arise as the students wade into a problem like the problems adults encounter in real jobs.
>
> Moreover, there are real-world outcomes of students' work. The soundness of the students' research, the degree to which they consider the full range of relevant factors, the cogency with which they present their recommendations, and the savvy with which they deal with the powers-that-be will determine whether their recommendations are accepted. The motivation to perform each task well does not rest solely on a grade but is intrinsic to the enterprise—the better a task is carried out, the more likely a successful final outcome. These elements are all important for effective education.[2]

Learning Through Integrated Simulations

Once they complete two months of courses in geology and math, seventh grade students at Orange Grove Middle School in Tucson, Arizona, are divided into six simulated mining companies. The student officers of each company must make decisions about which mines to lease and which to keep in production, basing their decisions on what they have learned about geology. The students use their newly acquired math skills to allocate their company's operating capital between production, public relations, marketing, pollution control, and R&D. The exercise is constructed so that student decisions cause supply, demand, and pricing of metals to vary as the exercise progresses.

In another simulation, Orange Grove students first study topics such as land management, recreation theory, social systems, geography, ecological community theory, and politics. Then they utilize their newly acquired knowledge to design a public park with a multimillion-dollar budget. In designing the park, the students have to avoid a threatened lawsuit by not desecrating a nearby Indian burial site, include features to make the park attractive to users, avoid damage to the environment, and still develop and operate the park within their budget.[3]

Learning from Water Wheels

At Lakeland Regional High School in Wanaque, New Jersey, students spent two years designing a nineteenth-century water wheel for a historical park. Over the two-year period the students had to research the history of water wheels and water wheel design, make their own drawings and templates, design the water wheel using computer graphics and design tools, select and test materials, and actually build a full-size working replica of the water wheel for the park.[4]

Only a few years ago, these same students would have been attending a class known as industrial arts. They would have been taught how to use drafting machines, wood lathes, and table saws, and they would have produced toolboxes, birdhouses, and bookshelves. Instead, they were receiving technology education in computer-aided drafting, computer-aided manufacturing, laser photography, and robotics.

Realism Is the Key

Experiments in the new education, like those described above, vary greatly in scope and content, but they have one characteristic in common. All of the experiments seek to make the learning experience more realistic—to make it a closer approximation to the real work experience. One type of new education experiment that a number of education reformers are advocating takes this "make it real" approach a step further. It is a blending of the traditional college-bound curriculum with more traditional vocational education and apprenticeship.

Smoothing The School-To-Work Transition

To a large extent, America's educational institutions have created a two-tiered system. College-bound kids are given some preparation for the future, while the non-college-bound get little preparation at all. Those who fail to obtain a college degree are frequently left to spend most of their twenties, perhaps most of their life, drifting from menial job to menial job and in and out of employment. To change that two-tier approach, a number of educational reformers and officials of the Clinton administration are advocating widespread adoption of "tech-prep" (technical-preparation) programs paired with apprenticeships for non-college-bound students. The Clinton administration proposal seeks, among other things, to

- spend $1.2 billion over five years as seed money to create more than 100,000 apprenticeship slots with employers;
- create a national skills standards board to promote the development of industry skill standards;
- create certificates for students meeting these standards to help companies judge a job applicant's skills; and
- combine on-the-job skill training with high school and community college so that apprentices are not locked into just one narrow technical track, but can pursue either technical work or a college degree.[5]

The Clinton administration proposal is essentially designed to support work-to-school efforts already under way in a number of states. One such program that is advocated by the Atlanta-based Southern Regional Education Board (SREB) is typical of this new approach to vocational education. Since the late 1980s, the SREB has been pushing southern high schools to adopt a tech-prep curriculum that combines a traditional college-bound curriculum of English, science, and math with hands-on learning typical of vocational education. The idea is to convert vocational education programs from being a baby-sitting situation and a dumping ground for the non-college-bound students to a program of rigorous preparation for work. By 1994, the SREB had convinced 329 high schools in nineteen states to adopt the following goals and principles for vocational education:

- Vocational learning must emphasize intellectual skills as well as teach students skills they will need on the job. Students must know how to perform tasks that use thinking, estimation, reasoning, and judgment.
- Vocational education must stress a number of skills within an area rather than teach a student to do one job. Students must "learn how to learn."
- Developing good vocational skills requires two years of training beyond high school. Community colleges play an important part in this reform.
- Students should go to job sites to understand how the technologies they are learning are applied to the real world. By linking study and work through partnerships and apprenticeship programs, the theoretical aspects of education quickly become real.
- Business leaders and workers must help teachers and administrators plan vocational programs. These groups must be in constant communication.
- Rather than learn only specific skills, students must be versed in all aspects of a particular area. To be capable of adapting to a changing workplace, students must know the full history and practice of a trade or industry.[6]

An example of a typical tech-prep program based on these principles is in place in the Lexington County (Swansea), South Carolina, school system. First, the general education program—the typical curriculum followed by most non-college-bound students—has been eliminated. Students are given only two options, college preparation or the new technical preparation. Students who choose the tech-prep program of study take courses in algebra, physics, chemistry, biology, along with in-depth instruction in communication in the workplace. The instruction is tied closely to occupational clusters such as health, drafting, industrial occupations, and business education. Most importantly, the instruction is interdisciplinary. Sandy Sarvis, assistant superintendent for instruction in the Lexington County schools, explained the interdisciplinary approach in a 1993 *Forbes* magazine article:

> Our tech-prep math teacher works with our college-prep science teacher, and their classes all work together studying the building trades. The geometry teacher offers a lesson in angles; the science teacher shows how a building was constructed using these angles in lumber and brick. . . . Students begin to see the whole picture. We help kids make sense of learning by teaching math, science and English in ways they recognize. They begin to understand why these subjects are important.[7]

Do such tech-prep curriculums work? Sarvis argues that they do, citing statistics from the Lexington County school district. Prior to implementation of the tech-prep program, Lexington County had a high school dropout rate of 7.7 percent. Since the introduction of tech prep, the dropout rate has been cut to just 1 percent. Additionally, the number of students going on to some type of post-secondary education has increased from 35.6 percent to 58 percent, and achievement test scores of students have improved. The percentage of students scoring in the fiftieth percentile on standardized national tests in science has gone from 25 percent to 50 percent, from 41 to 50 percent in English, and from 38 to 55 percent in reading comprehension.[8]

Sarvis commented on the success of the program as follows:

> This program works because of high expectations for all of our students. We expect all students to learn advanced skills in math, science and communication. We taught our teachers how to work in teams and encourage students to think critically and creatively to solve problems.[9]

Tech-prep curricula also work because they pair academic instruction with real-world work experience through some type of formal or informal apprenticeship program. For example, Banta Printing in central Wisconsin participates in a tech-prep–apprenticeship program with the local high school. Kids in the program attend school two days a week and work at Banta Printing three days a week over a period of two years. During that time they are rotated through all parts of the printing operation, including pre-press, binding, stripping, photography, and distribution, under the tutelage of a mentor. At each stage the student's work experience is coordinated with his or her academic instruction, so the student is applying what he or she is learning. For example, students are required to employ math skills to estimate paper needs, to use their training in English composition to write reports for their mentors, and to use their study of filtration using inks in the printing process as an integrated part of their instruction in chemistry.[10]

An Education For The Twenty-First Century

Promising educational experiments, such as those we discussed earlier in this chapter, and school-to-work transition programs, such as those advocated by the Southern Regional Education Board and the Clinton administration, offer the prospect that we may be finding our way out of the education crisis. That doesn't mean that we have accomplished a great deal to date. We are far, far from making real, measurable progress. For most young Americans very little has changed. The good news is that for some young Americans and older Americans with skill and knowledge deficiencies, things are beginning to change.

It is ironic in a way that some of the real improvements we are making are coming about as the result of the innovative application of new educational technology. We say "ironic," because it was the rapid and widespread introduction of technology into the workplace in the 1970s and 1980s that, to a large extent, precipitated our education crisis. Now we are finding a way to employ technology to help us solve some of our educational problems. Technology is leading us to create a new type of classroom, a revolutionary new learning experience for students, and it very likely will lead us to rethink the role of schools and the relationship of schools to the future. That's another part of the education story, and it is something we address in more detail in the next chapter.

CHAPTER 17 The Promise of Technology

Until recently, our experience with technology in American schools had not been too promising. In the 1980s, we went from almost no computers in American schools to over 2 million. Yet by the end of the decade, the whole effort seemed to have had little impact on student performance. In 1989, a *Business Week* article noted that "after a decade of enthusiasm, there's still not clear consensus about the role, value, or effectiveness of computers in schools. Well-thought-out goals are still lacking. Gains in achievement have proved modest at best. And, in many schools, initial fervor has given way to 'benign neglect.' "[1] Fortunately, that is now beginning to change. As we enter mid-1990s, computers and other technology appear to be coming of age in schools across the nation. The technology that exists today compared to the technology available only a few years ago is extraordinary. The promised technology of the next few years is exciting.

Edutainment

It's called "edutainment" and it is showing up in schools and homes across the United States. This new software mixes fun and learning and finally may be turning the computer into a true high-tech learning tool. The key to the new programs is that they are interactive and go far beyond the drill/practice deadly dull flash card programs of only a few years ago. Some of the more well-known programs are

- **SimCity:** Students (and their parents) try their hand at constructing and running a modern city. They lay out industrial parks and commercial and residential areas; they build roads, bridges, and mass transportation systems; and they balance the health cost and environmental impact of coal-fired versus nuclear energy. All the while, they have to deal with a city population that wants a good transportation system, low crime, sports arenas, and entertainment complexes, but just like most Americans, they don't want to raise taxes to pay for such a lifestyle. The program even throws in an occasional earthquake, fire, flood, airplane crash, tornado, nuclear-reactor meltdown, shipwreck, or even monster attack just for interest.
- **Where in the World Is Carmen Sandiego:** Kids answer geography questions to capture a globe-trotting thief.
- **Math Blaster:** Students solve math problems to blow up space trash.
- **Oregon Trail:** Players plan and undertake a trip to Oregon experiencing the same challenges and having to make the same decisions about such things as what food to carry and which rivers to ford as the pioneers did in the 1840s.

SimCity, Oregon Trail, and the others mentioned above represent just a few of the titles available. In fact, by 1994, there were an estimated 700 edutainment titles on the market, with some 250 to 300 being introduced each year. For many experts, edutainment was finally delivering on the promise of technology. One study found that students with access to interactive software learned 30 to 50 percent faster than those exposed only to drill and practice or other more conventional methods of instruction.[2]

Networks

Edutainment software represents one part of the technology breakthrough. The other involves networks and communication systems that are allowing students and teachers to reach far beyond the classroom walls and undertake learning in a truly global context. A host of electronic networks are being developed. For example, by 1993, ten thousand elementary school children in the United States were participating in a National Geographic Kids Network that allowed students who were conducting experiments to share their data with other students doing similar work in other parts of the world. AT&T ran a social studies and literature program that electronically linked some 35,000 kids in twenty-three nations. They could use the network to send messages to each other and to conduct research for their school projects.

The High-Tech Classroom

How does this new technology change the experiences our children have at school? How does it change the way the classroom looks and feels? *Business Week* provided a glimpse of the twenty-first-century classroom in a 1993 article.[3] The article followed the fictional Jackie and José on a typical day. On this particular Tuesday, Jackie and José don't head to a regular classroom, but to a high-tech Mediated Learning Center, where they have access to instruction in a variety of formats, including text, graphics, animation, simulation, and full-motion audio and video.

Jackie and José are both working on their algebra using interactive instructional software. Their first step is to take a pre-test. Based upon the results, the computer takes each student to his or her best starting place—lesson seven for Jackie and lesson six for José. The students progress through their lessons at their own pace and get regular feedback on their progress. Of course, this isn't just straightforward, linear software. There isn't just one sequence of exercises and one course for navigating the topic. Rather, the software presents a variety of unique pathways to learning so the student can tailor the experience and move ahead at his or her own pace. Also, when Jackie and José feel they need more help, they can access video clips of the nation's best teachers explaining topics by simply clicking on a help key.

José, who absorbs information better in short spurts, gets up after about half an hour and leaves. He will return to the point at which he left off later in the day. He takes with him a printout of computer-generated readings and exercises that were identified in the course of his session and are geared to his particular strengths and weaknesses. Jackie, who prefers to work longer stretches, stays on in the lab for another two hours. Where are the teachers while Jackie and José are working on their computers? The teachers are working with other students, either individually or in small groups; they are teaching classes on material that is not well suited for the technology-mediated instruction; and they are developing new curricula.

The classroom of tomorrow is unlike any classroom we have known. Traditionally, learning was a passive process in which students read textbooks or listened to teachers lecture. Students had no involvement in the structure of the course or where or how the information was presented. In contrast, the learning environment of tomorrow will be highly interactive and will engage the student in the entire learning process. Students will use a variety of instructional resources and software that will allow them to control the pace and sequence of instruction to fit their individual needs. They will be able to work interactively with a computer on a topic, problem, or exercise for as long as it takes for them to master the topic fully. While they are working, they will receive regular feedback on their progress with detailed direction on how they should proceed. One-on-one or in small groups, they will receive tutoring from teachers or teaching assistants. When they leave their learning sessions, students will take with them interactive textbooks that will be more like individual study guides than the textbooks we have today.

Freeing Learning From Time And Space

We used to think of learning as something that occurred at a specific place and time and in a particular sequence. The new technology of learning is changing all of that. Bernard Avishai, a former associate editor of the *Harvard Business Review*, put it this way:

> The point is, technologies . . . will . . . transform the structure of schools. These could well become networked hives of specialized, team-based, computer-supported mentoring. The structural patterns that connect various educational programs, in all kinds of buildings—or at home, for that matter—may themselves be like . . . stars . . . and spiders' webs.
>
> Students might attend a supervised program at a public building one day and a teleconferenced program at a neigh-

bor's telecomputer the next; one day, the program might be a lecture or a discussion of a film run by a nonprofit teaching organization; the next, it might be an interactive program put on the network by a for-profit software developer. Nor will the students have to be children. . . . Everybody will have to keep learning.[4]

Indeed they will. And the school itself will change, expand, and grow. In fact, the school may become the centerpiece institution that links all of us not just with the educational system, but with work, government, community support groups, and, most importantly, each other.

The Twenty-First-Century Learning Campus

After the January 1994 earthquake in Los Angeles, the *Los Angeles Times* speculated about the city's and the state's future in a special report entitled "The Next Los Angeles: Reinventing Our Future." Part of the "reinvention," the report prophesied, was a reinvented school system—a "Cyber School," in the newspaper's terms. The Cyber School would be not just a high-tech learning center, but a center of community and social services, with much longer operating hours and a greatly expanded mission. While the crystal ball gazing of the *Los Angeles Times* may not be entirely accurate, it comes close to the transformation we are likely to see in schools, not just in Los Angeles, but across the nation. Here are some of the key features of this new type of school.

- **The Community Center:** First and foremost we will see a return to the school playing an integral role in the community. The public school will become a kind of community center offering both eight A.M. to three P.M. instruction and a full range of community and social services for all age groups.
- **Longer Operating Hours:** Since the school will be providing so many additional services, it will be open longer each day and will stay open on weekends and holidays. Libraries, interactive learning centers, science labs, and other study facilities will be open late at night and on weekends and available for use not just by students but by working parents and

community groups too. Figure 17.1 shows what the schedule of a typical day might look like.

FIGURE 17.1

**Typical Schoolday
Schedule of Events
of a Community School of the Future**

6 A.M. —Child-care and elder-care center opens

7 A.M. —Work carpool departs from parking lot

8 A.M. —School starts

10 A.M.—Speaking English as a second language

Noon —Lunch

1 P.M. —Prenatal-care clinic open at School Health Center

2 P.M. —Storytelling at elder-care center for third graders and senior citizens

3 P.M. —Intramural sports, grades four to six

3 P.M. —After-school child-care center open
–7 P.M.

6 P.M. —Parenting class with individual counseling
–8 P.M.

6 P.M. —Childbirth class at School Health Center
–7 P.M.

7 P.M. —Village coffee shop open in cafeteria with entertainment
–10 P.M. and dance lessons

8 P.M. —Community school governing body meets to discuss plans for annual neighborhood carnival, operating report for community recycling center operated on school grounds, and school budget for the coming year

8 P.M. —Speaking English as a second language
–10 P.M.

10 P.M.—Voluntary cleanup crew
–11 P.M.

- **The Self-Governing School:** The new school has a remarkable degree of independence. A principal is selected by a committee of parents, teachers, and district administrators. Together with this parent-teacher council he or she is then given lump sum annual funds and allowed to decide how the money should be spent. For accountability, the state or the school district sets clear performance goals that are used to measure the effectiveness with which the schools are run.

- **A Single Learning Campus:** Instead of scattering schools throughout the community, all age groups, from pre-school through twelfth grade, attend mini-schools grouped on the same learning campus. This community learning center provides continuity for students as they move through the system. From time to time, students will leave this campus to take special training at colleges and universities affiliated with the community school or to gain work experience through apprenticeship programs with private firms.

- **Teaching Staff:** The teaching staff will consist of a mixture of master teachers, instructors, and teacher's aides who will work together in teams to provide instruction and to coach students. These teams will be multicultural and bilingual, and students and teaching teams will stay together for as long as three years.

- **Technology:** The community campus–learning center will have a full complement of technology to support instruction and to streamline administrative tasks. Additionally, the campus–learning center computers will be linked to national and international learning/information networks. Through these networks, students, teachers, parents, and everyone in the community will have instant access to information anywhere in the world.

- **Services:** The school/campus isn't just a learning center. It is a full community center offering child care, elder care, immunization clinics, aid to families, childbirth and parenting classes, social services, and so on.

The Revolution In American Education

Tech-prep programs and apprenticeships; edutainment software and mediated learning centers; the "Cyber School"—these all represent revolutionary changes to America's educational systems. Will they move beyond the experimental stage and become the day-to-day education reality for most Americans? Probably, at least in some form. Will they work? No one can be entirely sure, but the results from early experiments seem to indicate that now we may have finally learned how to create educational systems that can produce a highly skilled or at least a significantly "up-skilled" workforce. The individuals turned out by the revolutionized educational system will be capable and demanding employees, and they will be in demand for their skills and knowledge. They will be employees who cannot be managed. They will be employees who must be led.

PART VII

THE NEW LEADERSHIP

The Boss. We know who he is and what he is like, and it is always or almost always a *he*. No women need apply. He is the one who issues the orders, calls the shots, makes the decisions, and tells us what to do to solve the problems. He takes names and kicks the lower-rear portion of underlings' anatomies. He punishes. He never asks for advice but frequently asks questions. They aren't really questions: they are more like mini-examinations in which the questioned had better know the answers or else. The Boss knows that he is always right and that, with the right amount of intimidation, he can get everyone else to agree that, indeed, he is. He can be brilliant and charming at times, but he can also explode in a rage, screaming and swearing at incompetence, both real and imagined. In the blink of an eye, he can switch from being kind and even compassionate to being brutal.

Regardless of mood, he demands ultimate loyalty—actually, *fealty* is a better word. He plays head games and has a sadistic penchant for psychological oppression, particularly the kind that comes from humiliating people in front of their peers. He does whatever he has to do to get what he wants, regardless of how his behavior affects other people. Having a rigid superego, he is relentlessly demanding and is impossible to please, especially since he rarely makes his exaggerated expectations clear. His antics are legendary and frequently even funny in a morbid sort of way. For example, the Boss is the one who

- writes a memo threatening to fire anyone who adjusts the office thermostat;
- issues a directive that employees who take time off to attend a funeral must show a copy of the obituary to verify their relationship to the deceased;
- makes his subordinates bark like dogs to receive their paychecks; and even
- demands an immediate meeting with a subordinate, then keeps the luckless and terrified underling waiting for hours or even days for the meeting to occur before suddenly deciding not to have the meeting at all.

The Boss is the one who routinely rejects everyone's work the first time it is presented to him on the premise that no one's first efforts could ever possibly live up to his own exalted standards. He loves to start meetings at five P.M. and have them run until midnight or later just for the fun of it. He has no home life to speak of and assumes that no one who works with him should have a home life either. When he is angry, as he frequently is, he expresses his displeasure by slamming doors, throwing telephones or anything else that is handy, pounding on the table at meetings, and kicking the chairs of errant subordinates, thus forcing the unlucky occupant to hang on to their body and sanity for dear life.[1]

The Boss has been variously described as tough; a sadistic bully; an impossible tyrant; a rabid perfectionist; an ego-squashing, tongue-lashing tail-kicker; a hot-tempered control freak; or just a plain cold, calculating, mean-spirited SOB. He is also now being described as passé.

We are beginning to realize that "Boss Behavior," particularly in its most brutal and extreme form, doesn't work anymore. The workplace of tomorrow demands something quite different. We don't know exactly what the leader of tomorrow will be like, but we can be certain that he or she won't behave like the Boss from Hell we have been describing.

As we approach the end of the twentieth century, we are developing new concepts of leadership. We are beginning to speak of the possibility of the leader being a "servant" and a "selfless steward" rather than a "commander," "boss," or "tyrannical SOB." We are beginning to develop a picture of a leader who is no longer the symbolic head of the organization. Instead, we are beginning to view the leader as symbolizing the organization's heart, or even its soul. And we are changing our ideas about what a leader does. The new leader doesn't plan, watch, control, direct, or evaluate like the leader of the past. He or she isn't the solution giver and doesn't prescribe what is best for others. The new leader isn't so much a teacher or coach as a facilitator—a facilitator of change, learning, and self-management. Perhaps the best term that captures the essence of the new leadership is this: the new leader is a *servant*.

The Leader As A Servant

The idea of servant leadership isn't new. It was first voiced by Robert K. Greenleaf, a former director of management research at AT&T, in a 1970 essay entitled "The Servant as Leader." Greenleaf's basic philosophy of leadership was simple.[2] The leader, argued Greenleaf, exists only to serve his followers. They, in turn, grant him their allegiance in response to his servant nature.

Greenleaf credited his ideas about the servant leader to the German-Swiss Nobel prize–winning writer Hermann Hesse. Hesse wrote a novel entitled *Journey to the East* in the 1930s. In this novel, Hesse tells the story of a group of men who go on a mysterious journey sponsored by the League, a secret society. They are accompanied by a servant, Leo, who not only performs menial chores but entertains and sustains the others on the journey with good spirits and song. In the course of the journey, Leo suddenly disappears. After Leo's disappearance the others discover that they can't go on without him, and the group falls apart. Years later, the narrator of Hesse's story searches for Leo and visits the seat of the League. Greenleaf wrote, "There he discovers that Leo, whom he had known first as *servant*, was in fact the titular head of the Order, its guiding spirit, a great and noble *leader.*" Greenleaf built his philosophy of servant leadership from the foundation of this simple story.

What are the characteristics of the servant leader? Here are a few drawn from Greenleaf's writings:

- Servant leaders are servants first. They don't aspire to lead as much as they aspire to learn. They aren't driven by the need for power or material possession so much as the need to serve.
- Servant leaders lead first by listening. They seek, in the words of the prayer of St. Francis, not so much to be understood as to understand. Whom do servant leaders listen to? Their followers, of course. Robert Taylor, dean of the University of Louisville business school says, "The servant leader doesn't have answers, he has questions."
- Servant leaders help people to articulate their own goals. Part of the listening and questioning the servant leader does is intended to figure out (or better yet, help his or her followers figure out) the will of the group. Whether it is called "vision," "purpose," or "mission," the servant leader seeks to articulate clearly and to have the group reach consensus on a direction or raison d'être.
- The servant leader inspires trust. Followers are confident of the servant leader's values, commitment, integrity, and concern. The most important of the servant leader's values is, of course, the value he or she places on people and the faith that doing what is good for people *will* pay off in the end.
- Finally, the servant leader takes people and their work seriously and is devoted to their personal development. This emphasis goes beyond employee involvement, participation, and empowerment to something much deeper and more fundamental. Ultimately the hope of the servant leader is that everyone will realize his or her potential not only to be self-managing but to be self-led—that everyone can aspire to and become servants and leaders.

In his book *Managing from the Heart,* Hyler Bracey, president of the Atlanta Consulting Group, describes the servant leader as a leader-manager who honors five unspoken employee requests:

- hear and understand me
- even if you disagree with me, please don't make me wrong

- acknowledge the greatness within me
- remember to look for my loving intentions
- tell me the truth with compassion

In *Leadership Jazz*, Herman Miller chairman Max Dupree lists the following twelve characteristics as key to anyone wishing to become a servant leader:

1. **Integrity**
2. **Vulnerability**
3. **Discernment**
4. **Awareness of the human spirit** (understanding the cares, yearnings, and struggles of the human spirit)
5. **Courage in relationships** (ruthless honesty and willingness to face up to tough decisions)
6. **Sense of humor**
7. **Intellectual energy and curiosity**
8. **Respect for the future, regard for the present, understanding of the past** (ability to move constantly between the present and the future)
9. **Predictability**
10. **Breadth** (or vision)
11. **Comfort with ambiguity**
12. **Presence** (being approachable, having the willingness to ask and answer questions)

Peter Block's *Stewardship: Choosing Service Over Self-Interest*, further describes the essence of servant leadership, what Block calls "stewardship," as "the willingness to be accountable for the well-being of the larger organization by operating in service, rather than in control, of those around us." "The underlying value," Block continues, "is about deepening our commitment to service" by

- seeking a balance of power in the organization;
- having the primary commitment be one to the larger community;
- having each person in the organization join in defining purpose and deciding what kind of culture the organization will become; and
- ensuring that rewards are distributed in a balanced and equitable manner.

This new-age concept of servant leadership, stewardship, and so on is, of course, a far cry from the Theory-X, Machiavellian, Leona Helmsley, Attila-the-Hun, boss-as-psycho approaches to which we have become accustomed. It is not exactly the kind of leadership paradigm we might expect to develop in an environment of stress, uncertainty, and upheaval. Yet Chris Lee and Ron Zemke suggested in a 1993 *Training* magazine article that Greenleaf planted a slow-growing seed back in 1970, and the result of that planting now seems to be bearing fruit.

In reality, we probably won't see a form of leadership in most American organizations that perfectly mirrors Greenleaf's philosophies. That may be going a bit too far. Most American businesses and business leaders are not yet ready to make redemption, rather than profit, the purpose of the business, as the most extreme servant leader might be tempted to do. We are likely, however, to see a definite movement in the direction of the servant leader. Why? Because change—rapid, discontinuous, fearful, gut-wrenching change—will continue to be there for all of us to face, and what we have done to lead change or manage change in the past hasn't worked very well. We are being forced into servant leadership, or something very close to it, because it is the only kind of leadership that seems to work when the only certainty is change, change, change, change, change, and change again.

CHAPTER 18

The Leader as a Facilitator of Change

The leader of tomorrow will be a master facilitator of change. More precisely, the future leader will be a purveyor of reality—a doggedly determined disciple of personal, organizational, and societal truth. He or she will be almost evangelically committed to rooting out the ways people limit or deceive themselves from seeing what is and will insist that everyone within his or her realm of influence continually challenge espoused and unespoused theories about what things are, what things mean, and why things are the way they are. The leader of tomorrow recognizes that the changes of the past were different from the changes of today and tomorrow. Old change-management paradigms don't work anymore. The nature of change itself has changed and so must our response.

The Nature Of Change Has Changed

The change we face is different now. It is not just that change comes at a faster pace or that it is more turbulent or complex than the kind of change we have known in the past. The kind of change we frequently experience today and the kind that will be increasingly prevalent tomorrow is different in another way. Much of today's change and most of tomorrow's will be non-linear, unpredictable, and discontinuous. In the past, the past itself provided rules, guidance, and instruction for dealing with the future. If the future couldn't be forecasted precisely, at least the past and present provided a basis for a reasonably accurate guess as to what the future might be like. No more. The only certainty is that revolutionary, sweeping, unexpected, breakpoint change will occur and will do so on a regular basis. In such a world, a central task for the leadership of any organization is to help individuals and the organization as a whole come to grips with the reality of a future that can only be partially foreseen, if it is foreseeable at all. In short, a principal challenge for leaders in the new workplace is to enable people to march confidently forward, accepting, if not becoming totally comfortable with, the knowledge that the consequence of each subsequent step they take can never be fully known in advance of their taking the step. It is a level of self-confidence and comfort with uncertainty, unpredictability, and relentless forward movement that is foreign to our nature, but it is a skill or character trait that all participants in the workplace of the new millennium will have to acquire.

Entering The Green Room

Most members of American organizations have been taught to avoid change. Whether we realize it or not, we have been emotionally conditioned to react negatively to change, particularly sharp, unpredictable, and sudden change. Our reaction is entirely natural, given our experiences. It is a learned anxiety, and it is a type of anxiety we will all have to work to overcome.

What is this "learned anxiety"? Edgar Schein, professor of management at the MIT Sloan School of Management, describes a classical example of emotional conditioning and learned anxiety in a 1993 *Sloan Management Review* article.[1] Schein notes that if you put a dog on a black platform in a green room, ring a bell, and give the dog a painful shock anytime it tries to get off the platform, the dog, being reasonably intelligent and sensitive to pain, will quickly learn that it is better to stay on the platform than to venture into the unknown. From then on, just ringing the bell will be sufficient to keep the dog on the platform. Eventually it won't be necessary even to ring the bell. The dog will learn that the green room is to be avoided at all costs, and if it has sufficient food and water, it will live happily on the black platform forever.

Our learned habits, beliefs, values, assumptions, and ways of doing things in organizations represent our black platforms. They are comfortable and secure, and in most organizations employees have been taught that getting off the black platform—venturing into the green room of change—can be painful. Schein writes:

> In the organizational world, the green room can be something that the company once tried that did not work, or it can be anything new in an organization. . . .
>
> For example, if employees have been through several traumatic reorganizations that involved downsizing or other painful events, they may come to treat all proposed change programs or reorganizations as bells that signal once again that they are being forced into a green room. Or, equally restrictive, if employees remember that certain past strategies have not worked well, they will treat those strategies as green rooms and will avoid them or cower anxiously, they will not produce the new behavior that the change agent or coach is anxious to reward.

How do we learn to overcome this anxiety we feel toward change? The answer, Schein notes, is a paradox.

The Necessary But Paradoxical Anxieties Of Change

We now know that there are certain necessary but paradoxical anxieties that are integral to change. Resistance to change, as Schein suggests, is an emotionally conditioned and learned response. Having been punished for changing or trying to change in the past, we dare not change in the future. Our anxiety with change keeps us paralyzed and fearful. The paradox is that most people cannot overcome their anxiety with changing unless they develop an even greater anxiety with not changing. It isn't enough for our leader simply to entice us with vivid descriptions of how nice the green room has become. Rarely are such promises of tomorrow sufficient to make us give up the comfort of today. We will stubbornly cling to what we know. In fact, most of us won't venture into the green room unless we first become uncomfortable with our black platform and feel guilty about staying on it. Schein writes:

> The organization members must come to perceive that their current ways of doing things are no longer working. There is

not enough food on the black platform, or it is beginning to rock dangerously, or something else bad is happening on it or to it. Change managers must make disconfirming data highly visible to all members of the organization, and such data must be convincing. Just saying that the organization is in trouble because profit levels are down, market share is being lost, customers are complaining, costs are too high, or good people are leaving is not enough. Employees and managers at all levels must believe the data, and that requires *intense communication and economic education* which has often been lacking in organizations. Employees often simply do not understand or do not believe it when management says, "We are in trouble."[2]

This lesson of leadership and change is well established. We now know that order, equilibrium, stability, and simplicity are the enemies of change. The leader who wishes to push his people off the black platform must first create disorder, disequilibrium, and instability. Most importantly, he or she must not reduce or simplify information and communication but rather push the organization into information overload. Jack Welch's experiences at GE provide a good example.

The GE Experience

In 1981, when Jack Welch became CEO at GE, the company had a host of problems. Its earnings growth was only average. It had problems with cash flow. GE's core business was growing slowly, if at all. The company's productivity growth rate was only 1 percent to 2 percent a year, and its operating margins were inadequate. Perhaps worse, GE was inwardly focused and not very innovative. Its bureaucracy was slow to make decisions and its managers were forever engaged in turf struggles. In Edgar Schein's terms, GE had too many managers and employees sitting comfortably in the middle of one big, wide, and deep "black platform." Welch quickly realized that the situation required a revolution. But first he had to wake the organization by taking control of its police, media, and educational system and using them to interject reality and spread discomfort.

Noel Tichy, a professor of business at the University of Michigan and a consultant who helped Welch revolutionize GE, described Welch's facilitation of change as follows:

Revolutionaries overturn the current system and replace it with one of their own devising. They . . . grab the police, media, and education system, as Welch did.

The Police: GE's internal auditing staff, considered by many inside the company as the Gestapo and headed by the top finance executive. Welch eliminated many financial measures and forced people to look at comparisons with competitors, not just budgets. He redirected the auditors' focus to serving GE's businesses rather than controlling them.

The Media: Welch took control of all his forms of communication, from board communications to security analyst presentations, using his own words and ideas when writing speeches for internal audiences.

The Schools: The GE Blue Books (management training guides), although not used for 15 years, had still left their cultural imprint. They were symbolically burned. Welch said that there were no more "textbook" answers. Leaders must write their own. He took direct control of Crotonville, the GE training facility. He continues to appear personally every two weeks at Crotonville to interact in classes and direct the overall curriculum for everyone from new hires to senior executives.[3]

In a 1989 interview, Welch reflected on his experiences at GE and described what he believed were a leader's responsibilities. Welch said:

Above all else, . . . good leaders are open. They go up, down, and around their organization to reach people. They don't stick to the established channels. They're informal. They're straight with people. They make a religion out of being accessible. They never get bored telling their story.

Real communication takes countless hours of eyeball to eyeball, back and forth. It means more listening than talking. It's not pronouncements on a videotape, it's not announcements in a newspaper. It is human beings coming to see and accept things through a constant interactive process aimed at consensus. And it must be absolutely relentless. . . .

I mean facing reality, seeing the world as it is rather than as you wish it were. We've seen over and over again that businesses facing market downturns, tougher competition, and more demanding customers inevitably make forecasts that are much too optimistic. This means they don't take advantage of the opportunities change usually offers. Change in the marketplace isn't something to fear; it's an enormous opportunity to shuffle the deck, to replay the game. Candid managers—leaders—don't get paralyzed about the "fragility" of the organization. They tell people the truth. That doesn't scare them because they realize their people know the truth anyway. . . .

. . . The point is, what determines your destiny is not the hand you're dealt; it's how you play the hand. And the best way to play your hand is to face reality—see the world the way it is—and act accordingly.[4]

The Real Purpose Of "Reality Seeking"

Facing reality is, indeed, the first step to change. This "reality seeking," though, is more than simply nudging, or perhaps we should say bludgeoning, the troops into adopting new work processes, technology, and organizational forms. There are a number of new ideas about learning and personal growth that are bound closely to "reality seeking." It is subtle and typically unexpressed, but it is there. It is psychological, philosophical, and in some respects even spiritual. It has to do with something Peter Senge and his colleagues at the Systems Thinking and Organization Learning Program at MIT's Sloan School of Management call "personal mastery."

Personal Mastery And Commitment To The Truth

In his book *The Fifth Discipline*, Peter Senge describes "personal mastery" as a discipline of personal growth and learning. He writes:

People with high levels of personal mastery are continually expanding their ability to create the results in life they truly seek. From their quest for continual learning comes the spirit of the learning organization.

. . . Personal mastery goes beyond competence and skills, though it is grounded in competence and skills. It goes beyond spiritual unfolding or opening, although it requires spiritual growth. It means approaching one's life as a creative work, living life from a creative as opposed to [a] reactive viewpoint.[5]

Senge notes that to achieve personal mastery, a person must, among other things, learn how to see current reality more clearly.[6] Senge calls this search for current reality a "commitment to the truth." He writes:

> Commitment to the truth does not mean seeking the "Truth," the absolute final word or ultimate cause. Rather, it means a relentless willingness to root out the ways we limit or deceive ourselves from seeing what is, and to continually challenge our theories of why things are the way they are. It means continually broadening our awareness, just as the great athlete with extraordinary peripheral vision keeps trying to "see more of the playing field."[7]

Ultimately, the goal of the servant leader is not just to facilitate immediate change, but to liberate the innate capacity of each individual to learn and to become excited about new imaginings. Once engendered, such excitement about individual learning will lead to faster and deeper organization learning, to breaking mental modes, to innovation, to the creation of value with the customer, and ultimately to profits and growth. Of course, the willingness to change and to embrace change as a real and welcome part of life has to be sustained. Something else, though, is required for that to happen.

Disorder, disequilibrium, instability, and crisis—even the perception of impending doom—create in most of us a level of anxiety and sense of guilt sufficient to cause us to begin to change, but they are rarely sufficient to sustain that change, much less to induce us to love change itself. While it is true that anxiety and guilt will cause us to begin moving off the black platform and into the green room, it is also true that we will be ever watchful of the black platform. At the first sign that the platform is no longer shaking—that the crisis and instability that engendered our anxiety and guilt in the first place might be abating—we will cease changing and return to our comfort zone.

Avoiding the pain of the present is rarely enough motivation for us to undertake radical or lasting change, nor is it sufficient for us to learn to appreciate change itself. We need a much better reason.

As someone once said, people don't climb mountains in order to avoid pain in the valley. They climb mountains to realize the joy they believe can be theirs only if they reach the summit. The servant leader understands this second principle of facilitating change. That is why the leader's second step in facilitating change is creation of the shared vision—our own personal and collective notion of what the summit of the mountain truly can be like.

CHAPTER 19 Facilitating the Shared Vision

Let us suppose that we were asked for one all-purpose bit of advice for management, one truth that we were able to distill from the excellent companies research. We might be tempted to reply, "Figure out your value system. Decide what your company stands for. What does your enterprise do that gives everyone the most pride? Put yourself out ten or twenty years in the future: what would you look back on with the greatest satisfaction?"[1]

Of course, when Tom Peters and Bob Waterman wrote these lines in the early 1980s, they weren't the first management consultants and business writers to suggest that leaders needed to inspire their troops with a compelling vision. Many other writers had offered similar advice to America's business leaders long before Peters and Waterman began work on their famous 1982 best-seller *In Search of Excellence.* Maybe it was just that Peters and Waterman presented the argument for *vision and values* so well, or maybe it was just that their book was so widely read. Regardless, Peters and Waterman's "one all-purpose piece of advice" was widely followed. In the 1980s, it seemed that every CEO had to give his or her company a *vision, mission, set of values, statement of purpose, philosophy, credo,* call it what you will. Every company had to have something to post on the walls of corporate headquarters. Teams of underlings were sent off to create a vision for their company. We got such clear, crisp, gut-grabbing, awe-inspiring statements as

---

The Corporation is committed to providing innovative engineering solutions to specialized problems where technology and close attention to customer service can differentiate it from mass production or job shop operations.

---

or

We provide our customers with retail banking, real estate, finance, and corporate banking products which will meet their credit, investment, security and liquidity needs.

---

or

[The company] is in the business of applying micro-electronics and computer technology in two general areas: computer-related hardware, and computer enhancing services, which include computation, information, education, and finance.

---

or

[We] are the best in the business. We are made a unique company through employee involvement. We promote from within regardless of race, religion, creed, or educational background. Only through Attitude, Pride, and Enthusiasm will both our employees and our company prosper and grow. We not only demand excellence of ourselves, we demand excellence of our employees as well. [Our] explosive growth is due to the partnership between the employees and the company. [We] are committed to rewarding employees who "Make it happen!"[2]

They were all so bland and boring. The only thing most of them motivated employees to do was yawn. The reality for most American companies in the 1980s and early 1990s was that the creation and communication of a vision accomplished little. Employees weren't inspired or motivated. The workforce didn't develop a clearer sense of direction. The best efforts of people weren't mobilized toward a common goal. None of the expected benefits of a vision were realized. It was all a waste of time, effort, and the paper on which the vision statements were printed.

Given our experiences with visioning efforts in the recent past, it is somewhat ironic that the creation of a shared vision is becoming one of the most important, and in some ways *the* most important, task of leadership in the new organization. Why? Because it is next to impossible to have an energetic, creative, innovative, flexible, competency-driven company without a vision. Peter Senge states the matter clearly, "You cannot have a learning organization without a shared vision."[3] In a world of chaos and rapid change, a company that continues without a clear and consistent vision risks much, as Margaret Wheatley points out in her book *Leadership and the New Science:*

> If we have not bothered to create a field of vision that is coherent and sincere, people will encounter other fields, the ones we have created unintentionally or casually. It is important to remember that *space is never empty.* If we don't fill it with coherent messages, if we say one thing but do another, then we create dissonance in the very *space* of the organization. As employees bump up against contradicting fields, their behavior mirrors those contradictions. We end up with what is common to many organizations, a jumble of behaviors and people going off in different directions, with no clear or identifiable pattern. Without a coherent, omnipresent field, we cannot expect coherent organizational behavior. What we lose when we fail to create consistent messages . . . is not just integrity. We lose the partnership of a field-rich space that can help bring form and order to the organization."

As we approach the end of the twentieth century, it has become obvious that the very thing most American companies have failed to do well in the past—create a consistent, inspiring, shared vision—has become vital to their survival in the future. The new organization will be dysfunctional if those working in it don't share a common purpose, mission, and values. Fortunately, we have found a way to help large groups of people reach consensus on a common purpose and desired future state. The technique is called the "future search conference" and it dates from a chance meeting between two Britons, one a CEO and the other a social scientist, over thirty years ago. The results of that meeting are now having a profound effect on what American business leaders do and how mission, purpose, and direction is set for American companies.

The Fortunate Meeting At A Pub

One evening in 1960, Sir Arnold Hall, CEO of the Bristol Siddeley Aircraft Engine Company, met Eric Trist, a social scientist, in a London pub. Hall was introduced to Trist by a mutual friend, John Chandos, who had been doing some public relations work for Hall's firm. In the course of the conversation that followed that evening, Hall described the multiple problems his company was facing. Bristol Siddeley had been created in the 1950s through the merger of two companies—Armstrong-Siddeley, a piston engine company, and Bristol Aero Engines, a world-class jet pioneer. Hall faced a classic problem. The two companies had been merged on paper, but they had no common mission, strategy, or plans. The executives from the two former firms were having difficulty working together, to put it mildly. One social scientist who worked with Bristol Siddeley at the time recalled that the two companies were "as alike as chalk and cheese. Their corporate philosophies were incompatible and they were contemptuous of each other."[4] This inability of executives from the two newly merged companies to work together was particularly serious, since Bristol Siddeley was, at the time, in a high-stakes race with Rolls Royce to become number one in jets.

After listening to Hall's concerns for some time, Trist said that he thought he and his colleagues at the famous Tavistock Institute could help. Hall accepted the offer, and shortly after that first chance meeting, Trist and Hall met for lunch to discuss what could be done. Trist brought along Fred Emery, with whom he had done some groundbreaking work on new workplace and team practices, particularly the use of self-managed teams. Trist later recalled, "The discussion, wide-ranging and sophisticated, also showed [the Bristol Siddeley executives] had developed no particular ways of working together as a group, nor had they used modern methods of management." Trist and Emery proposed a week-long residential seminar at Bistol Siddeley's staff college at Bradford near Warwick, England. Sir Arnold proposed inviting a panel of eminent experts—"great minds," as he put it—to the conference to stimulate thinking about leadership and strategy formulation. Trist and Emery resisted. They wanted to have the executives spend the week in a "dialogue" that could "unlock the internal forces of the group." Obviously the CEO and social scientists couldn't have been further apart on their expectations for the conference. Yet they eventually reached a compromise.

The compromise was simple. Emery and Trist would run the conference as an active group exercise with plenty of dialogue and discussion. Sir Arnold would bring in his outside experts to give lectures before dinner each evening, and the experts would remain after dinner for an open-ended discussion. "The 'great minds' would be allowed in," Emery later recalled, "when they would least disrupt the continuity of the group's work. They would be selected and briefed so that they acted to induce the group to move faster and more widely in directions we had already established."

Bristol Siddeley's conference was held at Bradford House, Warwick, England, on July 10–16, 1960. The company's eleven top executives in design, production, finance, and marketing attended. At the conference, the executives discussed three major topics in the following global-to-specific order:

1. What was the state of the industry in the world at large, and what would the future be like over the next fifteen years?
2. What had the aviation industry become, and how was it likely to develop?
3. In relationship to these, what was the state of Bristol Siddeley, and how should it prepare to develop itself?

In a report issued shortly after the conference ended, Trist and Emery wrote that it "was probably successful." They were being modest in their appraisal. In reality the conference accomplished a great deal. Marvin Weisbord describes the results of the Bristol Siddeley conference in his book *Discovering Common Ground* as follows:

Despite the mixed mode, anxiety and novelty, ... the aircraft merger partners made both social and technical breakthroughs. The two cultures discovered their common ground, AND they made critical strategic choices. "By the end of the week they were certainly thinking like one group; and not at all like Siddeley or Bristol men," recalled Emery. "They radically re-defined the business they were in: from pursuing the top-end of the big jets to mobile combustion power generation across the spectrum of internal and external combustion engines." In fact, top management had been on the verge of rolling out an expert strategy directly contradicting the plan that finally emerged.

Finally, there was a major new product breakthrough. As Emery recalled it in 1990, they came up with "the design concept for an airbus for short, dense inter-city routes ... four small engines with the plane certified for landing on two; modular replacement of engines for over-haul; high wing for easy ground loading; small engines meant very low noise levels. That plane became the BA 146 which is Britain's winning product today."

After the conference, Trist and Emery wrote a long action research paper, the Bradford report, giving a detailed account of both the content and processes they used at the Bristol Siddeley conference. Their report has been called one of the key documents in the history of management. Indeed it is, because it documents the first of what would come to be called "future search conferences."[5] Since then, such conferences have been held throughout the world for businesses, government agencies, communities, labor groups, health care organizations, and educational institutions. They have been refined for thirty years by hundreds of researchers, academics, and practitioners. As a result, they have now become one of the most promising vehicles for creating a shared vision for the organization. They have also become one of the key leadership practices for the new workplace.

The Future Search Conference

There are a number of different models for future search conferences. Below is a description that captures the essence of what it is like to attend such a conference.

You receive an invitation to attend a meeting usually reserved for those several levels above you in the hierarchy— even more unusual is the fact that this business meeting is being held in the largest hotel in town.

When you arrive at the meeting you realize that this is going to be unlike any meeting you've ever attended before. It is a meeting to decide the future direction for your organization and there are 500 people in attendance! All levels and functions are represented, seated in mixed table groups of 8 people . . . some of the people at your table you have never even heard of, let alone met.

You are involved in a real and meaningful way in creating your organization's future. You have been waiting years for the opportunity to share your ideas, to have your voice heard. And heard it is, for 3 days as you learn about competitive issues, challenges, and whole system strategies. Collaborating, you make informed decisions and reach agreements that enable the whole organization to better serve all of its stakeholders—customers, corporate suppliers, yourselves, and leaders of your organization.

In the end you recognize this entire experience as basic common sense. Bring together all the interested and affected parties to a change, provide them with the right information and an opportunity to work together interactively—be they 5 or 500—and they will create their collective future. Most important, they will then be empowered to do the right thing to make that future a reality. Nothing more than basic common sense.[6]

A Typical Future Search Conference

A typical future search conference involves from thirty to as many as several hundred participants in a systematic search for consensus on an achievable future for themselves and the organization. The conference is usually held away from the work site, at a hotel or a resort-like location, and is staffed by two to three facilitators who have training and experience in conducting such conferences. While the actual agenda for each conference varies, a typical agenda might look something like the agenda shown in Figure 19.1.

FIGURE 19.1

The Future Search Conference
AGENDA
DAY ONE

I. Opening/Welcome/Introductions

II. World Trends

    1. Whole group:
       • Brainstorm world trends; record on flip chart

    2. Breakout groups (8 to 10 people each):
       • Identify desirable and probable future scenarios

    3. Group presentations

LUNCH

III. Trends That Affect Our Organization

    1. Whole group:
       • Brainstorm trends; record on flip chart

    2. Breakout groups (8 to 10 people each):
       • Identify desirable and probable future scenarios

    3. Group presentations

FIGURE 19.1 CONTINUED

The Future Search Conference
AGENDA
DAY TWO

IV. The Evolution of Our Organization

1. Whole group:
   • Develop timeline of history of our organization
   • Identify significant events
   • Brainstorm strengths and weaknesses

2. Breakout groups (8 to 10 people each):
   • Sort out Prouds and Sorries; things to keep about the organization and things to discard and leave behind as the organization goes forward

3. Group presentations

LUNCH

V. The Future of Our Organization

1. Breakout groups (8 to 10 people each):
   • Create newspaper article about the organization as if writing 5 years from now
   • List our organization's proudest accomplishments

2. Group presentations

3. Whole group:
   • Consolidate lists
   • Search for commonalities
   • Prioritize: Each participant has $10 to spend on their priority items

---

FIGURE 19.1 CONTINUED

The Future Search Conference
AGENDA
DAY THREE

VI. Action Planning

   1. Breakout groups (8 to 10 people each):
      • Develop action plan for top priority items; individuals choose items to work on

   2. Group presentations of action plans

LUNCH

VII. Top Management Staff Meeting (FISHBOWL)

   1. Top management team holds public staff meeting to discuss actions proposed, next steps, how to monitor progress, etc. Whole group watches and listens. Open chair available to anyone for up to 2 minutes.

VIII. Closing

   1. Senior leader of our organization facilitates discussion on how well conference met the expectations of the participants and what participants are willing to do to make a difference.

As shown in the sample agenda, future searches typically start with a broad-brush look at world trends. The participants are asked to brainstorm how things have changed over the last few decades and what trends they discern. Participants are asked to think of the "waves washing over them," that is, the trends that originate elsewhere and continue onward past the point where the participants encounter them. The group's ideas are recorded on flip chart paper that is posted around the room. Oguz Baburoglu and Andy Garr, two consultants who have led a number of future search conferences, note that

this scanning of the environment sets the tone of the conference. This method of starting shows participants that their
ideas will be registered without discrimination based on status
or affiliation. They can see that their perception is legitimately
a part of the whole group.[7]

The whole-group brainstorming session is followed by a breakout session at which groups of eight to ten participants discuss
and reach consensus on what they see as the desirable and probable global trends. The groups choose their own recorder and pre-
senter and decide for themselves how they wish to hold their
discussion and reach consensus. This phase concludes with each
small group reporting back to the larger group. This phase of the
search conference accomplishes three things:

1. participants begin to see themselves as part of the same
   shared world, with many common concerns, hopes, and
   needs
2. collectively the participants begin to evaluate the world in
   which they live
3. the participants begin to experience collective action and
   decision making as a group

The next few phases of the conference become increasingly
more focused and specific. After taking a look at global trends, the
participants next focus just on those trends that are currently im-
pacting their organization. Finally, the conference participants
look internally at the evolution of their own organization and what
they like and dislike about their organization—what are called the
"prouds and sorries." All of this information gathering typically
throws the participants into information overload. The entire experience for the participants becomes chaotic, messy, and frustrating. Yet out of this chaos emerges creative ideas and a group
commitment toward a common future vision. Marvin Weisbord describes this strange complacency-to-confusion-to-renewal cycle
that occurs in future search conferences this way:

People arrive [at the conference] curious, expectant, eager,
mystified, open—and anxious. This is, after all, a strange
group, an unfamiliar methodology, and a formidable task.

Each person has an agenda, though [he or she] may not know what it is or how to work with it. That is part of the discovery.

We build lists, compare world views, listen, and seek to make order from chaos. No person has the whole. Each is tuned into different events. But you remember what I have forgotten, and together we build a very rich portrait. Each discovery brings heightened anxiety and a release of energy. Early on people report being both confused by the multiple images, impressions, diversity, and eager to go deeper, explore more, find new action channels.

In future search conferences, we usually plunge furthest into . . . confusion . . . when we make a group "mind map" of external trends affecting "X"—the focus of our search. Groups grow agitated as the map grows and grows. Gradually the realization sinks in that *this*—all of it—constitutes a mutual portrait of our world. It is complex, interconnected, hopeless, hopeful, unmanageable, inescapable. At the end of the map-making most groups fall speechless. My word for it is "awe.". . .

That is entirely the right place to be. We get out when we take charge of the map. Every person touches it as they indicate the issues [he or she] most want[s] to work with. Then, they start a dialogue with peers on what they are doing now and what they wish to do in the future. Within an hour, the anxiety becomes pure energy. We are moving toward renewal. We have touched down on common ground.[8]

The Vision As A Force Field

Future search conferences provide a process for involving large groups of people in creating their own collective vision of the future and what their organization can and should be like. The visions that result from these conferences aren't just bland, meaningless words on paper. They are vibrant, emotional commitments. The visions produced by future search conferences are rarely, if ever, statements of destination, such as "this organization will grow by 'x' amount by the year 2000 and achieve 'xx' market share." Instead, the visions produced by these conferences are more like guideposts or commonly accepted notions of what is right and wrong, acceptable and unacceptable, important and unimportant, notions that tie people together and provide a sense of oneness and wholeness about their endeavors. The shared vision is more of a feeling shared by all members of the group than a set of facts or body of knowledge. Perhaps Margaret Wheatley explained it best.

In her book *Leadership and the New Science*, Wheatley describes some work on customer service she undertook for a retail chain. In the course of working with the company, Wheatley said she asked employees of the chain to visit several stores. When these employees compared their notes after visits to a large number of stores, something unusual emerged. Wheatley writes:

> To a person, we agreed that we could "feel" good customer service just by walking into the store. We tried to get more specific by looking at visual clues, merchandising layouts, facial expressions—but none of that could explain the sure sense we had when we walked into the store that we would be treated well. Something else was going on. Something else was in the air. We could feel it, we just couldn't describe *why* we felt it.[9]

Eventually, says Wheatley, she came to think of that strange something that they all felt in certain stores as a kind of force field that filled the stores they visited and helped to structure the employees' activities and generate service behavior. Because of that customer-service force field, employees knew instinctively what to do and what not to do. Few controls and policies, if any, were necessary. Good service, as defined by the right behaviors, was guaranteed every time because of that customer-service force field/vision.

When the members of an organization develop a shared vision, they create such a force field. When they do, the leadership of the business is no longer restricted to just involving employees or empowering them. The shared vision allows the leadership of the new organization to do something that has never been done before. Now the leadership can genuinely set employees free to be as creative and innovative as they wish, with no controls, no restraints, and no conditions. Employees can become self-led. Facilitating this self-leadership is the last and most critical task of the new leader.

CHAPTER 20

From Self-Management to the Dawn of Self-Leadership

When Delco Remy opened a new plant in Fitzgerald, Georgia, in 1975, it did something that was relatively rare at that time. Instead of organizing the plant along traditional lines, it created a plant structure in which practically all production and support employees were on teams, and it assigned these teams responsibility and accountability for their own self-management. The operating teams had a laundry list of duties to perform which typically would have been performed by managers, supervisors, or support personnel—certainly not by employees themselves. For example, the Delco Remy teams at Fitzgerald were required to

- handle their own quality control;
- do all maintenance and make minor repairs on machines;
- keep track of their own time cards;
- handle all housekeeping responsibilities;
- engage in regular problem-solving activities;
- monitor their own safety compliance;
- prepare and review capital and operating budgets;
- determine staffing levels;
- advise management on equipment layout and requirements for new equipment;
- recruit employees; and
- even decide on layoffs.

Although such self-managed teams were rare in the 1970s, the idea for self-management wasn't new. Eric Trist and Fred Emery (yes, the same Trist and Emery who were involved in developing future search conferences) did research on self-managed teams in England in the 1950s. Procter & Gamble implemented some team systems in the United States in the 1960s, and practically every major U.S. company, including giants like GM, Ford, Motorola, AT&T, and General Electric, to name just a few, experimented with self-managed teams at selected locations in the 1970s and 1980s. Until now, the experience of most American companies with self-management has been limited to a few isolated experiments, but that is changing. We are beginning to see a much wider movement toward self-management.

We are beginning to see self-management used in companies and places where we have never seen them used before. Once, self-managed teams were found only in manufacturing companies, and only in a few of their plants. Now we are seeing self-managed teams in service companies, and in both manufacturing and service organizations the practice is becoming more common. Additionally, we are seeing a change in the size of the companies experimenting with self-managed teams. Once it was mostly the large companies that conducted the experiments. Now medium-size and even small, start-up companies are practicing self-management.

In 1975, as we said, a plant organized like the Delco Remy's Fitzgerald plant was rare, experimental, and considered very odd. It will be considered anything but rare, experimental, or odd by the turn of the century. In fact, self-management is becoming very much the norm in most American businesses. For example, Charles Manz and Henry Sims, authors of *Business Without Bosses*, estimate that 40 to 50 percent of the U.S. workforce will work in self-managed teams by the end of this decade. What is more, we are even seeing the emergence of a form of organizing and operating businesses that goes beyond self-management. We are beginning to create not just self-managed teams, but self-*leading* teams. In the process, we are drastically and forever changing the role of leaders and followers in American organizations. In fact the terms "leader" and "follower" soon may lose their meaning, as each person becomes not one or the other, but both.

Leading Self-Managed Teams

The term "self-management" carries with it the notion that somehow managers disappear, and by extension, leadership becomes unnecessary when self-managed teams are introduced. That's not entirely true. Managers and supervisors continue to exist, albeit in smaller numbers, and leadership is still important, though no longer vested in just one or a few individuals. In fact, self-management requires more leaders, not less. Such teams need leadership from inside and outside the group.

Leadership Within Self-Managed Teams

David Barry, a professor of management at Syracuse University, studied fifteen self-managed teams in manufacturing, government agencies, and educational institutions over a three-year period in the 1980s to determine the kind of leadership practices the teams followed. Barry identified at least four different leadership roles and behaviors that were required by these self-managed teams for them to function effectively.[1] They were as follows:

1. **Envisioning leadership.** Someone had to facilitate idea generation and innovation in the team and help team members think conceptually and creatively.
2. **Organizing leadership.** Someone had to help the group focus on details, deadlines, efficiency, and structure so that the team could get its work done. These people had, in Barry's terms, an "exacting nature" and were constantly pushing the group to make things predictable and clear, get the task done, and not waste time.
3. **Spanning leadership.** These people were good at maintaining relationships with outside groups and people. Their skills, notes Barry, include networking, presentation management, developing and maintaining a strong team image with outsiders, intelligence gathering, locating and securing critical resources, bargaining, finding and forecasting areas of outside resistance, being sensitive to power distributions, and being politically astute. The spanning leader provided the group with a constant source of reality checks concerning the receptivity of the outside world to what the group proposed or did.
4. **Social leadership.** The social leader was good at uncovering the needs and concerns of individuals in the group, ensuring that everyone had the opportunity to present his or her views, injecting humor when it was needed to relieve group tensions, and generally taking care of the social and

psychological needs of group members or, at least, ensuring that these needs weren't ignored by the group.

All of these leadership roles were important, but, said Barry, they didn't have equal importance at every stage of the team's activities. Each stage called for a different mix of leadership. All types were still present, but usually there was one primary form of leadership and one secondary form that stood out. Since it was rare that any single team member performed more than one type of leadership role, there were normally at least two leaders active at any given time. If the team was to succeed, these leaders' activities had to complement each other. For example, when a team was just getting started, social and spanning leadership were most important to help the team members get acquainted and acquire the resources they needed to start functioning. Later, as the team began to set goals and get organized, envisioning and organizing leadership became more important.

It was very important that a team have the right mix of leadership at every stage of its development. Barry cites the experiences of two of the teams he studied.

Team 1

The first team, Team 1, was a five-person, self-managed team in an electronics firm. All of the members of this team had engineering backgrounds, but they brought to the team different skills, personalities, and orientations. For example, Ann was cool and forceful and had spent the last year studying marketing. Henry was an engineering genius and very inventive but a social misfit. Ken was older, easygoing, and philosophical. Chuck was neat, precise, methodical, and, in addition to engineering, had experience in cost accounting. Jeff was the extrovert of the group and had many friends throughout the company.

Team 1 got off to a good start the first week, and distinct leadership roles began to emerge. Barry writes:

> Ken exhibited social leadership by starting off the first meeting with the suggestion that members give each other some background information about one another's experiences and expectations of the team. From then on, the discussion became animated as each person opened up. Later that week, the team met for four hours at Jeff's house; again, Ken

demonstrated social leadership by making sure that Henry and Chuck, who were the quieter members, got their ideas out and that Jeff, who was the most vocal member of the team, did not monopolize the conversation. At the conclusion of the meeting, Ann began to exert spanning leadership by volunteering to set up a number of site visits with other companies that might be interested in the product ideas the team was considering.

Following Ann's suggestion, the team began visiting other companies. Ann, as she promised, made the contacts with the outside firms. Henry came up with ideas the group could try out on those they visited. Chuck made the travel arrangements and kept track of expenses. He also queried clients about which products and systems were inadequate and made careful records of their responses. Jeff kept the team member's spirits up with humor and talked up the team's activities with other managers in the company. Ken spent a lot of time getting the others to share what they were learning and to summarize the team's progress.

As the team moved on through development and prototyping, the members of the team continued to perform their various leadership roles. The team was together for over two years and was highly successful, developing three new products in the first year alone, including one that revolutionized the industry. It was quite a contrast to what happened in Team 2.

Team 2

Team 2 also had five team members and was in the same electronics firm. However, Team 2 lasted only a few months and was considered a failure by both the company management and team members. Like Team 1, all of the members of Team 2 were engineers. Scott and Frank were quiet, organized, and methodical. Neither had been on a self-managed team before. Russ was friendly and outgoing and cultivated important contacts within the company. He liked power and came across to others as very directive. Bill had a lot of contacts outside the company, and Kevin was the athletic member of the team. Kevin had been captain of most of his sports teams, liked lots of activity, and was a self-proclaimed enemy of formal analysis and planning. It was hardly an ideal mix, as Barry notes in his description of Team 2's first meeting:

From the very first meeting, the team evidenced discord. Frank and Scott opened by stating that the whole idea of an SMT [self-managed team] was stupid. Scott voiced doubts about whether such a team could work very fast, while Frank stated that he did not like working in groups. Russ interjected by saying that the team had to work together for better or worse. He then argued that the team would be best served if one person was in charge and then went on to give reasons why he should be the team's leader. Kevin agreed with the need for one leader but argued that he could do a better job. Later, the group became further polarized as Bill supported Kevin while Scott sided with Russ; Frank remained neutral. The meeting ended with Bill saying that he had another appointment to catch and Russ pushing for another meeting later that week.

During subsequent meetings, things got worse. Kevin and Russ got into a heated argument about a product idea. The argument erupted into a series of sessions during which they blamed each other for the team's lack of progress. Bill was frequently absent from meetings, and when he did show up, he would often leave before the meeting ended. Frank and Scott sat in the meetings and said little. Within two months it was well known throughout the company that Team 2 was having problems. Upper management suggested to the team that they bring in an outside facilitator to help them deal with the conflict. The team refused, and one month later, management disbanded the team.

The Proper Mix

What made the difference between Team 1 and Team 2? Team 1 had all the different leadership styles from the start, as well as members who naturally and easily exhibited those styles. Team 2 didn't have such a mix. Most importantly, Team 2 didn't have an effective social leader who could help the team cope with conflicts that arose or develop an appreciation of the talents potentially resident in the team.

Based upon Barry's research and that of others studying self-managed teams, we now know that the success of such teams depends to a large extent on our ability to staff them with the proper mix of talent and make sure that the mix includes from the beginning and retains over time the full range of leadership styles. So who is responsible for ensuring that the teams are properly staffed? That's one of the key roles of external leaders.

Leadership External to the Self-Managed Team

He or she has been called a "boundary manager," "coach," "champion," "supporter," "resource provider," "consultant," "facilitator," "communicator," and even an "unleader." We prefer the title "coordinator," so that is what we will use here. Regardless of what title he or she is given, we know the coordinator plays a pivotal role in the success of self-managed teams. Yet until recently, we haven't been entirely sure what that role should be. We have spent the better part of two decades trying to answer a question that has plagued advocates of self-managed teams from the beginning: "If the teams are supposed to lead themselves, then what is a coordinator [external leader] supposed to do?" We still have no definitive answers, but some themes are emerging. First, as we have suggested, the coordinator has a critical role to play in selecting people for the self-managed teams in order to ensure that the teams have the proper balance of technical talent and internal leadership skills. In this respect, the coordinator acts like the general manager or coach of a sports team, putting together athletes with the right mix of talent and making sure that the team has strong players at every position.

A second key role of the coordinator is to provide external support to the team. Here the coordinator helps the team's spanning leader locate and acquire resources, provides technical and other training to the team or arranges for it to be provided, advises the team on technical issues or helps the team to identify and acquire the technical support it needs, and helps resolve disputes that occur within teams or between teams. The support role always requires a delicate balancing act on the part of the coordinator. If he or she intervenes in the team's operations and affairs too much, the team ceases to function as a self-managed team. If the coordinator fails to intervene or waits too long to intervene when problems occur, then the team can fail. This balancing act leads to the final key role of the coordinator. The ultimate objective of the coordinator is to push the team and team members toward ever greater independence and ultimately to something beyond self-management—something we are now beginning to call self-*leadership*.

Self-Leadership

There is a fundamental difference between self-*management* and self-*leadership*. Self-managed people take responsibility for controlling their own behavior *within boundaries set by others*. Self-led people decide for themselves what *is* and *is not* worth pursuing and then set their own goals and expectations, arrange their own feedback systems to tell them how they are performing, and gain natural or intrinsic reinforcement from what they accomplish.

Self-led people are not just self-controlled, they are self-motivated. They aren't pushed to performance by external forces. They are pulled to excellence by their own internal needs, drives, and desires. Ultimately, the most important task of the new leader/coordinator is the fostering among groups and individuals this self-leadership. The ultimate task of the leader/coordinator is to help teams assume greater and greater levels of responsibility, accountability, and control so that they become not self-managed teams, but self-led teams. While we don't have any such teams yet, we have a sense of what they would be like, and the most advanced of self-managed teams are increasingly becoming self-led.

Self-Leading Teams

Self-leading teams are different from self-managed teams in several key respects. Like self-managed teams, self-leading teams are small groups of individuals, usually four to twelve people. Team members make their own job assignments, determine how they will accomplish their production goals, solve their own quality problems, address social problems within their groups, carry out most of the traditional managerial and supervisory tasks, and generally have wide discretion about how they perform their work. Like self-managed teams, self-directed teams usually perform some natural, whole, value-adding piece of the work or process flow. So far, in almost all respects, self-leading teams and self-managed teams are very similar. The key difference is not in what self-leading teams do as much as the discretion they exercise over what they do.

Charles Manz, co-author of *Business Without Bosses*, has been a prominent advocate of self-leading teams. Some key differences he finds between self-managed and self-leading teams are shown in Figure 20.1.[2]

FIGURE 20.1

SELF-MANAGED TEAMS	SELF-LEADING TEAMS
Meet standards and goals set by others.	Set their own standards and goals.
Make decisions on *how* work should be performed.	Make decisions not only on *how* work is to be performed, but on *what* work is to be done and *why* it is done through participation in events such as future search conferences.
Team members are provided with technical, problem-solving, process analysis, and social skills training.	Team members receive self-leadership and management skills training in addition to the training they would have received as part of a self-managed team.
Team members are provided with information relevant to their own group's performance.	Team members are provided with information concerning organizational strategy and management in addition to information relevant to their own group's performance.
Teams are provided with leaders that serve as facilitators/coaches.	Team members decide for themselves the type of leaders they will have and who they will be.
Team members interact with other organizational employees within and outside their group.	Team members interact with customers and suppliers outside their organization.

Manz points out that self-leading teams structure themselves, function, and have the discretionary authority common to groups with which we are already familiar, such as professional partnerships, academic departments in universities, small theater companies, and volunteer groups. In essence, self-leading teams are the nodes of the spider's-web organizations we discussed earlier in this book. They take us much further along the path to a truly egalitarian workplace than ever before. At their most extreme, self-leading teams obliterate the long-standing barrier between labor and management and invite the work team members and their representatives to play a much larger role in the governance of the business organization than we have ever known in this country. To say that this movement toward self-leadership is a revolutionary and potentially highly volatile change is to put it mildly. As we said, we don't have true self-led teams yet, so there isn't a real example we can provide. However, there is a business that comes close to being self-led. The name of that company is W. L. Gore & Associates.

W. L. Gore

W. L. Gore & Associates was founded by Wilbert L. ("Bill") Gore in 1958.[3] Gore had worked on a du Pont team to develop applications for Teflon (polytetrafluoroethylene, or PTFE). He had a knowledge of computers and transistors and became convinced that, given the insulating properties of Teflon, there would be a market for Teflon-coated computer cable if it could be produced. Gore set out to make just such a cable, working in his home lab at night.

For several months, Gore had little success. Then, thanks to a suggestion he received from his son, who had seen how 3M had applied the Teflon coating to sealant tape, Gore made a breakthrough. He produced a Teflon-coated ribbon cable. Unfortunately, when he showed his invention to du Pont, the company wasn't interested. Du Pont wanted to remain a supplier of raw materials. It had no desire to become a fabricator, at least not for the product Gore was suggesting. Gore was left to go it alone.

Forty-five years old and with five kids to raise, Gore left du Pont, mortgaged his house, and, over the objections of all of his friends, started his own company in the late 1950s. By 1993, Gore & Associates was an $800 million manufacturer of a wide range of Teflon-based electronic, medical, fabric, and industrial products, including its best-known product Gore-Tex. The company had forty-four plants worldwide and 5,600 associates.

W. L. Gore & Associates still carries the indelible stamp of its founder. Gore created a unique company based on the principles of team systems that Gore learned from his experiences at du Pont. Here are some of the key features that reflect, as you will see, much of what we have been talking about in this book.

1. **No Titles and No Hierarchy.** W. L. Gore & Associates has a president and a secretary-treasurer only because it is required to do so for purposes of incorporation. Other than

that, however, no one has a title, and there is no hierarchy. The company structure is totally flat.

2. **Get Big by Being Small.** None of Gore's forty-four plants has more than two hundred employees. The philosophy at W. L. Gore & Associates is that they can get big but still maintain the close-knit and interpersonal atmosphere of a small company. So far they are succeeding.

3. **No Employees, Just Associates.** The company has no employees, only associates, and it always capitalizes the word in its literature. All associates receive a salary, participate in company profit sharing, and earn stock in the company through an Associates' Stock Ownership Program, which is legally similar to employee stock ownership plans used by other companies.

4. **No Bosses.** W. L. Gore & Associates has no managers, supervisors, or bosses. Instead, every associate has one or more sponsors. In fact, candidates for a job at W. L. Gore have to find a sponsor before they can be hired. That means finding someone in the company who agrees to take a personal interest in you and who will serve as your coach and advocate. There are three kinds of sponsors:

   • the starting sponsor, who helps a new associate get started on his first job or on a new job within the company
   • the advocate sponsor, who sees to it that the associate gets credit and recognition for his or her accomplishments
   • the compensation sponsor, who sees to it that the associate is fairly paid (this sponsor serves as the associate's advocate before a compensation team, which is composed of individuals from the associate's work area; the compensation team reviews and sets the associate's compensation annually)

5. **The Lattice Structure.** The company uses what it calls a lattice structure. It is similar to a spider's-web organization, with many cross-level and cross-functional teams forming and reforming constantly as they are needed. Gore referred to the structure as "teams without formally designated teams." Regardless, lines of communication are direct and open. Anyone can talk to anyone at any time without having to go through an intermediary. People set their own objectives and make their own commitments. It is all very informal.

6. No Bosses, Just Lots of Leaders. While there are no bosses, there are a lot of leaders. In fact, in internal memos Gore described ten types of leaders he felt were necessary:

1) The associate who is recognized by a team as having a special knowledge or experience. . . . This kind of leader gives the team guidance in a special area.

2) The associate the team looks to for coordination of individual activities in order to achieve the agreed-upon objectives of the team. The role of this leader is to persuade team members to *make the commitments* necessary for success (commitment seeker).

3) The associate who proposes necessary objectives and activities and seeks agreement and team *consensus on objectives*. . . .

4) The leader who evaluates the relative contributions of team members (in consultation with other sponsors) and reports these contribution evaluations to a compensation committee. . . .

5) The leader who coordinates the research, manufacturing and marketing of one product type within a business, interacting with team leaders and individual associates who have commitments regarding the product type. The leaders are usually called *product specialists*. They are respected for their knowledge and dedication to their products.

6) *Plant leaders* who coordinate activities of people within a plant.

7) *Business leaders* who help coordinate activities of people in a business.

8) *Functional leaders* who help coordinate activities of people in a "functional" area.

9) *Corporate leaders* who help coordinate activities of people in different businesses and functions and who try to promote communication and cooperation among all associates.

10) *Intrapreneuring associates* who *organize new teams* for new businesses, new products, new processes, new devices, new marketing efforts, new or better methods of all kinds. These leaders invite other associates to "sign up" for their project.

Bill Gore saw plenty of opportunities for leadership and he saw lots of leaders. Everyone could be a leader. He went on to write:

It is clear that leadership is widespread ... and that it is continually changing and evolving. . . . Leaders are not authoritarians, managers of people, or supervisors who tell us what to do or forbid us from doing things; nor are they "parents" to whom we transfer our own self-responsibility. However, they do often advise us of the consequences of actions we have done or propose to do. Our actions result in contributions, or lack of contributions, to the success of our enterprise. Our pay depends on the magnitude of our contributions. This is the basic discipline of our lattice organization.

7. **An Environment of Self-Leadership.** Gore wrote, "All our lives most of us have been told what to do, and some people don't know how to respond when asked to do something—and have the very real option of saying no—on their job. It's the new Associate's responsibility to find out what he or she can do for the good of the operation." Such an approach of non-management could be unnerving to those who had never experienced it before.

The folklore of the company tells the story of one Jack Dougherty, a bright young MBA graduate from the College of William and Mary. Jack joined W. L. Gore & Associates right out of school. Dressed in his best blue suit, he met Bill Gore his first day on the job. Looking Gore squarely in the eye and firmly shaking his hand, Jack told him that he was ready for anything. But Jack wasn't ready for what happened next. Gore reportedly replied, "Why don't you look around and find something you'd like to do." It took Dougherty several frustrating weeks, but finally he found something to do. He started loading fabric into a machine that laminates Gore-Tex membrane to other fabrics. "It was Jack's way of learning the business. And by 1982, he had become responsible for all advertising and marketing for the fabrics group."

Of course that's all folklore. Today, new associates receive several weeks of training before they are ushered to their office or work station and turned loose to find something to do—to make commitments and explore opportunities. Some find the lack of direction and structure frustrating and decide they can't stay. Those who do stay eventually figure out what they are good at and how they can contribute. It all gets very exciting, but, as Anita McBride, an associate in Phoenix says, "It's not for everybody. . . ."

8. **Unstructured R&D.** Gore believed that every associate could be creative, so research and development, like everything else, is totally unstructured. While the company holds a number of patents, it has no R&D department. Instead any associate with an idea can request a piece of raw PTFE (Teflon) with which to experiment. Every associate is encouraged to develop ideas and follow them to their conclusion. That's how Fred Eldreth, an associate at W. L. Gore's Newark, Delaware, plant, who had only a third-grade education, came up with a new design for a machine that is now used to wrap thousands of yards of wire a day. He developed the design over a weekend.

From Labor To Action And On To The World Beyond Workplace 2000

W. L. Gore & Associates is approaching the kind of organization we have been describing. It isn't yet an organization that has gone beyond Workplace 2000, but it comes close to being one. That is the case with an ever-increasing number of American businesses. The business revolution that started in the 1980s is continuing.

In the late 1980s, the United States was a nation in economic retreat. The quality of American-made products was so bad that the label "Made in the USA" was more of a hindrance than a help to a company wishing to sell either in domestic or in foreign markets. The level of service most American companies provided their customers was so atrocious that poor service became the predominant reason they lost customers. In fact, more customers deserted American companies for reasons of poor treatment than for poor quality or high costs. To make matters worse, American businesses were agonizingly slow in developing new products and bringing them to market. For example, American automakers took two years longer, on average, to move new models from concept to market than their Japanese counterparts, and U.S. high-tech companies found that their Japanese counterparts could bring new and more technologically advanced products to market twice as fast and at half the cost. The country that had dominated the global marketplace for decades was in precipitous decline. The world's economic heavyweight had become a paunchy pushover that was being laughed at, ridiculed, and soundly beaten by its fleet-footed global competitors from Asia and elsewhere. Yet even in the face of the country's generalized competitive malaise, America had its success stories.

In the early-to-mid-1980s, Motorola, Xerox, Harley-Davidson, General Electric, Ford, and a few other American companies began to change. They tossed out many of their most treasured business traditions and reinvented themselves. They downsized, restructured, and began to pursue total quality aggressively. But that wasn't all they did. They launched a revolution to reshape the American workplace totally. As we enter the middle of the 1990s, the workplace revolution that these leading American companies began has touched practically every working American. In the early 1990s, less than 5 percent of U.S. companies were engaged in this workplace revolution. Now, practically all of them are, and one-third to one-half have completed or almost completed at least the first stage of this workplace transformation. The remaining are struggling to complete the first stages of the transformation by the end of this decade.

America's workplace revolution began as a fight for survival in a strange new, chaotic, rapidly changing, and totally uncertain business environment of the 1980s. In order to survive, American businesses were forced to rediscover product quality and to reengineer their factories, but what happened in America's factories was only a small part of the story.

America's companies soon discovered that reengineering factories wasn't enough. They were forced to look outside the factory doors for other potential causes of their competitiveness problems. When they did, they found bloated bureaucracies, cumbersome managerial hierarchies, and antiquated, overly generous personnel practices that drove sales and administrative expenses relentlessly upward and systematically devoured whatever cost savings were generated from process improvements in the factories. As it turned out, America's real bloating and sluggishness wasn't in its factories so much as in its big company offices. American business finally realized that just reinventing its factories wouldn't be enough. The whole business not only had to be restructured, but had to be redesigned. The American workplace had to be fundamentally and permanently altered. Incremental change wasn't sufficient. It required a revolution. Workplace 2000 was the beginning of that revolution. Going beyond Workplace 2000 is the continuation. Workplace 2000 was largely about reengineering the business. Going beyond Workplace 2000 is about reconceptualizing the entire nature of work. Both stages of our workplace revolution are concerned with profits and competitiveness, of course, but they involve much more. They go deeper to address fundamental questions about who we are, what we do, and how we live our lives.

Hannah Arendt, the teacher, writer, and political philosopher, described three fundamental human activities—labor, work, and action—in her book *The Human Condition. Labor*, she said, is what a person does to survive. She defined *work* as what we do beyond what was necessary for survival in order to contribute to the world around us. *Action*, however, is something much more. It is what we do beyond labor or work that gives meaning to our lives.

For most of this century, our *work* has actually been, in Arendt's terms, *labor*. It has been what we did to survive, and it has taken an awful toll. In Studs Terkel's terms, *work* for most Americans has been largely about the experience of violence to the spirit as well as to the body: ". . . about ulcers as well as accidents, about nervous breakdowns as well as kicking the dog around."[4] In the last few years the terrible experience of work that has been so common for so long has begun to change at least for some Americans. With the revolution of Workplace 2000, we started turning *labor* into something more—into something beyond what we did simply to survive. Now, as we move beyond Workplace 2000, we have the promise of something even greater. We have the hope of finally finding resolution to the conflicts between work and the rest of our lives. More importantly, we may finally be finding ways to build *meaning* into what we do. And that ultimately is the promise of the world beyond Workplace 2000.

Appendix: The Scans Competencies

The Skills Required For Workplace 2001

The Three-Part Foundation

Basic Skills: Reads, writes, performs arithmetic and mathematical operations, listens, and speaks.

   A. **Reading**—locates, understands, and inteprets written information in prose and in documents such as manuals, graphs, and schedules
   B. **Writing**—communicates thoughts, ideas, information, and messages in writing; and creates documents such as letters, directions, manuals, reports, graphs, and flow charts
   C. **Arithmetic-Mathematics**—performs basic computations and approaches practical problems by choosing appropriately from a variety of mathematical techniques
   D. **Listening**—receives, attends to, interprets, and responds to verbal messages and other cues
   E. **Speaking**—organizes ideas and communicates orally

Thinking Skills: Thinks creatively, makes decisions, solves problems, visualizes, knows how to learn, and reasons.

   A. **Creative Thinking**—generates new ideas
   B. **Decision Making**—specifies goals and constraints, gen-

erates alternatives, considers risks, and evaluates and chooses best alternative

C. **Problem Solving**—recognizes problems and devises and implements plan of action

D. **Seeing Things in the Mind's Eye**—organizes, and processes symbols, pictures, graphs, objects, and other information

E. **Knowing How to Learn**—uses efficient learning techniques to acquire and apply new knowledge and skills

F. **Reasoning**—discovers a rule or principle underlying the relationship between two or more objects and applies it when solving a problem

Personal Qualities: Displays responsibility, self-esteem, sociability, self-management, and integrity and honesty.

A. **Responsibility**—exerts a high level of effort and perseveres towards goal attainment

B. **Self-Esteem**—believes in own self-worth and maintains a positive view of self

C. **Sociability**—demonstrates understanding, friendliness, adaptability, empathy, and politeness in group settings

D. **Self-Management**—assesses self accurately, sets personal goals, monitors progress, and exhibits self-control

E. **Integrity-Honesty**—chooses ethical courses of action

The Five Competencies
Competency #1: Resources

Allocates Time. Selects relevant, goal-related activities, ranks them in order of importance, allocates time to activities, and understands, prepares, and follows schedules.

Examples:

- construct a timeline chart, e.g., Gantt, PERT
- understand the concept of a critical path
- estimate the time required to complete a project by task
- use computer software, e.g., Harvard Project Planner, to plan a project

Allocates Money. Uses or prepares budgets, including cost and revenue forecasts; keeps detailed records to track budget performance; and makes appropriate adjustments.

Examples:

- estimate costs
- prepare a multiyear budget using a spreadsheet
- do a cost analysis

Allocates Material and Facility Resources. Acquires, stores, and distributes materials, supplies, parts, equipment, space, or final products in order to make the best use of them.

Examples:

- lay out a workspace document with narrative and graphics using desktop publishing software
- demonstrate understanding of first-in-first-out (FIFO) and just-in-time (JIT) inventory systems
- design a request for proposal (RFP) process

Allocates Human Resources. Assesses knowledge and skills and distributes work accordingly, evaluates performance, and provides feedback.

Examples:

- develop a staffing plan
- write a job description
- conduct a performance evaluation

Teaching RESOURCES

English/Writing: Write a proposal for an after-school career lecture series that schedules speakers, coordinates audiovisual aids, and estimates costs.

Mathematics: Develop a monthly family budget, taking into account expenses and revenues, and—using information from the budget plan—schedule a vacation trip that stays within the resources available.

Science: Plan the material and time requirements for a chemistry experiment, to be performed over a two-day period, that demonstrates a natural growth process in terms of resource needs.

Social Studies/Geography: Design a chart of resource needs for a community of African Zulus. Analyze the reasons why three major cities grew to their current size.

History: Study the Vietnam War, researching and making an oral presentation on the timing and logistics of transport of materials and troops to Vietnam and on the impact of the war on the federal budget.

How RESOURCES Competency is used on the job

A chef is required to *allocate money* when performing a cost analysis on menu items in order to turn a profit. This involves calling purveyors and seaching for the freshest products, as well as assessing the costs of various elements of preparation. To allocate money as required in this task, the chef must

- identify, search for, and collect information concerning the freshness and costs of available meats and produce
- assess or project customer demand for the product
- estimate costs (such as for labor, ingredients, and garnishes), cooking-weight loss, and revenues (such as by using a computer-spreadsheet program)

The Five Competencies
Competency #2: Information

Acquires and Evaluates Information. Identifies need for data, obtains it from existing sources or creates it, and evaluates its relevance and accuracy.

Examples:

- develop a form to collect data
- research and collect data from appropriate sources (library, on-line data bases, field research)
- develop validation instrument for determining accuracy of data collected

Organizes and Maintains Information. Organizes, processes, and maintains written or computerized records and other forms of information in a systematic fashion.

Examples:

- develop a filing system for storing information (printed or computerized)
- develop an inventory record-keeping system
- develop a bill-processing system

Interprets and Communicates Information. Selects and analyzes information and communicates the result to others using oral, written, graphic, pictorial, or multimedia methods.

Examples:

- produce a report using graphics to interpret and illustrate associated narrative information
- make an oral presentation using several different media to present information (overheads, slides, film, audio)
- develop material for communicating information to be used during a teleconference call

Uses Computers to Process Information. Employs computers to acquire, organize, analyze, and communicate information.

Examples:

- use a computer spreadsheet, e.g., Lotus 1-2-3, to develop a budget
- use a computer graphics program, e.g., Harvard Graphics, to prepare overheads for a report
- use on-line computer databases, e.g., Lexus, New York Times, ERIC, to research a report

Teaching INFORMATION

English/Writing: Identify and abstract passages from a novel to support an assertion about the values of a key character.

Mathematics: Design and carry out a survey, analyzing data in a spreadsheet program using algebraic formulas. Develop table and graphic display to communicate results.

Science: In an entrepreneurship project, present statistical data on a high-tech company's production/sales. Use computer to develop statistical charts.

Social Studies/Geography: Using numerical data and charts, develop and present conclusions about the effects of economic conditions on the quality of life in several countries.

History: Research and present papers on effect of Industrial Revolution on class structure in Britain, citing data sources used in drawing conclusions.

How INFORMATION Competency is used on the job

A travel agent *uses on-line computer* terminals to provide a variety of customer services (e.g., retrieving customer-request information, planning itineraries, and booking airline tickets). Elements of information skills implicit in this description include

- using an on-line computer database to access information
- selecting and evaluating information
- interpreting information for the customer
- communicating alternative choices for the customer
- ensuring the accurate conversion of information into the chosen format (e.g., hotel and airline tickets)

The Five Competencies
Competency #3: Interpersonal

Participates as a Member of a Team. Works cooperatively with others and contributes to group with ideas, suggestions, and effort.

Examples:

- collaborate with group members to solve a problem
- develop strategies for accomplishing team objectives
- work through group-conflict situation

Teaches Others. Helps others learn.

Examples:

- train a colleague on-the-job

- explore possible solutions to a problem in a formal group situation

Serves Clients/Customers. Works and communicates with clients and customers to satisfy their expectations.

Examples:

- demonstrate an understanding of who the customer is in a work situation
- deal with a dissatisfied customer in person
- respond to a telephone complaint about a product

Exercises Leadership. Communicates thoughts, feelings, and ideas to justify a position; and encourages, persuades, convinces, or otherwise motivates an individual or group, including responsibility challenging existing procedures, policies, or authority.

Examples:

- use specific team-building concepts to develop a work group
- select and use an appropriate leadership style for different situations
- use effective delegation techniques

Negotiates. Works towards an agreement that may involve exchanging specific resources or resolving divergent interests.

Examples:

- develop an action plan for negotiating
- write strategies for negotiating
- conduct an individual and a team negotiation

Works with Cultural Diversity. Works well with men and women and with a variety of ethnic, social, or educational backgrounds.

Examples:

- demonstrates an understanding of how people with differing cultural/ethnic backgrounds behave in various situations (work, public places, social gatherings)

- demonstrate the use of positive techniques for resolving cultural/ethnic problem situations

Teaching INTERPERSONAL SKILLS

English/Writing: Discuss the pros and cons of the argument that Shakespeare's *Merchant of Venice* is a racist play and should be banned from the school curriculum.

Mathematics: Present the results of a survey to the class and justify the use of specific statistics to analyze and represent the data.

Science: Work in a group to design an experiment to analyze the lead content in the school's water. Teach the results to an elementary school class.

Social Studies/Geography: In front of a peer panel, debate whether to withdraw U.S. military support from Japan. Simulate urban planning exercise for Paris.

History: Study America's Constitution and roleplay negotiation of the wording of the free states–slave states clause by different signers.

How INTERPERSONAL SKILLS are used on the job

A plastic molding machine operator *works as a member of a team* on a production floor in order to identify problems and ensure that everyone works at a consistent speed. In order to perform this task effectively, the machine operator must

- coordinate activities and movements with other group members to optimize production
- communicate needs to group members
- listen and respond to needs of group members
- identify, discuss, and resolve problems through cooperative group efforts

The Five Competencies
Competency #4: Systems

Understands Systems. Knows how social, organizational, and technological systems work and operates effectively within them.

Examples:

- draw and interpret an organization chart
- develop a chart that illustrates an understanding of stocks and flows
- draw a diagram that illustrates a technological problem definition and problem-solving process

Monitors and Corrects Performance. Distinguishes trends, predicts impact of actions on system operations, diagnoses deviations in the function of a system/organization, and takes necessary action to correct performance.

Examples:

- generate a statistical process control (SPC) chart
- develop a forecasting model
- develop a monitoring process

Improves and Designs Systems. Makes suggestions to modify existing systems to improve products and services, and develops new or alternative systems.

Examples:

- draw a diagram showing an improved organizational system based on Dr. W. Edwards Deming's 14 points
- choose a situation needing improvement, break it down, examine it, propose an improvement, and implement it

Teaching SYSTEMS Competency

English/Writing: Develop a computer model that analyzes the motivation of the hero of Shakespeare's *Hamlet*. Plot the events that increase or decrease Hamlet's motivation to avenge the death of his father by killing Claudius.

Mathematics: Develop a system to monitor and correct the heating/cooling process in a computer laboratory, using principles of statistical process control.

Science: Build a model of human population growth that includes the impact of the amount of food available on birth and death rates, etc. Do the same for a growth model for insects.

Social Studies/Geography: Analyze the accumulation of capital in industrialized nations in systems terms (as a reinforcing process with stocks and flows).

History: Develop a model for the social forces that led to the American Revolution. Then explore the fit between the model and other revolutions.

How SYSTEMS Competency is used on the job

A traffic, shipping, and receiving clerk may be required to *improve or design a system.* This job involves

- determining more efficient ways to stack merchandise
- observing the processes involved in loading, unloading, and moving merchandise
- developing ideas for performing these activities more efficiently
- sharing the ideas with the supervisor, and implementing changes which ultimately save money or prevent damage to merchandise

The clerk must carefully observe existing processes and develop an idea for improving the system. He or she needs to be able to communicate the idea clearly to others by preparing and explaining, for example, a diagram that illustrates how the redesigned system would be an improvement.

The Five Competencies
Competency #5: Technology

Selects Technology. Judges which set of procedures, tools, or machines, including computers and their programs, will produce the desired results.

Example:

- read equipment descriptions and technical specifications to select equipment to meet needs

Applies Technology to Task. Understands the overall intent and the proper procedures for setting up and operating machines, including computers and their programming systems.

Example:

- set up/assemble appropriate equipment from instructions

Maintains and Troubleshoots Technology. Prevents, identifies, or solves problems in machines, computers, and other technologies.

Examples:

- read and follow instructions for troubleshooting and repairing relevant equipment
- read and follow maintenance instructions for keeping relevant equipment in good working order

Teaching TECHNOLOGY Competency

English/Writing: Write an article showing the relationship between technology and the environment. Use word processing to write and edit papers after receiving teacher feedback.

Mathematics: Read manuals for several data-processing programs and write a memo recommending the best programs to handle a series of mathematical situations.

Science: Calibrate a scale to weigh accurate portions of chemicals for an experiment. Trace the development of this technology from earliest uses to today.

Social Studies/Geography: Research and report on the development and functions of the seismograph and its role in earthquake prediction and detection.

History: Analyze the effects of wars on technological development. Use computer graphics to plot the relationship of the country's economic growth to periods of peace and war.

How TECHNOLOGY Competency is used on the job

A graphics designer must *select technology*, determining which tools could best accomplish the work required to meet the goals of a project. Among the activities to be performed are

- reviewing the customer's ideas (e.g., by reading a description of project requirements)
- evaluating the graphics methods or tools to be used (e.g. by reading technical specifications)
- choosing a particular tool or method to produce rough drafts
- using this tool or method to produce rough drafts
- look at rough drafts and alternative methods to decide which is the best technology for the customer's project

At the heart of these activities is the ability to read a requirements description and technical specifications and come up with a match. In essence, the graphics designer is engaging in technological problem solving.

Notes

Chapter 1

1. Gary Hamel and C. K. Prahalad, "Corporate Imagination and Expeditionary Marketing," *Harvard Business Review*, July-August, 1991, p. 87.

2. Marco Iansiti, "Real-World R&D: Jumping the Product Generation Gap," *Harvard Business Review*, May-June 1993, pp. 138–147.

3. Fumio Kodama, "Technology Fusion and the New R&D," *Harvard Business Review*, July-August 1992, p. 70.

Chapter 3

1. For a useful discussion of each of these, see Yoram Wind and Vijay Mahajan's "Designing Product and Business Portfolios," *Harvard Business Review*, January-February 1981, pp. 155–165.

2. This discussion is based upon Michael E. Porter's *Competitive Advantage: Creating and Sustaining Superior Performance* (New York: Free Press, 1985).

3. This discussion is based on an article by Richard Normann and Rafael Ramirez, "From Value Chain to Value Constellation: Designing Interactive Strategy," *Harvard Business Review*, July-August 1993, pp. 65–77.

4. Ibid., p. 68.

Chapter 4

1. Robert M. Grant, "The Resource-Based Theory of Competitive Advantage: Implications for Strategy Formulation," *California Management Review*, Spring 1991, pp. 129–130.

Chapter 5

1. Joseph G. Morone, *Winning in High-Tech Markets: The Role of General Management* (Boston: Harvard Business School Press, 1993), p. 176–177.

2. Ibid., p. 178.

3. For more information on GTE and NEC, see C. K. Prahalad and Gary Hamel's "The Core Competence of the Corporation," *Harvard Business Review*, May-June 1990, p. 80.

PART III

1. John W. Verity, "Deconstructing the Computer Industry," *Business Week*, November 23, 1992, p. 90.

2. John A. Byrne, "Belt-tightening the Smart Way," *Business Week*, Special Issue: Enterprise 1993, p. 34.

3. Ibid.

Chapter 6

1. Lisa Baggerman, "The Futility of Downsizing," *Industry Week*, January 18, 1993, p. 27.

2. Ibid.

3. Ronald Henkoff, "Cost Cutting: How to Do It Right." *Fortune*, April 9, 1990, p. 40.

4. Robert M. Tomasko, "Restructuring: Getting It Right," *Management Review*, April 1992, p. 10.

5. Ibid.

6. Ibid., p. 13.

7. Ibid., p. 15.

8. Robert Howard, "The CEO as Organizational Architect: An Interview with Xerox's Paul Allaire," *Harvard Business Review*, September-October 1992, p. 108.

9. Tomasko, "Restructuring: Getting It Right," p. 15.

Chapter 7

1. Homa Bahrami, "The Emerging Flexible Organization: Perspectives from Silicon Valley," *California Management Review*, Summer 1992, p. 37.

2. Ibid.

3. Ibid., p. 46.

4. Harvey E. Wagner, "The Open Corporation," *California Management Review*, Summer 1991, pp. 43–54.

5. Peter Drucker, *Post-Capitalist Society* (New York: Harper-Collins, 1993), p. 54.

6. For more on the way information technology is changing, see Don Tapscott and Art Caston's *Paradigm Shift: The Promise of Information Technology* (New York: McGraw-Hill, 1993).

7. David Kirkpatrick, "Groupware Goes Boom," *Fortune*, December 27, 1993, p. 100.

8. Ibid., pp. 100–101.

9. Peter Coy, "Start with Some High-Tech Magic . . . ," *Business Week*, Special Issue: Enterprise 1993, pp. 24–25.

Chapter 8

1. Myron Magnet, "The American Family," *Fortune*, August 10, 1992, pp. 42–47.

2. Susan Caminiti, "Who's Minding American Kids?" *Fortune*, August 10, 1992, pp. 50–53.

3. Pat Wingert and Barbara Kantrowitz, "The Day Care Generation," *Newsweek*, Special Issue: Winter-Spring 1990, pp. 86–92; and

Arleen Leibowitz, Jacob Alex Klerman, and Linda J. Waite, "Employment of New Mothers and Child Care Costs: Differences by Children's Age," *Journal of Human Resources*, Winter 1992, pp. 112–133.

4. Kenneth Labich, "Can Your Career Hurt Your Kids?" *Fortune*, May 20, 1991, pp. 38–56.

5. Ibid.

6. Wingert, "The Day Care Generation," pp. 86–92.

7. "Report Raises Questions on Day Care," *Atlanta Journal*, January 24, 1994, p. A5.

8. Louis Richman, "Struggling to Save Our Kids," *Fortune*, August 10, 1992, pp. 34–40.

9. Ronald Henkoff, "Kids Are Killing, Dying, Bleeding," *Fortune*, August 10, 1992, pp. 62–69.

10. Ibid., p. 64.

11. Ibid.

12. Merit Systems Protection Board, *Balancing Work Responsibilities and Family Needs: The Federal Civil Service Response*, November 1991, p. 24. Washington, D.C.: U.S. Government Printing Office.

Chapter 9

1. Sue Shellenbarger, "Data Gap: Do Family-support Programs Help the Bottom Line? The Research Is Inconclusive," *Wall Street Journal*, June 21, 1993, p. R6.

2. Richard Louv, "Should Corporations Care About Child Care?" *Business and Society Review*, Winter 1992, p. 56.

3. Richard D. McMormick, "Family Affair," *Chief Executive*, May 1992, p. 30.

4. Maureen Milford, "Businesses and Employees Ask . . . Who's Responsible?" Wilmington, Delaware, *News Journal*, March 23, 1992, p. D10.

5. Jeff L. Lefkovich, "Business Responds to Elder-Care Needs," *HR Magazine*, June 1992, pp. 103–108.

6. Charles S. White, Marilyn M. Helms, and Judy C. Nixon, "A Survey of Child Care Needs and Benefits," *Employee Benefits Journal*, June 1992, pp. 28–30.

7. Ibid.

8. Ibid.

Chapter 10

1. Sue Shellenbarger, "Lessons from the Workplace: How Corporate Policies and Attitudes Lag Behind Workers' Changing Needs," *Human Resource Management*, 31:3 (1992), pp. 157–158.

2. Ibid., p. 159.

3. Merit Systems Protection Board, *Balancing Work Responsibilities and Family Needs: The Federal Civil Service Response*, November 1991, pp. 36–37. Washington, D.C.: U.S. Government Printing Office

4. Ibid., p. 48.

5. Susan Chira, "Family Leave Is Law; Will Things Change?" *New York Times*, August 15, 1993, p. E3.

6. Ibid.

7. Sue Shellenbarger, "So Much Talk, So Little Action," *Wall Street Journal*, June 21, 1993, p. R4.

8. Ibid.

Chapter 11

1. Charles S. Rodgers, "The Flexible Workplace: What Have We Learned?" *Human Resource Management*, 31:3 (1992), p. 187.

2. Ibid.

3. Brian O'Reilly, "Is Your Company Asking Too Much?" *Fortune*, March 20, 1990, p. 46.

4. Richard Louv, "Should Corporations Care About Child Care?" *Business and Society Review*, Winter 1992, p. 64.

5. Lotte Bailyn, "Issues of Work and Family in Different National Contexts: How the United States, Britain, and Sweden Respond," *Human Resource Management*, 31:3 (1992), p. 203.

Chapter 12

1. This discussion of learning is based upon a model for linking individual and organizational learning offered by Daniel H. Kim in his article "The Link Between Individual and Organizational Learning," *Sloan Management Review*, Fall 1993, pp. 37–50.

2. Patricia A. Galagan, "The Search for the Poetry of Work," *Training & Development*, October 1993, p. 35.

3. While Orr was studying technicians, he could have been studying almost any group of workers engaged in a common work activity, since the results would have been virtually the same.

4. John Seely Brown and Paul Duguid, "Organizational Learning and Communities-of-Practice: Toward a Unified View of Working, Learning, and Innovation," *Organization Science*, 2:1 (1991) p. 44.

Chapter 13

1. This description is based upon William N. Isaacs's article, "Taking Flight: Dialogue, Collective Thinking, and Organizational Learning," *Organizational Dynamics*, Autumn 1993, pp. 34–38.

2. The description of Royal Dutch–Shell is based upon Pierre Wack's articles "Scenarios: Uncharted Waters Ahead" (*Harvard Business Review*, September-October 1985, pp. 73–89) and "Scenarios: Shooting the Rapids" (*Harvard Business Review*, November-December 1985, pp. 139–150).

3. Peter Senge, *The Fifth Discipline: The Art & Practice of The Learning Organization* (New York: Doubleday Currency, 1990), p. 181.

Chapter 14

1. Fred Kofman and Peter M. Senge, "Communities of Commitment: The Heart of Learning Organizations," *Organizational Dynamics*, Autumn 1993, pp.13–14.

2. Ibid., pp. 16–17.

3. This discussion of system archetypes is based upon Peter Senge's book *The Fifth Discipline: The Art & Practice of The Learning Organization* (New York: Doubleday Currency, 1990).

PART VI

1. See Joseph H. Boyett and Henry P. Conn, *Workplace 2000: The Revolution Reshaping American Business* (New York: NAL/Dutton, 1991), pp. 266–273.

2. "Business and Education: The Demand for Partnership," *Business Week*, May 2, 1988, pp. 123–135.

3. "Illiteracy Magnified as US Heads into 21st Century," *Prodigy*, December 17, 1993.

4. Nancy J. Perry, "School Reform: Big Pain, Little Gain," *Fortune*, November 29, 1993, p. 130.

5. Jerome Cramer and Leanna Landsmann, "The School/Business Connection: Preparing America's Students for the Workplace," *Forbes*, Special Advertising Supplement: November 22, 1993, p. 129.

6. Michael Lotito, "A Call to Action For U.S. Business and Education," *Employment Relations Today*, Winter 1992–93, p. 379.

Chapter 15

1. The Secretary's Commission on Achieving Necessary Skills, U.S. Department of Labor, *Teaching the SCANS Competencies* (Washington, D.C.: U.S. Government Printing Office, 1993), p. 6.

2. The Secretary's Commission on Achieving Necessary Skills, U.S. Department of Labor, *What Work Requires of Schools: A SCANS Report for America 2000* (Washington, D.C.: U.S. Government Printing Office, June 1991), p. 11.

Chapter 16

1. "A Mall for Learners," *NEA Today*, March 1994, p. 15.

2. The Secretary's Commission on Achieving Necessary Skills, U.S. Department of Labor, *Teaching the SCANS Competencies* (Washington, D.C.: U.S. Government Printing Office, 1993), p. 16.

3. Ibid., p. 45.

4. Ibid., p. 49.

5. Christina Del Valle, "From High Schools to High Skills," *Business Week*, April 26, 1993, pp. 110–112.

6. Jerome Cramer and Leanna Landsmann, "The School/Business Connection," *Forbes*, Special Advertising Supplement: November 22, 1993, p. 2.

7. Ibid., p. 4.

8. Ibid.

9. Ibid.

10. Ibid., p. 8.

Chapter 17

1. Joseph H. Boyett and Henry P. Conn, *Workplace 2000: The Revolution Reshaping American Business* (New York: NAL/Dutton, 1991), p. 286.

2. Larry Armstrong, "The Learning Revolution: Technology is Reshaping Education—At Home and At School," *Business Week*, February 28, 1994: pp. 80–88.

3. "The Future of Technology in Education: Tomorrow's Classroom," *Business Week*, November 15, 1993, Special Advertising Section (no page numbers).

4. Bernard Avishai, "What Is Business's Social Compact?" *Harvard Business Review*, January-February 1994, p. 47.

PART VII

1. For some real Boss-as-SOB models, see Brian Dumaine's article "America's Toughest Bosses."

2. See Chris Lee and Ron Zemke's "The Search for Spirit in the Workplace," *Training*, June 1993, pp. 21–28; Walter Kiechel III's "The Leader as a Servant," *Fortune*, May 4, 1992, pp. 121–122; and Peter Block's "Should We Quit Looking for Leaders?" *Industry Week*, June 7, 1993, pp. 33–36.

Chapter 18

1. Edgar Schein, "How Can Organizations Learn Faster? The Challenge of Entering the Green Room," *Sloan Management Review*, Winter 1993, p. 87.

2. Ibid., p. 88.

3. Noel Tichy, "Revolutionize Your Company," *Fortune*, December 13, 1993, pp. 117–118.

4. Warren Bennis, ed., *Leaders on Leadership* (Boston: Harvard Business Review Books, 1992) pp. 16–17. *Fortune* magazine has called Jack Welch "the leading master of corporate change in our time." Between 1981, when he became CEO of GE, and 1994, Welch cut 200,000 employees from GE's payroll, nearly tripled the company's net income, and added $67.6 billion to its market value. See *Fortune*, "A Master Class in Radical Change," December 13, 1993, p. 82.

5. Peter Senge, *The Fifth Discipline: The Art & Practice of The Learning Organization* (New York: Doubleday Currency, 1990), p. 141.

6. These "other things" are "personal vision" and "creative tension." Senge and his colleagues argue that a person will learn, grow, and develop if he or she (1) has a clear sense of what is important or desirable and (2) sees present reality clearly. The creative tension is between the reality of what is and the possibilities of what could be.

7. Senge, *The Fifth Discipline*, p. 159.

Chapter 19

1. Thomas J. Peters and Robert H. Waterman, Jr., *In Search of Excellence: Lessons from America's Best-Run Companies* (New York: Harper & Row, 1982), p. 279.

2. James C. Collins and Jerry I. Porras, "Organizational Vision and Visionary Organizations," *California Management Review*, Fall 1991, p. 31.

3. Peter Senge, *The Fifth Discipline: The Art & Practice of the Learning Organization* (New York: Doubleday Currency, 1990), p. 209.

4. Marvin R. Weisbord, *Discovering Common Ground: How Future Search Conferences Bring People Together To Achieve Breakthrough Innovation, Empowerment, Shared Vision, and Collaborative Action* (San Francisco: Berrett-Koehler Publishers, 1992), p. 21.

5. They are also called "search conferences," "collaborative communities," "visioning meetings," "future searches," or "strategic futures conferences." While not identical, these types of conferences are all derived from the same common base of experiments, beliefs, and theories, and all date back to the work of Trist and Emery.

6. This description was provided by Kathleen D. Dannemiller and Robert W. Jacobs in their article "Changing the Way Organizations Change: A Revolution of Common Sense," *Journal of Applied Behavioral Science*, 28:4, December 1992, pp. 480–481.

7. Weisbord, *Discovering Common Ground*, pp. 73–81.

8. Ibid., pp. 101–103.

9. Margaret Wheatley, *Leadership and the New Science: Learning About Organizations from an Orderly Universe* (San Francisco: Berrett-Koehler Publishers, 1992), pp. 52–53.

Chapter 20

1. David Barry, "Managing the Bossless Team: Lessons in Distributed Leadership," *Organizational Dynamics*, Summer 1991, pp. 31–47.

2. Charles C. Manz, "Self-Leading Work Teams: Moving Beyond Self-Management Myths," *Human Relations*, 45:11 (1992), p. 1130.

3. For a more detailed discussion of W. L. Gore & Associates, see Frank Shipper and Charles C. Manz's "Employee Self-Management Without Formally Designated Teams: An Alternative Road to Empowerment," *Organizational Dynamics*, Winter 1992, pp. 48–61. A similar description can be found in Charles C. Manz and Henry P. Sims, Jr.'s, *Business Without Bosses: How Self-Managing Teams Are Building High-Performing Companies* (New York: John Wiley & Sons, 1993).

4. Studs Terkel, *Working* (New York: Pantheon, 1972), p. xiii.

Bibliography

Introduction

Boyett, Joseph H., and Conn, Henry P. *Workplace 2000: The Revolution Reshaping American Business* (New York: NAL/Dutton, 1991), pp. 266–273.

Filipczak, Bob. "It's Just a Job," *Training*, April 1994, pp. 21–27.

Geber, Beverly. "Retrain Who to Do What?" *Training*, January 1993, pp. 27–34.

Gordon, Jack. "Into the Dark: Rough Ride Ahead for American Workers." *Training*, July 1993, pp. 21–29.

Judis, John B. "Why Your Wages Keep Falling." *Training*, April 1994, p. 39.

Reich, Robert B. "Jobs: Skills Before Credentials." *Training*, April 1994, p. 38

Part I: The Pursuit of Innovation

Abetti, Pier A. "Technology: A Key Strategic Resource." *Management Review*, February 1989, pp. 37–41.

Ali, Abdul; Kalwani, Manohar U.; and Kovenock, Dan. "Selecting Product Development Projects: Pioneering Versus Incremental Innovation Strategies." *Management Science*, March 1993, pp. 255–274.

Altany, David R. "Frank Ryder: Inventor, Entrepreneur, Dreamer." *Industry Week*, May 3, 1993, pp. 31–36.

Benson, Tracy E. "The Learning Organization: Heading Toward

Places Unimaginable." *Industry Week*, January 4, 1993, pp. 35–38.

Berk, Sherrill. "Managing Technology for a Competitive Edge: An AMA Survey." *Management Review*, February 1989, pp. 49–58.

Bessen, Jim. "Riding the Marketing Information Wave." *Harvard Business Review*, September-October 1993, pp. 150–160.

Bohl, Don L. "Winning the New Product Race." *Industry Forum*, March 1990, p. 1.

Bouwen, Rene, and Fry, Ronald. "Organizational Innovation and Learning: Four Patterns of Dialog Between the Dominant Logic and the New Logic." *International Studies of Management & Organization*, Winter 1991, pp. 37–51.

Branscomb, Lewis M. "Does America Need a Technology Policy?" *Harvard Business Review*, March-April 1992, pp. 24–31.

Brown, John Seely. "Research That Reinvents the Corporation." *Harvard Business Review*, January-February 1991, pp. 102–175.

Burke, Michael I. "How Quality Is Factored into the Design Process." *Automotive Engineering*, October 1989, pp. 65–77.

Capon, Noel; Farley, John U.; Lehmann, Donald R.; and Hulbert, James M. "Profiles of Product Innovators Among Large U.S. Manufacturers." *Management Science*, February 1992, pp. 157–169.

Carey, John; Gross, Neil; Maremont, Mark; and McWilliams, Gary. "Moving the Lab Closer to the Marketplace." *Business Week*, Special Issue, Reinventing America 1992, pp. 164–171.

Case, John. "Sources of Innovation." *INC*, June 1989, p. 29.

Cleland, David I., and Bursic, Karen M. "Simultaneous Engineering Tears Down Organizational Walls." *Industry Forum*, November 1991, pp. 1–2.

"Continuous Improvement and Simultaneous Engineering." *Automotive Engineering*, October 1989, pp. 59–63.

Covucci, David. "Is Your Company Ready for Innovation?" *Management Review*, February 1989, pp. 17–18.

Crosby, Philip B. *Completeness: Quality for the 21st Century* (New York: Dutton, 1992).

———. *The Eternally Successful Organization* (New York: McGraw-Hill, 1988).

———. *Quality Is Free: The Art of Making Quality Certain* (New York: McGraw-Hill, 1979).

———. *Quality Without Tears* (New York: McGraw-Hill, 1984).

Davidson, Kenneth M. "How Should the U.S. Encourage Innovation?" *Journal of Business Strategy*, March-April 1992, pp. 58–61.

"Design: The Power Behind Concurrent Engineering." *Design News*, February 22, 1993, pp. 25–26.

DeYoung, H. Garrett. "Making R&D Pay Off Better and Quicker." *Electronic Business*, December 1992, pp. 61–64.

Diebold, John. *The Innovators: The Discoveries, Inventions, and Breakthroughs of Our Time* (New York: Truman Talley Books, 1990).

Droz, Dan. "Prototyping: A Key to Managing Product Development." *Journal of Business Strategy*, May 1992, pp. 34–38.

Drucker, Peter. "The Five Deadly Business Sins." *Wall Street Journal*, October 21, 1993, p. A18.

Frey, Donald N. "The Duality Principle." *Chief Executive*, January-February 1992, pp. 64–67.

"Future View: Manufacturing Management in Crisis." *Manufacturing Engineering*, January 1992, pp. 31–43.

"Future View: Tomorrow's Manufacturing Technologies." *Manufacturing Engineering*, January 1992, pp. 76–88.

Gannes, Stuart. "The Good News About U.S. R&D." *Fortune*, February 1, 1988, pp. 48–56.

Garvin, David. "Building a Learning Organization." *Harvard Business Review*, July-August 1993, pp. 78–91.

Hamel, Gary, and Prahalad, C. K. "Corporate Imagination and Expeditionary Marketing." *Harvard Business Review*, July-August 1991, p. 87.

Harris, Robert G., and Mowery, David C. "Strategies for Innovation: An Overview." *California Management Review*, Spring 1990, pp. 7–16.

Hequet, Marc. "Creativity Training Gets Creative." *Training*, February 1992, pp. 41–46.

Higgins, James M. "The Value-Added Analysis: A Seventh Pathway to Marketing Innovation." *Planning Review*, November-December 1992, p. 19.

Hise, Richard T., and McDaniel, Stephen W. "What Is the CEO's Role in New Product Efforts?" *Management Review*, February 1989, pp. 44–48.

Iansiti, Marco. "Real-World R&D: Jumping the Product Generation Gap." *Harvard Business Review*, May-June 1993, pp. 138–147.

"Innovation in America." *Business Week*, Special 1989 Bonus Issue.

"Innovation: The Global Race." *Business Week*, Special Issue, June 15, 1990.

Jacobson, Gary. "Carlson's Timeless Lessons on Innovation." *Management Review*, February 1989, pp. 13–16.

Jasinowski, Jerry. "The Magic of Small Manufacturers: Right Now, They're Collecting All the Gold." *Industry Week*, August 19, 1991, p. 35.

Kay, Allen. "Why Fish Didn't Discover Water." *Across the Board*, June 1991, pp. 11–13.

Keithley, Joseph P. "Customer-Driven Design." *Design News*, December 7, 1992, p. 186.

Kelley, Robert, and Caplan, Janet. "How Bell Labs Creates Star Performers." *Harvard Business Review*, July-August 1993, pp. 128–139.

Kim, Daniel H. "The Link Between Individual and Organizational Learning." *Sloan Management Review*, Fall 1993, pp. 37–50.

King, Nigel. "Modelling the Innovation Process: An Empirical Comparison of Approaches." *Journal of Occupational and Organizational Psychology* 65 (1992), pp. 89–100.

Kodama, Fumio. "Technology Fusion and the New R&D." *Harvard Business Review*, July-August 1992, pp. 70–78.

Krause, Irv, and Liu, John. "Benchmarking R&D Productivity." *Planning Review*, January-February 1993, pp. 16–21.

"The Learning Organization Made Plain." *Training & Development*, October 1991, pp. 37–44.

Lefebvre, Louis-A.; Lefebvre, Elizabeth; and Poupart, Robert. "The Shape of the New Winner: Innovativeness and the Strategic Edge in Small Firms." *National Productivity Review*, Summer 1990, pp. 313–320.

Lengnick-Hall, Cynthia A. "Innovation and Competitive Advantage: What We Know and What We Need to Learn." *Journal of Management* 18 no. 2, (1992), pp. 399–429.

Levinthal, Daniel. "An Investment in Learning." *Chief Executive*, November-December 1992, pp. 63–64.

Magrath, Allan J. "Six Pathways to Marketing Innovation." *Planning Review*, November-December 1992, pp. 12–19.

Manheim, Amy Lowen. "The Need for a Strategic Marketing Plan for U.S. Technology." *The G.A.O. Journal*, Summer 1990, pp. 19–23.

Manu, Franklyn A. "Innovation Orientation, Environment and Performance: A Comparison of U.S. and European Markets." *Journal of International Business Studies*, Second Quarter 1992, pp. 333–359.

McGough, Robert, and Wrubel, Robert. "Second Chance: How U.S. Companies Are Outflanking Japanese Consumer Electronics Giants." *FW*, April 28, 1992, pp. 22–28.

McWilliams, Gary. "A Notebook That Puts Users Ahead of Gimmicks." *Business Week*, September 27, 1993, pp. 92–96.

Meade, E. Kidder. "Simultaneous Engineering in Action." *Production*, October 1989, pp. 68–70.

Mechlin, George F., and Berg, Daniel. "Evaluating Research—ROI is not Enough." *Harvard Business Review*, September-October 1980, pp. 3–99.

Mitchell, Russell. "How Ford Hit the Bull's Eye with Taurus." *Business Week*, June 30, 1986, pp. 69–70.

———. "Masters of Innovation: How 3M Keeps Its New Products Coming." *Business Week*, April 10, 1989, pp. 58–63.

Mitsch, Ronald A. "Three Roads to Innovation." *Journal of Business Strategy*, September-October 1990, pp. 18–21.

Moore, James F. "Predators and Prey: A New Ecology of Competition." *Harvard Business Review*, May-June 1993, pp. 75–86.

Nayak, P. Ranganath. "Product Innovation Practices in Europe, Japan, and the U.S." *Journal of Business Strategy*, May 1992, pp. 62–63.

Nonaka, Ikujiro. "Redundant, Overlapping Organization: A Japanese Approach to Managing the Innovation Process." *California Management Review*, Spring 1990, pp. 27–38.

———. "The Knowledge-Creating Company." *Harvard Business Review*, November-December 1991, pp. 96–104.

Nulty, Peter. "The Soul of an Old Machine." *Fortune*, May 21, 1990, pp. 67–72.

Nussbaum, Bruce. "Hot Products: Smart Design Is the Common Thread." *Business Week*, June 7, 1993, pp. 54–57.

Patterson, Marvin L. "Accelerating Innovation: A Dip into the Meme Pool." *National Productivity Review*, Autumn 1990, pp. 409–418.

Pavitt, Keith. "What We Know about the Strategic Management of Technology." *California Management Review*, Spring 1990, pp. 17–26.

Pearson, Andrall E. "Corporate Redemption and the Seven Deadly Sins." *Harvard Business Review*, May-June 1992, pp. 65–75.

Peters, Tom, and Austin, Nancy. *A Passion for Excellence* (New York: Random House, 1985).

Pine, B. Joseph, II. *Mass Customization: The New Frontier in Business Competition* (Boston: Harvard Business Review Press, 1993).

Pine, B. Joseph, II; Victor, Bart; and Boynton, Andrew C. "Making Mass Customization Work." *Harvard Business Review*, September-October 1993, pp. 108–119.

Power, Christopher. "Flops." *Business Week*, August 16, 1993, pp. 76–80.

———. "How to Get Closer to Your Customers." *Business Week*, Special Issue, Enterprise (1993), pp. 42–45.

Power, Christopher; Kerwin, Kathleen; Grover, Ronald; Alexander, Keith; and Hof, Robert D. "Flops: Too Many New Products Fail. Here's Why—And How to Do Better." *Business Week*, August 16, 1993, pp. 76–82.

Reiner, Gary. "Winning the Race for New Product Development." *Management Review*, August 1989, pp. 52–53.

Rosenfeld, Lawrence, W. "Using Knowledge-Based Engineering." *Production*, November 1989, pp. 74–76.

Rosenfelder, Gerald S. "How to Stay at the Forefront of Technological Innovations." *Journal of Business Strategy*, May-June 1991, pp. 44–46.

Russell, Robert D. "Innovation in Organizations: Toward an Integrated Model." *Review of Business*, Fall 1990, pp. 19–47.

Senge, Peter M. "Mental Models." *Planning Review*, March-April 1992, pp. 5–10.

Shepetuk, Alexander J. "Is Your Product Development Process a Tortoise or a Hare?" *Management Review*, March 1991, pp. 25–27.

Sheridan, John H. "Agile Manufacturing: Stepping Beyond Lean Production." *Industry Week*, April 10, 1993, pp. 30–46.

Sisodia, Rajendra S. "Why Companies Kill Their Technologies." *Journal of Business Strategy*, January-February 1992, pp. 42–48.

Smith, Geoffrey. "Corning Laboratories: A Warm Feeling Inside." *Business Week*, October 25, 1991, p. 158.

Sonnenberg, Frank K. "Strategies for Creativity." *Journal of Business Strategy*, January-February 1991, pp. 50–53.

Sonnenberg, Frank K., and Goldberg, Beverly. "It's a Great Idea, But . . ." *Training & Development*, March 1992, pp. 65–68.

Sullivan, Jeremiah J. "Japanese Management Philosophies: From the Vacuous to the Brilliant." *California Management Review*, Winter 1992, pp. 66–87.

"Survival of the Swiftest." *Manufacturing Engineering*, January 1992, pp. 20–22.

Szakonyi, Robert. *Managing New Product Technology*, American Management Association Management Briefing, 1988.

Tanner, Ronald. "Paying the Price for New Ideas." *Intrapreneur*, September 1989, pp. 44–47.

Valentino, Daniel, and Christ, Bill. "Teaming Up for Market: Cheaper, Better, Faster." *Management Review*, November 1989, pp. 46–49.

Vasilash, Gary S. "The American Manufacturing Challenge: Being Like the Tortoise—and the Hare." *Production*, December 1989, pp. 54–61.

———. "Designing the Car of the Decade." *Production*, April 1990, pp. 54–56.

———. "Honda's Brilliant Mistake." *Production*, June 1992, pp. 34–39.

Vogt, Carlton F., Jr. "Concurrent Engineering: Industry's Best Hope." *Design News*, March 25, 1991, pp. 23–24.

Weimer, George A. "Is an American Renaissance at Hand?" *Industry Week*, May 4, 1992, pp. 48–51.

Wheelwright, Steven C., and Clark, Kim B. "Creating Project Plans to Focus Product Development." *Harvard Business Review*, March-April 1992, pp. 70–82.

Zakond, Alan. "The Two Sides of the Innovation Equation." *Management Review*, February 1989, pp. 19–21.

Zangwill, Willard I. "When Customer Research Is a Lousy Idea." *Wall Street Journal*, March 8, 1993, p. A12.

Part II: The New Strategy

Anderson, Richard E. "Strategic Integration: How John Deere Did It." *Journal of Business Strategy*, July 1992, pp. 21–26.

Barney, Jay. "Firm Resources and Sustained Competitive Advantage." *Journal of Management* 17:1 (1991), pp. 99–120.

Bartmess, Andrew, and Cerny, Keith. "Building Competitive Advantage Through a Global Network of Capabilities." *California Management Review*, Winter 1993, pp. 78–103.

Barton, Laurence. "The Use of Scenario-Based Planning." *IM*, November-December 1991, pp. 8–11.

Belohlav, James A. "Quality, Strategy, and Competitiveness." *California Management Review*, Spring 1993, pp. 55–67.

"Capabilities-Based Competition." *Harvard Business Review*, May-June 1992, p. 162–171.

Conner, Kathleen R. "A Historical Comparison of Resource-Based Theory and Five Schools of Thought Within Industrial Organization Economics: Do We Have a New Theory of the Firm?" *Journal of Management* 17:1 (1991), pp. 121–154.

Coyne, Kevin P. "Achieving a Sustainable Service Advantage." *Journal of Business Strategy*, January-February 1993, pp. 3–10.

Davidow, William H., and Malone, Michael S. *The Virtual Corporation: Structuring and Revitalizing the Corporation for the 21st Century.* (New York: Edward Burlingame Books/Harper Business, 1992).

———. "The Virtual Corporation." *California Business*, November 1992, pp. 34–42.

deRoulet, David G. "Designing—and Sustaining the Gains from—a Service Strategy." *Journal of Business Strategy*, January-February 1993, pp. 21–30.

DeSouza, Glenn. "Designing a Customer Retention Plan." *Journal of Business Strategy*, March-April 1992, pp. 24–28.

Dickson, Peter Reid. "Toward a General Theory of Competitive Rationality." *Journal of Marketing* 56 (January 1992), pp. 69–83.

Egelhoff, William G. "Great Strategy or Great Strategy Implementation—Two Ways of Competing in Global Markets." *Sloan Management Review*, Winter 1993, pp. 37–50.

Ewaldz, Donald B. "How Integrated Should Your Company Be?" *Journal of Business Strategy*, July-August 1991, pp. 52–55.

Fiol, C. Marlene. "Managing Culture as a Competitive Resource: An Identity-Based View of Sustainable Competitive Advantage." *Journal of Management* 17:1 (1991), pp. 191–211.

Freeman, John, and Boeker, Warren. "The Ecological Analysis of Business Strategy." *California Management Review* XXVI no. 3, (1984), pp. 73–86.

Fuller, Joseph B.; O'Conor, James; and Rawlinson, Richard. "Tailored Logistics: The Next Advantage." *Harvard Business Review*, May-June 1993, pp. 87–98.

Gartrell, Kenneth D. "Innovation, Industry Specialization, and Shareholder Wealth." *California Management Review*, Spring 1990, pp. 87–101.

Grant, Robert M. "The Resource-Based Theory of Competitive Advantage: Implications for Strategy Formulation." *California Management Review*, Spring 1991, pp. 114–135.

Hamel, Gary, and Prahalad, C. K. "Strategic Intent." *Harvard Business Review*, May-June 1989, pp. 63–76.

———. "Strategy as Stretch and Leverage." *Harvard Business Review*, March-April 1993, pp. 75–84.

———. "Corporate Imagination and Expeditionary Marketing." *Harvard Business Review*, July-August 1991, pp. 81–92.

Hansen, Gary S., and Wernerfelt, Birger. "Determinants of Firm Performance: The Relative Importance of Economic and Organizational Factors." *Strategic Management Journal* 10, (1989), pp. 399–411.

Hax, Arnoldo C. "Redefining the Concept of Strategy and the Strategy Formation Process." *Planning Review*, May-June 1990, pp. 34–40.

Hines, Gary. "Strategic Planning Made Easy." *Training & Development Journal*, April 1991, pp. 39–43.

Hitt, Michael A., and Ireland, R. Duane. "Relationships Among Corporate Level Distinctive Competencies, Diversification Strategy, Corporate Structure and Performance." *Journal of Management Studies* 23:4 (July 1986), pp. 401–416.

Johnson, Rick. "A Strategy for Service—Disney Style." *Journal of Business Strategy*, September-October 1991, pp. 38–43.

Lado, Augustine, A.; Boyd, Nancy G.; and Wright, Peter. "A Competency-Based Model of Sustainable Competitive Advantage: Toward a Conceptual Integration." *Journal of Management* 18:1 (1992), pp. 77–91.

Lele, Milind M. "Selecting Strategies That Exploit Leverage." *Planning Review*, January-February 1992, pp. 15–21.

———. "The Lessons of Strategic Leverage." *Journal of Business Strategy*, July-August 1992, pp. 38–45.

Leonard-Barton, Dorothy. "Core Capabilities and Core Rigidities: A Paradox in Managing New Product Development." *Strategic Management Journal* 13 (1992), pp. 111–125.

Lorange, Peter, and Roos, Johan. "Why Some Strategic Alliances Succeed and Others Fail." *Journal of Business Strategy*, January-February 1991, pp. 25–30.

Mahoney, Joseph T., and Pandian, J. Rajendran. "The Resource-Based View Within the Conversation of Strategic Management." *Strategic Management Journal* 13 (1992), pp. 363–380.

Mason, Julie Cohen. "Value: The New Marketing Mania?" *Management Review*, May 1992, pp. 16–21.

McDonald, Laura. "Setting New Standards for Customer Advocacy." *Journal of Business Strategy*, January-February 1993, pp. 11–15.

Meyer, Christopher. "2020 Vision." *Planning Review*, Special Issue, Conference Executive Summary, September-October 1992, pp. 39–41.

Miles, Raymond, and Snow, Charles C. "Fit, Failure and the Hall of Fame." *California Management Review* XXVI no. 3, (1984), pp. 10–28.

Miller, Danny. "The Generic Strategy Trap." *Journal of Business Strategy*, January-February 1992, pp. 37–41.

Morone, Joseph G. *Winning in High-Tech Markets: The Role of General Management* (Boston: Harvard Business School Press, 1993).

Nelson, Richard. "Recent Writings on Competitiveness: Boxing the Compass." *California Management Review*, Winter 1992, pp. 127–137.

Nonaka, Ikujiro. "The Knowledge-Creating Company." *Harvard Business Review*, November-December 1991, pp. 96–104.

Norman, Richard, and Ramirez, Rafael. "From Value Chain to Value Constellation: Designing Interactive Strategy." *Harvard Business Review*, July-August 1993, pp. 65–77.

Pascale, Richard T. "Perspectives on Strategy: The Real Story Behind Honda's Success." *California Management Review* XXVI no. 3, (1984), pp. 47–72.

Porter, Michael E. *Competitive Advantage: Creating and Sustaining Superior Performance* (New York: Free Press, 1985).

Prahalad, C. K., and Hamel, Gary. "The Core Competence of the Corporation." *Harvard Business Review*, May-June 1990, pp. 79–91.

Prairie, Patti. "An American Express/IBM Consortium Benchmarks Information Technology." *Planning Review*, January-February 1993, pp. 22–27.

Quinn, James Brian. *Intelligent Enterprise* (New York: Free Press, 1992).

Quinn, James Brian; Doorley, Thomas L.; and Paquette, Penny C. "Beyond Products: Services-Based Strategy." *Harvard Business Review*, March-April 1990, pp. 58–67.

Raynor, Michael E. "The Pitfalls of Niche Marketing." *Journal of Business Strategy*, March-April 1992, pp. 29–32.

———. "Quality as a Strategic Weapon." *Journal of Business Strategy*, September-October 1992, pp. 3–9.

Reichheld, Frederick F. "Loyalty-Based Management," *Harvard Business Review*, March-April 1993, pp. 64–73.

Reimann, Bernard C., and Ramanujam, Vasudevan. "Acting Versus Thinking: A Debate Between Tom Peters and Michael Porter." *Planning Review*, March-April 1992, pp. 36–43.

Reinertsen, Donald G., and Smith, Preston G. "The Strategist's Role in Shortening Product Development." *Journal of Business Strategy*, July-August 1991, pp. 18–22.

Robert, Michel. "Market Fragmentation Versus Market Segmentation." *Journal of Business Strategy*, September 1992, pp. 48–53.

———. "Why CEOs Have Difficulty Implementing Their Strategies." *Journal of Business Strategy*, March-April 1991, pp. 58–59.

Schiemann, William A. "Organizational Change Starts with a Strategic Focus." *Journal of Business Strategy*, January-February 1993, pp. 43–48.

Schmidt, Jeffrey A. "The Link Between Benchmarking and Shareholder Value." *Journal of Business Strategy*, May-June 1992, pp. 7–13.

Schoemaker, Paul J. H. "How to Link Strategic Vision to Core Capabilities." *Sloan Management Review*, Fall 1992, pp. 67–81.

Senge, Peter M. "Mental Models." *Planning Review*, March-April 1992, pp. 4–10.

Snyder, Amy V., and Ebeling, William H., Jr. "Targeting a Company's Real Core Competencies." *Journal of Business Strategy*, November-December 1992, pp. 26–32.

Stalk, George; Evans, Philip; and Shulman, Lawrence E. "Competing on Capabilities: The New Rules of Corporate Strategy." *Harvard Business Review*, March-April 1992, pp. 57–69.

Stalk, George, Jr. "Time-Based Competition and Beyond: Competing on Capabilities." *Planning Review*, Special Issue, Conference Executive Summary, September-October 1992, pp. 27–29.

Sterne, Diana. "Core Competencies: The Key to Corporate Advantage." *Multinational Business*, no. 3 (1992), pp. 13–20.

"Strategy and the Art of Reinventing Value." *Harvard Business Review*, September-October 1993, pp. 39–51.

Sullivan, Jeremiah J. "Japanese Management Philosophies: From the Vacuous to the Brilliant." *California Management Review*, Winter 1992, pp. 66–87.

Taylor, William. "Message and Muscle: An Interview with Swatch Tital Nicolas Hayek." *Harvard Business Review*, March-April 1993, pp. 99–110.

Teece, David J. "Economic Analysis and Strategic Management." *California Management Review*, XXVI no. 3, (1984), pp. 87–110.

Treacy, Michael, and Wiersema, Fred. "Customer Intimacy and Other Value Disciplines." *Harvard Business Review*, January-February 1993, pp. 84–93.

Tregoe, Benjamin B.; Zimmerman, John W.; Smith, Ronald A.; and Tobia, Peter M. "The Driving Force." *Planning Review*, March-April 1990, pp. 4–16.

Turpin, Dominique. "The Strategic Persistence of the Japanese Firm." *Journal of Business Strategy*, January-February 1992, pp. 49–52.

Valentino, Daniel J. "Do More of What You Do Best." *Across the Board*, November 1992, pp. 53–54.

Venkatesan, Ravi. "Strategic Sourcing: To Make or Not to Make." *Harvard Business Review*, November-December 1992, pp. 98–107.

"Virtual Corporation." *Forbes*, December 7, 1992, pp. 103–107.

Wack, Pierre. "Scenarios: Uncharted Waters Ahead. How Royal Dutch-Shell Developed a Planning Technique That Teaches Managers to Think About an Uncertain Future." *Harvard Business Review*, September-October 1985, pp. 73–89.

Watson, Gregory H. "How Process Benchmarking Supports Corporate Strategy." *Planning Review*, January-February 1993, pp. 12–15.

Wernerfelt, Birger. "A Resource-Based View of the Firm." *Strategic Management Journal* 5, (1984), pp. 171–180.

———. "From Critical Resources to Corporate Strategy." *Journal of General Management* 14:3, (1989), pp. 4–12.

Whelan, James, and Sisson, James D. "How to Realize the Promise of Strategic Planning." *Journal of Business Strategy*, January-February 1993, pp. 31–36.

Whiteley, Richard C. "Why Customer Focus Strategies Often Fail." *Journal of Business Strategy*, September-October 1991, pp. 34–37.

Williams, Jeffrey R. "How Sustainable Is Your Competitive Advantage?" *California Management Review*, Spring 1992, pp. 29–51.

Wind, Yoram, and Mahajan, Vijay. "Designing Product and Business Portfolios: Steps Leading to Construction of a Portfolio Model for Planning Strategy." *Harvard Business Review*, January-February 1981, pp. 155–165.

Wright, Peter; Nazemzadeh, Asghar; Parnell, John; and Lado, Augustine. "Comparing Three Different Theories of Competitive Strategies." *IM*, November-December 1991, pp. 12–16.

Youssef, Mohamed A. "Agile Manufacturing: A Necessary Condition for Competing in Global Markets." *Industrial Engineering*, December 1992, pp. 18–20.

Part III: The New Structures

Baggerman, Lisa. "The Futility of Downsizing: Layoffs Eliminate More Than Just Workforce." *Industry Week*, January 18, 1993, pp. 27–29.

Bahrami, Homa. "The Emerging Flexible Organization: Perspectives from Silicon Valley." *California Management Review*, Summer 1992, pp. 33–52.

Bartlett, Christopher A., and Ghoshal, Sumantra. "Matrix Management: Not a Structure, a Frame of Mind." *Harvard Business Review*, July-August 1990, pp. 138–145.

Benson, Tracy E. "Your Structure May Be Killing You." *Industry Week*, November 2, 1992, pp. 13–16.

Bottoms, David T. "Status: Cleaning Up the Mess." *Industry Week*, May 3, 1993, pp. 15–20.

Boynton, Andrew C., and Victor, Bart. "Beyond Flexibility: Building and Managing the Dynamically Stable Organization." *California Management Review*, Fall 1991, pp. 53–66.

Brown, Tom. "Is There a Future for BIGCO?" *Industry Week*, April 6, 1992, p. 27.

———. "Think in Reverse." *Industry Week*, July 19, 1993, pp. 14–22.

Byrne, John A. "Belt-Tightening the Smart Way." *Business Week*, Enterprise 1993, pp. 34–38.

Byrne, John A.; Brandt, Richard; and Port, Otis. "The Virtual Corporation: The Company of the Future Will Be the Ultimate in Adaptability." *Business Week*, February 8, 1993, pp. 98–103.

Case, John. "Return of the Giants: What Hollywood Can Teach Us About the End of the Entrepreneurial Era." *INC*, December 1989, pp. 33–34.

Chandler, Alfred D., Jr. "Corporate Strategy and Structure: Some Current Considerations." *Society*, March-April 1991, pp. 35–38.

"Collaborating to Compete." *Chief Executive*, November-December 1992, pp. 38–54.

Coy, Peter. "Start With Some High-Tech Magic . . ." *Business Week*, Enterprise 1993, pp. 24–32.

Davidow, William H., and Malone, Michael S. "The Virtual Corporation." *California Business*, November 1992, pp. 34–42.

Drucker, Peter. *Post-Capitalist Society* (New York: HarperCollins, 1993).

———. "Playing in the Information-Based 'Orchestra.'" *Wall Street Journal*, June 4, 1985.

———. "The Coming of the New Organization." *Harvard Business Review*, January-February 1988, pp. 45–53.

———. "The New Society of Organizations." *Harvard Business Review*, September-October 1992, pp. 95–104.

Ford, Robert C., and Randolph, W. Alan. "Cross-Functional Structures: A Review and Integration of Matrix Organization and Project Management." *Journal of Management* 18:2 (1992), pp. 267–294.

"Future View: A Game of Musical Factories." *Manufacturing Engineering*, January 1992, pp. 69–74.

Galagan, Patricia A. "Beyond Hierarchy: The Search for High Performance." *Training & Development*, August 1992, pp. 21–25.

Haeckel, Stephan H., and Nolan, Richard L. "Managing by Wire." *Harvard Business Review*, September-October 1993, pp. 122–132.

Hammer, Michael, and Champy, James. *Reengineering the Corporation* (New York: Harper Business, 1993).

Harari, Oren. "Imperatives for Deflating the Fat Organization." *Management Review*, June 1992, pp. 61–62.

Heenan, David O. "The Right Way to Downsize." *Journal of Business Strategy*, September-October 1991, pp. 4–7.

Heitman, Evelyn, and Zahra, Shaker A. "Examining the U.S. Experience to Discover Successful Corporate Restructuring." *IM*, January-February 1993, pp. 7–10.

Henkoff, Ronald. "Cost Cutting: How to Do It Right." *Fortune*, April 9, 1990, pp. 40–49.

Heyer, Steven J., and Lee, Reginald Van. "Rewiring the Corporation." *The Journal of Business Strategy*, July-August 1991, pp. 40–45.

Hirschhorn, Larry, and Gilmore, Thomas. "The New Boundaries of the 'Boundaryless' Company." *Harvard Business Review*, May-June 1992, pp. 104–115.

Howard, Robert. "The CEO as Organizational Architect: An Interview with Xerox's Paul Allaire." *Harvard Business Review*, September-October 1992, pp. 107–121.

Huber, Richard L. "How Continental Bank Outsourced Its 'Crown Jewels.' " *Harvard Business Review*, January-February 1993, pp. 121–129.

"Jack Welch on the Art of Thinking Small." *Business Week*, Enterprise 1993, pp. 212–216.

Jaques, Elliott. "In Praise of Hierarchy." *Harvard Business Review*, January-February 1990, pp. 127–133.

Kaestle, Paul. "A New Rationale for Organizational Structure." *Planning Review*, July-August 1990, pp. 20–27.

Kanter, Rosabeth Moss. "From Climbing to Hopping: The Contingent Job and the Post-Entrepreneurial Career." *Management Review*, April 1989, pp. 22–27.

———. "Ourselves Versus Ourselves." *Harvard Business Review*, May-June 1992, pp. 8–10.

Kindel, Sharen. "Network Outsourcing: Let Your People Go." *FW*, June 9, 1992, p. 38.

Kirkpatrick, David. "Groupware Goes Boom." *Fortune*, December 27, 1993, pp. 100–101.

Kreiner, Kristian. "The Postmodern Epoch of Organization Theory." *International Studies of Management & Organization* 22:2 (1992), pp. 37–52.

Lammers, Teri. "The New, Improved Organization Chart." *INC*, October 1992, pp. 147–149.

Lei, David, and Slocum, John W., Jr. "Global Strategy, Competence-Building and Strategic Alliances." *California Management Review*, Fall 1992, pp. 81–97.

Lesly, Elizabeth, and Light, Larry. "When Layoffs Alone Don't Turn the Tide." *Business Week*, December 7, 1992, pp. 100–101.

Miles, Raymond E., and Snow, Charles C. "Causes of Failure in Network Organizations." *California Management Review*, Summer 1992, pp. 54–72.

Nonaka, Ikujiro. "Redundant, Overlapping Organization: A Japanese Approach to Managing the Innovation Process." *California Management Review*, Spring 1990, pp. 27–38.

"Paradigm Shift: How Information Technology Is Reinventing the Enterprise." *Business Week*, October 25, 1993, Special Advertising Section.

Peters, Tom. *Liberation Management: Necessary Disorganization for the Nanosecond Nineties* (New York: Alfred A. Knopf, 1992).

———. "Rethinking Scale." *California Management Review*, Fall 1992, pp. 7–29.

———. "Going 'Horizontal' in Your Career." *Industry Week*, January 4, 1993, pp. 47–50.

———. *Thriving on Chaos: Handbook for a Management Revolution* (New York: Alfred A. Knopf, 1987).

Port, Otis. "The Responsive Factory." *Business Week*, Enterprise 1993, pp. 48–53.

Poynter, Thomas A., and White, Roderick E. "Making the Horizontal Organization Work." *Business Quarterly*, Winter 1990, pp. 73–77.

Prevost, Tom. "Management's Holy Grail: Organizational Restructuring." *CMA Magazine*, February 1992, pp. 23–25.

Quinn, James Brian; Doorley, Thomas L.; and Paquette, Penny C. "Technology in Services: Rethinking Strategic Focus." *Sloan Management Review*, Winter 1990, pp. 79–87.

Robert, Michel. "The Do's and Don'ts of Strategic Alliances." *Journal of Business Strategy*, March-April 1992, pp. 50–53.

Schnitt, David L. "Reengineering the Organization Using Information Technology." *Journal of Systems Management*, January 1993, pp. 14–42.

Smart, Tim. "How Jack Welch Brought GE to Life." *Business Week*, October 26, 1992, pp. 13–14.

Sprackland, Teri. "Mid-managers Seek Escape from Quality Squeeze." *Electronic Business*, October 7, 1991, pp. 83–84.

Stalk, George, Jr., and Hout, Thomas M. "Redesign Your Organization for Time-Based Management." *Planning Review*, January-February 1990, pp. 4–9.

Stevenson, Howard H., and Gumpert, David E. "The Heart of Entrepreneurship." *Harvard Business Review*, March-April 1985, pp. 85–94.

Stralkowski, C. Michael, and Billon, S. Alexander. "Partnering: A Strategic Approach to Productivity Improvement." *National Productivity Review*, Spring 1988, pp. 145–151.

Tapscott, Don, and Caston, Art. *Paradigm Shift: The Promise of Information Technology* (New York: McGraw-Hill, 1993).

Tomasko, Robert M. *Downsizing: Reshaping the Corporation for the Future* (New York: AMACOM, 1987).

———. "Running Lean, Staying Lean." *Management Review*, November 1987, pp. 32–38.

———. "Restructuring: Getting It Right." *Management Review*, April 1992, pp. 10–15.

Veit, Ken. "The Reluctant Entrepreneur." *Harvard Business Review*, November-December 1992, pp. 40–49.

Venkatesan, Ravi. "Strategic Sourcing: To Make or Not to Make." *Harvard Business Review*, November-December 1992, pp. 98–107.

Verity, John W. "Taking a Laptop on a Call." *Business Week*, October 25, 1993, pp. 124–125.

"Virtual Corporation." *Forbes*, December 1992, pp. 103–107.

"Virtual Corporations: Fast and Focused." *Business Week*, February 8, 1993, p. 134.

Wagner, Harvey E. "The Open Corporation." *California Management Review*, Summer 1991, pp. 46–60.

Walton, Richard E. "From Control to Commitment in the Workplace." *Harvard Business Review*, March-April 1985, pp. 77–84.

Westerman, Jewell G., and Sherden, William A. "Moving Beyond Lean and Mean." *Journal of Business Strategy*, September-October 1991, pp. 12–16.

Winby, Stuart. "Hewlett-Packard Is Redefining State-of-the-Art When It Comes to Teams." *Total Quality*, October 1992, p. 7.

Part IV: Responding to the Needs of a New Workforce

Ahlburg, Dennis, and DeVita, Carol. "New Realities of the American Family." *Population Bulletin*, August 1992, p. 2.

Allen, Frank Edward. "What Problem? Chief Executives May Not Sympathize with Work-Family Conflicts for a Simple Reason: They Rarely Have Them." *Wall Street Journal*, June 21, 1993, p. R7.

"The American Family During the 20th Century." *Monthly Labor Review*, March 1990, pp. 2–3.

"An American Family: Two Working Parents, Three Children—and What They Think of Their Daily Lives." *Wall Street Journal*, June 21, 1993, p. R11.

Bailyn, Lotte. "Issues of Work and Family in Different National Contexts: How the United States, Britain, and Sweden Respond." *Human Resource Management*, Fall 1992, pp. 201–208.

Bamford, Janet. "Changing Business as Usual." *Working Woman*, November 1993, p. 62.

Barnett, Rosalind C., and Rivers, Caryl. "The Myth of the Miserable Working Woman." *Working Woman*, February 1992, p. 62.

Beck, Melinda. "The Geezer Boom." *Newsweek* Special Issue, Winter-Spring 1990, pp. 62–68.

"Benchmark: Telecommuting on the Increase." *INC*, November 1993, p. 142.

Black, Kathryn Stechert. "Should You Work from Home?" *Working Mother*, June 1993, pp. 27–31.

Caminiti, Susan. "Who's Minding America's Kids?" *Fortune*, August 10, 1992, pp. 50–53.

Chira, Susan. "Family Leave Is Law; Will Things Change?" *New York Times*, August 15, 1993, p. E3.

Christensen, Kathleen. "Managing Invisible Employees: How to Meet the Telecommuting Challenge." *Employment Relations Today*, Summer 1992, pp. 133–143.

"The Civilized Workplace." *Royal Bank Letter*, March-April 1992.

Cohen, Julie. "Keeping Kids at Work." *Management Review*, January 1991, pp. 26–29.

——. "Managing Tomorrow's Workforce Today." *Management Review*, January 1991, pp. 17–21.

Covin, Teresa J., and Brush, Christina C. "A Comparison of Student and Human Resource Professional Attitudes Toward Work and

Family Issues." *Group & Organization Management*, March 1993, pp. 29–49.

Dollars & Sense. "All Work and No Play: Burnt-Out Americans Working More, Liking It Less." January-February 1992, pp. 12–15.

Dumas, Lynne S. "Comebacks After a Career Break." *Working Mother*, December 1993, pp. 36–38.

———. "Getting Ahead on the Mommy Track." *Working Mother*, December 1993, pp. 33–35.

Eichman, Caroline. "Surveys Reveal Needs for Work/Family Benefits—By Both Employees and Employers." *Employment Relations Today*, Winter 1992-93, pp. 389–395.

"Family Feud: What Should Companies Do About Easing Work-Family Conflicts?" *Wall Street Journal*, June 21, 1993, p. 9.

"Family Leave, Without Labor Pains." *Working Woman*, January 1992, pp. 27–30.

"Family Leave Issue Settled with Law: Employers Report Few Ill-Effects from Requirements." *Business Insurance*, December 27, 1993, p. 13.

Farrell, Christopher. "Where Have All the Families Gone?" *Business Week*, June 29, 1992, pp. 90–91.

Fierman, Jaclyn. "Are Companies Less Family-Friendly?" *Fortune*, March 21, 1994, pp. 64–67.

"Firms Adopt Work/Family Policies Slowly." *Christian Science Monitor*, February 18, 1994, p. 10.

Footlick, Jerrold. "What Happened to the Family?" *Newsweek*, Special Issue, Winter-Spring 1990, pp. 15–20.

Galen, Michele; Palmer, Ann Therese; Cuneo, Alice; and Maremont, Mark. "Work & Family: Companies Are Starting to Respond to Workers' Needs—and Gain from It." *Business Week*, June 28, 1993, pp. 80–88.

Gardner, Marilyn. "Work Strategies: The Compressed Workweek." *Working Mother*, March 1993, pp. 30–34.

———. "Child Care: The Search for Quality." *Working Mother*, January 1994, pp. 33–40.

Gonyea, Judith G., and Googins, Bradley K. "Linking the Worlds of Work and Family: Beyond the Productivity Trap." *Human Resource Management*, Fall 1992, pp. 209–226.

Grossman, Laurie M. "What About Us? Family-Support Programs May Have a Side Effect: Resentment Among Childless Workers." *Wall Street Journal*, June 21, 1993, p. R8.

Gunsch, Dawn. "DuPont Pays for High-Quality Child Care." *Personnel Journal*, July 1992, p. 16.

Harris, Diane. "Big Business Takes on Child Care." *Working Woman*, June 1993, pp. 50–51.

Hayghe, Howard V. "Family Members in the Work Force." *Monthly Labor Review*, March 1990. pp. 14–19.

Henkoff, Ronald. "Kids Are Killing, Dying, Bleeding." *Fortune*, August 10, 1992, pp. 62–69.

Hickey, Mary C. "The Case for Commuting." *Working Mother*, July 1993, pp. 22–26.

Hudson Institute. *Opportunity 2000: Creative Affirmative Action Strategies for a Changing Workforce.* (Indianapolis: Hudson Institute, September 1988).

————. *Workforce 2000: Work and Workers for the 21st Century* (Indianapolis: Hudson Institute, June 1987).

Hutter, Sarah. "Moms Reinvent the Workplace." *Working Mother*, July 1993, pp. 37–39.

Jacobs, Eva, and Shipp, Stephanie. "How Family Spending Has Changed in the U.S." *Monthly Labor Review*, March 1990, pp. 20–27.

Johnson, Arlene. "Fear of Flexing." *Across the Board*, May 1992, p. 55.

Jones, Maggie. "Giving Family Leave a Checkup." *Working Woman*, November 1993, p. 17.

Kimmel, Michael S. "What Do Men Want?" *Harvard Business Review*, November-December 1993, pp. 50–63.

Klein, Easy. "Tomorrow's Work Force." *D&B Reports*, January-February 1990, pp. 33–35.

Korenman, Sanders, and Neumark, David. "Marriage, Motherhood, and Wages." *Journal of Human Resources* 27:2, Spring 1992, pp. 233–255.

Labich, Kenneth. "Can Your Career Hurt Your Kids?" *Fortune*, May 20, 1991, pp. 38–56.

Lefkovich, Jeff L. "Business Responds to Elder-Care Needs." *HRMagazine*, June 1992, pp. 103–108.

Lehrer, Evelyn L. "The Impact of Children on Married Women's Labor Supply." *Journal of Human Resources* 28:3 Summer 1992, pp. 422–444.

Leibowitz, Arleen; Klerman, Jacob Alex; and Waite, Linda J. "Employment of New Mothers and Child Care Choice." *Journal of Human Resources* 27:1, Winter 1992, pp. 112–133.

Levitan, Sar A., and Gallo, Frank. "Work and Family: The Impact of Legislation." *Monthly Labor Review*, March 1990, pp. 34–40.

Lopez, Julie Amparano. "The Enforcers: Corporate Work-Family Cops Make Sure Managers Don't Fall Back on Their Traditional Ways." *Wall Street Journal*, June 21, 1993, p. R7.

Louv, Richard. "Should Corporations Care About Child Care?" *Business and Society Review*, Winter 1992, pp. 56–64.

Magnet, Myron. "The American Family, 1992." *Fortune*, August 10, 1992, pp. 42–47.

McCormick, Richard. "Family Affair." *Chief Executive*, May 1992, pp. 30–33.

Milford, Maureen. "Businesses and Employees Ask . . . Who's Responsible." Wilmington, Delaware, *News Journal*, March 23, 1992, p. D10.

Mishel, Lawrence, and Bernstein, Jared. *The State of Working America, 1992–93* (Washington, D.C.: Economic Policy Institute, 1993).

Mock, Cindee, and Bruno, Andrea. "The Expectant Executive and the Endangered Promotion." *Harvard Business Review*, January-February 1994, pp. 16–25.

Morgan, Hal, and Milliken, Frances J. "Keys to Action: Understanding Differences in Organizations' Responsiveness to Work-and-Family Issues." *Human Resource Management*, Fall 1992, pp. 227–248.

Morrison, Peter A. "Congress and the Year 2000: Peering into the Demographic Future." *Business Horizons*, November-December 1993, pp. 55–63.

Moskowitz, Milton, and Townsend, Carol. "The 85 Best Companies for Working Mothers." *Working Mother*, October 1991, p. 29.

———. "8th Annual Survey: 100 Best Companies for Working Mothers." *Working Mother*, October 1993, pp. 27–67.

———. "5th Annual Survey: The 75 Best Companies for Working Mothers." *Working Mother*, October 1990, pp. 31–64.

———. "7th Annual Survey: 100 Best Companies for Working Mothers." *Working Mother*, October 1992, pp. 33–90.

Muller, Jerry Z. "The Health of Nations: Adam Smith's Family Formula." *Washington Post*, September 27, 1992, p. C3.

Nelton, Sharon. "Coping with Work and Family Issues." *Nation's Business*, August 1992, p. 52.

———. "A Flexible Style of Management." *Nation's Business*, December 1993, pp. 24–31.

Noble, Barbara Presley. "We're Doing Just Fine, Thank You: The Medical Leave Act Has Had Little Negative Impact, Especially on Small Businesses." *New York Times*, March 20, 1994, p. 25.

O'Reilly, Brian. "Is Your Company Asking Too Much?" *Fortune*, March 12, 1990, pp. 39–46.

———. "How to Take Care of Aging Parents." *Fortune*, May 18, 1992, pp. 108–112.

O'Toole, Patricia. "Redefining Success." *Working Woman*, November 1993, p. 49.

Perry, Nancy J. "Why It's So Tough to Be a Girl." *Fortune*, August 10, 1992, pp. 82–84.

Powell, Gary N., and Mainiero, Lisa A. "Cross-Currents in the River of Time: Conceptualizing the Complexities of Women's Careers." *Journal of Management* 18:2 (1992), pp. 215–237.

"Report Raises Questions on Day Care." *Atlanta Journal/Atlanta Constitution*, January 24, 1994, p. A5.

Ribar, David C. "Child Care and the Labor Supply of Married Women." *Journal of Human Resources* 27:1, Winter 1992, pp. 134–165.

Richards, Peter. "Why It Pays to Pay on the Books." *Working Woman*, June 1993, pp. 52–53.

———. "A Blueprint for Reform. What Government, Business and Parents Should Do Now to Ensure Affordable, High-Quality Care for Kids." *Working Woman*, June 1993, pp. 54–55.

Richman, Louis S. "Struggling to Save Our Kids." *Fortune*, August 10, 1992, pp. 34–41.

Rodgers, Charles S. "The Flexible Workplace: What Have We Learned?" *Human Resource Management*, Fall 1992, pp. 183–199.

Rogers, Beth. "Companies Develop Benefits for Part Timers." *HRMagazine*, May 1992, pp. 89–90.

Scarr, Sandra, and Holcomb, Betty. "What's Best for Your Baby?" *Working Mother*, May 1993, pp. 68–70.

Schachner, Michael. "Colgate Wants to be 'Family Friendly' " *Business Insurance*, April 2, 1990, p. 14.

Schwartz, Felice N. "The Riddle of the Ring." *Across the Board*, April 1992, pp. 32–36.

Shalowitz, Deborah. "Managers Named for Work-Family Issues." *Business Insurance*, April 27, 1992, p. 12.

Shellenbarger, Sue. "The Aging of America Is Making 'Elder Care' a Big Workplace Issue." *Wall Street Journal*, February 16, 1994, p. A1.

————. "Employees Take Pains to Make Flextime Work." *Wall Street Journal*, August 18, 1992, p. B1.

————. "More Companies Experiment with Workers' Schedules." *Wall Street Journal*, January 13, 1994, p. B1.

————. "Data Gap. Do Family-Support Programs Help the Bottom Line? The Research Is Inconclusive." *Wall Street Journal*, June 21, 1993, p. R6.

————. "So Much Talk, So Little Action." *Wall Street Journal*, June 21, 1993, p. R1.

————. "Some Thrive, But Many Wilt Working at Home." *Wall Street Journal*, December 14, 1993, p. B1.

————. "When Can Dad Choose Family Over Work?" *Wall Street Journal*, October 25, 1993, p. B1.

————. "Lessons from the Workplace: How Corporate Policies and Attitudes Lag Behind Workers' Changing Needs." *Human Resource Management*, Fall 1992, pp. 157–169.

Somerville, Sylvia. "Family Leave May End Family-ness at Work." *Restaurant Hospitality*, October 1993, p. 69.

U.S. Department of Education, Office of Educational Research and Improvement. *Women at Thirtysomething: Paradoxes of Attainment.* (Washington, D.C.: U.S. Government Printing Office, June 1991).

U.S. Department of Labor, Offices of the Secretary, Women's Bureau. *Employers and Child Care: Benefiting Work and Family.* Washington, D.C.: U.S. Government Printing Office, 1989.

————. *Work and Family Resource Kit* (Washington, D.C.: U.S. Government Printing Office 1989).

U.S. Merit Systems Protection Board. *Balancing Work Responsibilities and Family Needs: The Federal Civil Service Response* (Washington, D.C.: U.S. Government Printing Office, November 1991).

Verespej, Michael. "Where People Come First." *Industry Week*, July 16, 1990, pp. 22–32.

Wetzel, James R. "American Families: 75 Years of Change." *Monthly Labor Review*, March 1990, pp. 4–13.

White, Charles S.; Helms, Marilyn M.; and Nixon, Judy C. "A Survey of Child Care Needs and Benefits." *Employee Benefits Journal*, June 1992, pp. 28–30.

Wiatrowski, William J. "Family-Related Benefits in the Workplace." *Monthly Labor Review*, March 1990, pp. 28–33.

Williamson, Alistair D. "Is This the Right Time to Come Out?" *Harvard Business Review*, July-August 1993, pp. 18–26.

Wingert, Pat, and Kantrowitz, Barbara. "The Day Care Generation." *Newsweek* Special Issue, Winter-Spring 1990, pp. 86–92.

Wohl, Faith. "Work and Family Demands Must Balance If Quality Is to Prevail." *Total Quality*, March 1992, p. 7.

Part V: Learning and the New Workplace

Argyris, Chris. "Double Loop Learning in Organizations." *Harvard Business Review*, September-October 1977, pp. 115–125.

——. "Education for Leading-Learning." *Organizational Dynamics*, Winter 1993, pp. 5–17.

Barton, Laurence. "The Use of Scenario-Based Planning for Management Executives." *IM*, November-December 1991, pp. 8–11.

Beach, Barbara Kres. "Learning with Roger Schank." *Training & Development*, October 1993, pp. 39–44.

Bouwen, Rene, and Fry, Ronald. "Organizational Innovation and Learning: Four Patterns of Dialog Between the Dominant Logic and the New Logic." *International Studies of Management & Organization*, 21:4 (1991), pp. 37–51.

Brown, John Seely, and Duguid, Paul. "Organizational Learning and Communities-of-Practice: Toward a Unified View of Working, Learning, and Innovation." *Organization Science*, February 1991, pp. 40–57.

Cohen, Michael D. "Individual Learning and Organizational Routine: Emerging Connections." *Organization Science*, February 1991, pp. 135–139.

Cole, Robert E. "Learning from Learning Theory: Implications for Quality Improvement of Turnover, Use of Contingent Workers, and Job Rotation Policies." *Quality Management Journal*, October 1993, pp. 9–25.

Dodgson, Mark. "Organizational Learning: A Review of Some Literatures." *Organization Studies*, 14:3 (1993), pp. 375–394.

Duck, Jeanie Daniel. "Managing Change: The Art of Balancing." *Harvard Business Review*, November-December 1993, pp. 109–118.

Epple, Dennis; Argote, Linda; and Devadas, Rukmini. "Organizational Learning Curves: A Method for Investigating Intra-Planet Transfer of Knowledge Acquired Through Learning by Doing." *Organization Science*, February 1991, pp. 58–70.

Fiol, C. Marlene, and Lyles, Marjorie A. "Organizational Learning." *Academy of Management Review*, 10:4 (1985), pp. 803–813.

Galagan, Patricia A. "Helping Groups Learn." *Training & Development*, October 1993, pp. 57–61.

———. "The Search for the Poetry of Work." *Training & Development*, October 1993, pp.33–37.

Garavaglia, Paul L. "How to Ensure Transfer of Training." *Training & Development*, October 1993, pp. 63–68.

Garvin, David A. "Building a Learning Organization." *Harvard Business Review*, July-August 1993, pp. 78–91.

Goss, Tracy; Pascale, Richard; and Athos, Anthony. "The Reinvention Roller Coaster: Risking the Present for a Powerful Future." *Harvard Business Review*, November-December 1993, pp. 97–108.

Hall, Gene; Rosenthal, Jim; and Wade, Judy. "How to Make Reengineering *Really* Work." *Harvard Business Review*, November-December 1993, pp. 119–132.

Hamel, Gary. "Competition for Competence and Interpartner Learning Within International Strategic Alliances." *Strategic Management Journal* 12 (1991), pp. 83–103.

Hodgetts, Richard M.; Luthans, Fred; and Lee, Sang M. "New Paradigm Organization: From Total Quality to Learning to World-Class." *Organizational Dynamics*, Winter 1994, pp. 5–19.

Huber, George P. "Organizational Learning: The Contributing Processes and the Literatures." *Organization Science*, February 1991, pp. 88–115.

Isaacs, William N. "Taking Flight: Dialogue, Collective Thinking, and Organizational Learning." *Organizational Dynamics*, Autumn 1993, pp. 24–39.

Kanter, Rosabeth Moss. *The Change Masters* (New York: Simon and Schuster, 1983).

Keleman, Ken S.; Lewis, L. Floyd, II; and Garcia, Joseph E. "Script Management: A Link Between Group Support Systems and Organizational Learning." *Small Group Research*, November 1993, pp. 566–582.

Kim, Daniel H. "The Link Between Individual and Organizational Learning." *Sloan Management Review*, Fall 1993, pp. 37–50.

King, Nigel. "Modeling the Innovation Process: An Empirical Comparison of Approaches." *Journal of Occupational and Organizational Psychology*, June 1992, pp. 89–100.

Kofman, Fred, and Senge, Peter M. "Communities of Commitment: The Heart of Learning Organizations." *Organizational Dynamics*, Autumn 1993, pp. 5–23.

"The Learning Organization: Heading Toward Places Unimaginable." *Industry Week*, January 4, 1993, pp. 35–38.

"The Learning Organization Made Plain." *Training & Development*, October 1991, pp. 37–44.

"Learning-Style Theories." *Personnel Journal*, September 1992, p. 91.

Leonard-Barton, Dorothy. "The Factory as a Learning Laboratory." *Sloan Management Review*, Fall 1991, pp. 23–38.

Levinthal, Daniel. "An Investment in Learning." *Chief Executive*, November-December 1992, pp. 63–64.

March, James G. "Exploration and Exploitation in Organizational Learning." *Organization Science*, February 1991, pp. 71–87.

March, James G.; Sproull, Lee S.; and Tamuz, Michal. "Learning from Samples of One or Fewer." *Organization Science*, 2:1 (1991), pp. 1–13.

Marsick, Victoria J.; Cederholm, Lars; Turner, Ernie; and Pearson, Tony. "Action-Reflection Learning." *Training & Development*, August 1992, pp. 63–66.

Martin, Roger. "Changing the Mind of the Corporation." *Harvard Business Review*, November-December 1993, pp. 81–94.

McGill, Michael E., and Slocum, John W., Jr. "Unlearning the Organization." *Organizational Dynamics*, Autumn 1993, pp. 67–79.

McGill, Michael E.; Slocum, John W., Jr.; and Lei, David. "Management Practices in Learning Organizations." *Organizational Dynamics*, Summer 1992, pp. 5–17.

Nonaka, Ikujiro. "The Knowledge-Creating Company." *Harvard Business Review*, November-December 1991, pp. 96–104.

Prokesch, Steven E. "Mastering Chaos at the High-Tech Frontier: An Interview with Silicon Graphics's Ed McCracken." *Harvard Business Review*, November-December 1993, pp. 135–144.

Schein, Edgar H. "On Dialogue, Culture, and Organizational Learning." *Organizational Dynamics*, Autumn 1993, pp. 40–51.

Senge, Peter M. "Mental Models." *Planning Review*, March-April 1992, pp. 4–10.

Simon, Herbert A. "Bounded Rationality and Organizational Learning." *Organization Science*, February 1991, pp. 125–134.

Sorohan, Erica Gordon. "We Do; Therefore, We Learn." *Training & Development*, October 1993, pp. 47–55.

"Training 101: The Psychology of Learning." *Training and Development*, June 1993, pp. 17–22.

Ulrich, Dave; Jick, Todd, and Von Glinow, Mary Ann. "High-Impact Learning: Building and Diffusing Learning Capability." *Organizational Dynamics*, Autumn 1993, pp. 52–66.

Wack, Pierre. "Scenarios: Shooting the Rapids." *Harvard Business Review*, November-December 1985, pp. 139–150.

———. "Scenarios: Uncharted Waters Ahead." *Harvard Business Review*, September-October 1985, pp. 73–89.

Weick, Karl E. "The Nontraditional Quality of Organizational Learning." *Organization Science*, February 1991, pp. 116–124.

Wenger, Etienne. "Communities of Practice: Where Learning Happens." *Benchmark*, Fall 1991, pp. 6–8.

Part VI: American Education: An Update

Agovino, Theresa. "Business Creative in New School Efforts." *Crain's New York Business*, November 25, 1991, p. 3.

American Association of University Women Educational Foundation. *How Schools Shortchange Girls*. Washington, D.C.: American Association of University Women, 1992.

American Society for Training and Development. "Training America: Learning to Work for the 21st Century." Alexandria, VA: ASTD, 1989.

Armstrong, Larry; Yang, Dori Jones; and Cuneo, Alice. "The Learning Revolution: Technology Is Reshaping Education—At Home and At School." *Business Week*, February 28, 1994, pp. 80–88.

Avishai, Bernard. "What Is Business's Social Compact?" *Harvard Business Review*, January-February 1994, pp. 38–48.

Batt, Rosemary, and Osterman, Paul. *A National Policy for Workplace Training: Lessons from State and Local Experiments* (Washington, D.C.: Economic Policy Institute, 1993).

———. *Workplace Training Policy: Case Studies of State and Local Experiments* (Washington, D.C.: Economic Policy Institute, January 1993).

Beales, Janet. "Job and School Under One Roof." *Nation's Business*, February 1993, pp. 55–56.

Boyer, Ernest L. "Creating the New American College." *Chronicle of Higher Education*, March 9, 1994, p. A48.

Boyett, Joseph H., and Conn, Henry P. *Workplace 2000: The Revolution Reshaping American Business* (New York: NAL/Dutton, 1991), pp. 266–273.

Bureau of Labor Statistics, U.S. Department of Labor. *Working Women: A Chartbook.* Washington, D.C.: U.S. Department of Labor, August 1991, Bulletin 2385.

"Business and Education: The Demand for Partnership." *Business Week*, May 2, 1988, pp. 123–135.

Celis, William, 3d. "New Education Legislation Defines Federal Role in Nation's Classrooms." *New York Times*, March 30, 1994, p. B7.

Corcoran, Elizabeth. "Learning Companies." *Scientific American*, February 1993, pp. 106–107.

Council on Competitiveness. *Elevating the Skills of the American Workforce.* Washington, D.C.: Council on Competitiveness, May, 1993.

Cramer, Jerome, and Landsmann, Leanna. "The School/Business Connection: Preparing America's Students for the Workplace." *Forbes*, November 22, 1993, pp. 129–140.

"Cyber School: The New Community Center." *Los Angeles Times.* February 13, 1994, p. T7.

"A Day in the Life of the School of the Future." *Los Angeles Times*, February 13, 1994, p. T7.

Del Valle, Christina. "From High Schools to High Skills." *Business Week*, April 26, 1993, pp. 110–112.

Eck, Alan. "Job-Related Education and Training: Their Impact on Earnings." *Monthly Labor Review*, October 1993, pp. 21–38.

"Educating the Workforce of the Future." *Harvard Business Review*, March-April 1994, pp. 39–51.

Evans, Julie A. "Lessons in Privatization." *School and College*, March 1993, pp. 20–24.

Filipczak, Bob. "Apprenticeships: From High School to High Skills." *Training*, April 1992, pp. 23–29.

———. "Bridging the Gap Between School and Work." *Training*, December 1993, pp. 44–47.

Froiland, Paul. "Action Learning: Taming Real Problems in Real Time." *Training*, January 1994, pp. 27–34.

———. "Who's Getting Trained?" *Training*, October 1993, pp. 53–60.

Futrell, Mary Hatwood. "National Education Reforms: Is America Moving Toward a National Curriculum?" *Phi Kappa Phi Journal*, Fall 1993, pp. 30–34.

"The Future of Technology in Education." *Business Week*, November 15, 1993, Special Advertising Section.

"Future View: Will the Workforce Work?" *Manufacturing Engineering*, January 1992, pp. 46–60.

"Glass Boxes: Lifting the Veil on Information." *Benchmark*, Spring 1989, pp. 12–15.

Gordon, Edward. "The Role of Training in the Retooling of the American Economic Machine." *Training Today*, 1992, pp. 8–9.

Gordon, Edward E. "Assessing Training Alternatives in Today's Corporations." *Training Today*, December 1986, p. 8.

————. "Managing the Diverse Skills of America's New Workforce." *Managing Diversity*, December 1991, p. 1.

Gordon, Edward E.; Ponticell, Judith A.; and Morgan, Ronald R. *Closing the Literacy Gap in American Business* (New York: Quorum Books, 1991).

Gordon, Jack. "In Search of . . . Lifelong Learning." *Training*, September 1989, pp. 25–34.

Hecker, Daniel E. "Reconciling Conflicting Data on Jobs for College Graduates." *Monthly Labor Review*, July 1992, pp. 3–12.

Hequet, Marc. "Creativity Training Gets Creative." *Training*, February 1992, pp. 41–45.

"How Businesses Search for Qualified Applicants: Trying to Bridge the Skills Gap." *Personnel Journal*, June 1992, Supplement, pp. 1–2.

"Illiteracy Magnified as U.S. Heads into 21st Century." *Prodigy*, December 17, 1993.

Kaeter, Margaret. "The Age of the Specialized Generalist." *Training*, December 1993, pp. 48–53.

Karp, H. B., and Sutton, Nancy. "Where Diversity Training Goes Wrong." *Training*, July 1993, pp. 30–34.

Kinni, Theodore B. "The Cannons of Fredon." *Industry Week*, August 16, 1993, pp. 33–36.

"Labor Month in Review." *Monthly Labor Review*, July 1992, p. 2.

"Labor Month in Review." *Monthly Labor Review*, August 1993, p. 2.

"Labor Month in Review." *Monthly Labor Review*, October 1993, p. 2.

"Learning How to Learn." *Benchmark*, Winter 1988, pp. 2–5.

Lotito, Michael J. "A Call to Action for U.S. Business and Education." *Employment Relations Today*, Winter 1992-93, pp. 379–387.

Lynch, Lisa M. *Strategies for Workplace Training: Lessons from Abroad* (Washington, D.C.: Economic Policy Institute, 1993).

Lytle, Victoria. "A Mall for Learners." *NEA Today*, March 1994, p. 15.

Martinez, Michelle Neely. "Disney Training Works Magic." *HR Magazine*, May 1992, pp. 53–57.

McKenna, Joseph F. "Youth's Got a Friend in Pennsylvania." *Industry Week*, February 1, 1993, pp. 16–20.

Mishel, Lawrence, and Bernstein, Jared. *The State of Working America, 1992–93*. (Washington, D.C.: Economic Policy Institute, 1993).

Moskal, Brian S. "Apprenticeships: A Few Good Crusaders." *Industry Week*, January 4, 1993, pp. 23–24.

Muson, Howard. "Schooled for Success." *Working Woman*, January 1992, pp. 33–38.

National Alliance of Business. "Youth 2000: A Call to Action." Washington, D.C.: National Alliance of Business, 1986.

"The New 3Rs: Rethinking, Restructuring, Revitalizing Learning." *Benchmark*, Fall 1991, pp. 2–5.

Northdurft, William E. *School Works: Reinventing Public Schools to Create the Workforce of the Future* (Washington, D.C.: Brookings Institute, 1989).

Office of Technology Assessment, U.S. Congress. *Adult Literacy and New Technologies: Tools for a Lifetime* (Washington, D.C.: U.S. Government Printing Office, July 1993).

O'Meara, Frank. "The Pedagogue's Decalogue." *Training*, January 1993, pp. 43–45.

O'Neil, John. "Making Sense of Outcome-Based Education." *Instructor*, January 1993, pp. 46–47.

Parker, Arnold. "The SCANS Challenge: Preparing Your Work Force for High Performance." *Employment Relations Today*, Winter 1992-93, pp. 367–377.

Perry, Nancy J. "School Reform: Big Pain, Little Gain." *Fortune*, November 29, 1993, pp. 130–162.

Rasell, Edith, and Rothstein, Richard, eds. *School Choice: Examining the Evidence* (Washington, D.C.: Economic Policy Institute, 1993).

Reich, Robert B. "Jobs: Skills Before Credentials." *Wall Street Journal*, February 2, 1994, p. A18.

Rigdon, Joan E. "Technological Gains Are Cutting Costs, and Jobs, in Service." *Wall Street Journal*, February 24, 1994, p. A1.

Ryan, Michael. "The Day They Threw Out the Textbooks." *Parade Magazine*, February 20, 1994, pp. 10–12.

Ryscavage, Paul. "Recent Data on Job Prospects of College-Educated Youth." *Monthly Labor Review*, August 1993, pp. 16–26.

Secretary's Commission on Achieving Necessary Skills, U.S. Department of Labor. *Learning a Living: A Blueprint for High Performance: A SCANS Report for America 2000*. April 1992.

———. *Teaching the SCANS Competencies* (Washington, D.C.: U.S. Government Printing Office, 1993).

———. *What Work Requires of Schools: A SCANS Report for America 2000*. June 1991.

Shelley, Kristina J. "The Future of Jobs for College Graduates," *Monthly Labor Review*, July 1992, pp. 13–21.

Thornburg, Linda. "Training in a Changing World: How Four Successful Companies Are Thinking About Training in Today's Fast-Paced Environment." *HRMagazine*, August 1992, pp. 44–47.

Treece, James B. "Up from the Factory Floor." *Business Week*, October 5, 1992, p. 66.

U.S. Department of Education, Office of Educational Research and Improvement, Programs for the Improvement of Practice. *School Change Models and Processes*. Washington, D.C.: U.S. Department of Education, October 1993.

U.S. Department of Education, Office of Educational Research and Improvement, National Center for Education Statistics. *The Condition of Education 1993*. Washington, D.C.: U.S. Department of Education, June 1993.

Washburn, Susan Z., and Franklin, Geralyn McClure. "A Modern Workplace in the Face of an Age-old Problem: Illiteracy." *IM*, January-February 1992, pp. 2–4.

Winerip, Michael. "In School." *New York Times*, November 24, 1993, p. B8.

Womack, James P., and Jones, Daniel T. "From Lean Production to the Lean Enterprise." *Harvard Business Review*, March-April 1994, pp. 93–103.

"Workers' Socioeconomic Woes Can Hinder Involvement Efforts." *Total Quality*, January 1992, p. 4.

Yaffe, Jerry. "Workforce Literacy in the Local Public Sector." *Public Personnel Management*, Spring 1992, pp. 227–260.

Yoshinda, Kosaku. "The Joy of Work: Optimizing Service Quality Through Education and Training." *Quality Progress*, November 1993, pp. 29–33.

Part VII: The New Leadership

Ancona, Deborah G., and Nadler, David A. "Top Hats and Executive Tales: Designing the Senior Team." *Sloan Management Review*, Fall 1989, pp. 19–28.

Axelrod, Dick. "Getting Everyone Involved: How One Organization Involved Its Employees, Supervisors, and Managers in Redesigning the Organization." *Journal of Applied Behavioral Science*, December 1992, pp. 499–509.

Bailey, Darrel, and Dupré, Susan. "The Future Search Conference as a Vehicle for Educational Change: A Shared Vision for Will Rogers Middle School, Sacramento, California." *Journal of Applied Behavioral Science*, December 1992, pp. 510–519.

Barry, David. "Managing the Bossless Team: Lessons in Distributed Leadership." *Organizational Dynamics*, Summer 1991, pp. 31–47.

Belasco, James A., and Stayer, Ralph C. "Why Empowerment Doesn't Empower: The Bankruptcy of Current Paradigms." *Business Horizons*, March-April 1994, pp. 29–41.

Bennis, Warren, ed. *Leaders on Leadership* (Boston: Harvard Business Review Books, 1992).

Bennis, Warren, and Nanus, Burt. *Leaders: The Strategies for Taking Charge* (New York: Harper & Row, 1985).

Block, Peter. "Should We Quit Looking for Leaders?" *Industry Week*, June 7, 1993, pp. 33–36.

Bracey, Hyler; Rosenblum, Jack; Sanford, Aubrey; and Trueblood, Roy. *Managing from the Heart* (New York: Delacorte Press, 1991).

Bragar, Joan. "The Customer-Focused Quality Leader." *Quality Progress*, May 1992, pp. 51–53.

Brown, Tom. "The 'New Science' of Leadership." *Industry Week*, January 18, 1993, pp. 14–22.

Bunker, Barbara Benedict, and Alban, Billie T. "Conclusion: What Makes Large Group Interventions Effective?" *Journal of Applied Behavioral Science*, December 1992, pp. 579–591.

Burns, James MacGregor. *Leadership* (New York: Harper & Row, 1978).

Carr, Clay. "Empowered Organizations, Empowering Leaders." *Training & Development*, March 1994, pp. 39–44.

Champlin, Dell. "Structural Change in U.S. Labor Markets." *Review of Social Economy*, Spring 1993, pp. 40–61.

Chen, Chao C., and Meindl, James R. "The Construction of Leadership Images in the Popular Press: The Case of Donald Burr and People Express." *Administrative Science Quarterly*, 36 (1991), pp. 521–551.

Chopra, Deepak. *Quantum Healing: Exploring the Frontiers of Mind and Body Science* (New York: Bantam Books, 1989).

Clement, Ronald W. "Culture, Leadership, and Power: The Keys to Organizational Change." *Business Horizons*, January-February 1994, pp. 33–39.

Collins, James C., and Porras, Jeffy I. "Organizational Vision and Visionary Organizations." *California Management Review*, Fall 1991, pp. 30–52.

Conger, Jay A. *The Charismatic Leader: Beyond the Mystique of Exceptional Leadership* (San Francisco: Jossey-Bass, 1989).

Dannemiller, Kathleen, and Jacobs, Robert W. "Changing the Way Organizations Change: A Revolution of Common Sense." *Journal of Applied Behavioral Sciences*, December 1992, pp. 480–498.

Davenport, Thomas H. *Process Innovation: Reengineering Work Through Information Technology* (Boston: Harvard Business School Press, 1993).

DePree, Max. *Leadership Is an Art* (New York: Dell Publishing, 1989).

———. *Leadership Jazz* (New York: Dell Trade Paperback, 1992).

Downham, Thomas A.; Noel, James L.; and Prendergast, Albert E. "Executive Development." *Human Resource Management*, Spring-Summer 1992, pp. 95–107.

"The Downside of Quality: Companies That Focus All Their Efforts on Improving Quality May Pay a Price." *Training & Development*, March 1992, pp. 11–12.

Drucker, Peter. *Post-Capitalist Society* (New York: HarperCollins, 1993).

Dumaine, Brian. "America's Toughest Bosses." *Fortune*, October 18, 1993, pp. 38–50.

Dunnette, Marvin D. "My Hammer or Your Hammer?" *Human Resource Management*, Summer-Fall 1993, pp. 373–384.

Edgley, Gerald J. "Type and Temperament." *Association Management*, October 1992, pp. 83–92.

"Five Views of Change." *Training & Development*, March 1992, pp. 34–37.

Frank, Michael S. "The Essence of Leadership." *Public Personnel Management*, Fall 1993, pp. 381–389.

Fuchs, Edward. "Total Quality Management from the Future: Practices and Paradigms." *Quality Management Journal*, October 1993, pp. 26–34.

Galagan, Patricia A. "Beyond Hierarchy: The Search for High Performance." *Training & Development*, August 1992, pp. 21–25.

Gardner, John W. *On Leadership* (New York: Free Press, 1990).

Ghoshal, Sumantra; Arnzen, Breck; and Brownfield, Sharon. "A Learning Alliance Between Business and Business Schools: Executive Education as a Platform for Partnership." *California Management Review*, Fall 1992, pp. 50–67.

Gilmore, Thomas N., and Barnett, Charles. "Designing the Social Architecture of Participation in Large Groups to Effect Organizational Change." *Journal of Applied Behavioral Science*, December 1992, pp. 534–548.

Ginnodo, William. "Commitment: Fuel for Improvement." *QPMA's Discovery*, March-April 1994, p. 1.

Gouillart, Francis J., and Sturdivant, Frederick D. "Spend a Day in the Life of Your Customers." *Harvard Business Review*, January-February 1994, pp. 116–125.

Graham, Kenneth R. "Books on Leadership and Its Development." *Human Resource Planning*, 15:1 (1992), pp. 107–117.

Handy, Charles. *The Age of Paradox* (Boston: Harvard Business School Press, 1994).

———. *The Age of Unreason* (Boston: Harvard Business School Press, 1989).

Harris, George T. "The Post-Capitalist Executive: An Interview with Peter F. Drucker." *Harvard Business Review*, May-June 1993, pp. 115–122.

Hegarty, W. Harvey. "Organizational Survival Means Embracing Change." *Business Horizons*, November-December 1993, pp. 1–4.

Hesse, Hermann. *The Journey to the East* (New York: Noonday Press, 1968) translated by Hilda Rosnev. First published in German under the title *Die Morgenlandfahrt*.

Hossack, Richard. "A New Style of Leadership." *Canadian Business Review*, Autumn 1993, pp. 30–33.

Houghton, James R. "Leadership's Challenge: The New Agenda for the '90s." *Planning Review* (Special Issue: Conference Executive Summary), September-October 1992, pp. 8–9.

Kanter, Rosabeth Moss. "Six Certainties for CEOs." *Harvard Business Review*, March-April 1992, pp. 7–8.

Katzenback, Jon R., and Smith, Douglas K. *The Wisdom of Teams* (Boston: Harvard Business School Press, 1993).

Keller, Robert T. "Transformational Leadership and the Performance of Research and Development Project Groups." *Journal of Management*, 18:3 (1992), pp. 489–501.

Kelly, Joe. "Executive Behavior: Classical and Existential." *Business Horizons*, January-February 1993, pp. 16–26.

Khalil, Tarek M. "Management of Technology Education for the 21st Century." *Industrial Engineering*, October 1993, pp. 64–65.

Kiechel, Walter, III. "The Leader as Servant." *Fortune*, May 4, 1992, pp. 121–122.

Kim, W. Chan, and Mauborgne, Renée A. "Parables of Leadership." *Harvard Business Review*, July-August 1992, pp. 123–128.

Klein, Donald C. "Simu-Real: A Simulation Approach to Organizational Change." *Journal of Applied Behavioral Science*, December 1992, pp. 566–578.

Kotler, Greta. "Approaches to Change." *Training & Development*, March 1992, pp. 41–42.

Kotter, John P. *The Leadership Factor* (New York: Free Press, 1988).

Land, George, and Jarman, Beth. "Breakpoint Change." *Training & Development*, March 1992, pp. 38–40.

Langeler, Gerard H. "The Vision Trap." *Harvard Business Review*, March-April 1992, pp. 46–55.

Lataif, Louis E. "MBA: Is the Traditional Model Doomed?" *Harvard Business Review*, November-December 1992, pp. 128–140.

Lee, Chris, and Zemke, Ron. "The Search for Spirit in the Workplace." *Training*, June 1993, pp. 21–28.

Linder, Jane C., and Smith, H. Jeff. "The Complex Case of Management Education." *Harvard Business Review*, September-October 1992, pp. 16–32.

London, Manuel, and Beatty, Richard W. "360-Degree Feedback as a Competitive Advantage." *Human Resource Management*, Summer-Fall 1993, pp. 353–372.

Madigan, Kathleen; Flynn, Julia; and Weber, Joseph. "Masters of the Game." *Business Week*, October 12, 1992, pp. 110–118.

Manz, Charles C. "Self-Leading Work Teams: Moving Beyond Self-Management Myths." *Human Relations*, 45:11, 1992.

Manz, Charles C., and Sims, Henry P., Jr. *Business Without Bosses: How Self-Managing Teams Are Building High-Performance Companies* (New York: John Wiley & Sons, 1993).

"A Master Class in Radical Change." *Fortune*, December 13, 1993, pp. 82–90.

McKenna, Joseph F. "Bob Galvin Predicts Life After Perfection." *Industry Week*, January 21, 1991, pp. 12–15.

———. "Close Encounters of the Executive Kind." *Industry Week*, September 6, 1993, pp. 13–18.

Meyer, Christopher. "2020 Vision." *Planning Review* (Special Issue: Conference Executive Summary), September-October 1992, pp. 39–41.

Mills, D. Quinn. "The Truth About Empowerment According to D. Quinn Mills." *Training & Development*, August 1992, pp. 31–32.

Nadler, David A., and Tushman, Michael L. "Beyond the Charismatic Leader: Leadership and Organizational Change." *California Management Review*, Winter 1990, p. 77–97.

Nahavandi, Afsaneh, and Malekzadeh, Ali R. "Leader Style in Strategy and Organizational Performance: An Integrative Framework." *Journal of Management Studies*, May 1993, pp. 405–425.

Nanus, Burt. *The Leader's Edge: The Seven Keys to Leadership in a Turbulent World* (Chicago: Contemporary Books, 1989).

———. "Visionary Leadership: How to Re-Vision the Future." *The Futurist*, September-October 1992, pp. 20–25.

Nichols, Martha. "Does New Age Business Have a Message for Managers?" *Harvard Business Review*, March-April 1994, pp. 52–60.

Nohria, Nitin, and Berkley, James D. "Whatever Happened to the Take-Charge Manager?" *Harvard Business Review*, January-February 1994, pp. 128–137.

Norris, Marilyn. "Warren Bennis on Rebuilding Leadership." *Planning Review* (Special Issue: Conference Executive Summary), September-October 1992, pp. 13–15.

O'Rourke, J. Tracy. "The Essence of Leadership." *Industry Week*, January 4, 1993, p. 43.

O'Toole, James, and Bennis, Warren. "Our Federalist Future: The Leadership Imperative." *California Management Review*, Summer 1992, pp. 73–90.

Pagonis, William G. "The Work of the Leader." *Harvard Business Review*, November-December 1992, pp. 118–126.

Paine, Lynn Sharp. "Managing for Organizational Integrity." *Harvard Business Review*, March-April 1994, pp. 106–117.

Peters, Thomas J., and Waterman, Robert H., Jr. *In Search of Excellence: Lessons from America's Best-Run Companies* (New York: Harper & Row, 1982), p. 279.

Peters, Tom. *Liberation Management: Necessary Disorganization for the Nanosecond Nineties* (New York: Alfred A. Knopf, 1992).

Pinsonnault, Jean-Francois. "Grading the Boss's Performance." *CMA Magazine*, June 1992, p. 10–12.

Prahalad, C. K., and Bettis, Richard A. "The Dominant Logic: A New Linkage Between Diversity and Performance." *Strategic Management Journal*, 7 (1986), pp. 485–501.

Raelin, Joseph A. "Theory and Practice: Their Roles, Relationship, and Limitations in Advanced Management Education." *Business Horizons*, May-June 1993, pp. 85–89.

Rieley, James B. "The Circular Organization: How Leadership Can Optimize Organizational Effectiveness." *National Productivity Review*, Winter 1993/94, pp. 11–19.

Rothschild, William E. "Avoid the Mismatch Between Strategy and Strategic Leaders." *Journal of Business Strategy*, 1993, pp. 37–42.

Rummler, Geary. "Managing the White Space." *Training & Development*, August 1992, pp. 26–30.

Schein, Edgar H. "How Can Organizations Learn Faster? The Challenge of Entering the Green Room." *Sloan Management Review*, Winter 1993, pp. 85–92.

Schlossberg, Howard. "Three Innovators Bemoan Lack of Leadership in Corporate America." *Marketing News*, May 10, 1993, pp. 1–2.

Schnake, Mel; Dumler, Michael P.; and Cochran, Daniel S. "The Relationship Between 'Traditional' Leadership, 'Super' Leadership, and Organizational Citizenship Behavior." *Group & Organization Management*, September 1993, pp. 352–365.

Scholtes, Peter R. "Total Quality or Performance Appraisal: Choose One." *National Productivity Review*, Summer 1993, p. 349.

Senge, Peter. *The Fifth Discipline: The Art and Practice of the Learning Organization* (New York: Doubleday Currency, 1990).

———. "The Leader's New Work: Building Learning Organizations." *Sloan Management Review*, Fall 1990, pp. 7–23.

Shani, A. B. (Rami); Grant, Robert M.; Krishnan, R.; and Thompson, Eric. "Advanced Manufacturing Systems and Organizational Choice: Sociotechnical System Approach." *California Management Review*, Summer 1992, pp. 91–111.

Shipper, Frank, and Manz, Charles C. "Employee Self-Management Without Formally Designated Teams: An Alternative Road to Empowerment." *Organizational Dynamics*, Winter 1992, pp. 48–61.

Steinburg, Craig. "Taking Charge of Change." *Training & Development*, March 1992, pp. 26–32.

Stewart, Thomas A. "Rate Your Readiness to Change." *Fortune*, February 7, 1994, pp. 106–110.

Tichy, Noel M. "Revolutionize Your Company." *Fortune*, December 13, 1993, pp. 114–118.

Tichy, Noel M., and Sherman, Stratford. "Walking the Talk at GE." *Training & Development*, June 1993, pp. 26–35.

Toffler, Alvin. *Power Shift: Knowledge, Wealth, and Violence at the Edge of the 21st Century* (New York: Bantam Books, 1990).

Uchitelle, Louis. "Male, Educated and in a Pay Bind." *New York Times*, February 11, 1994, p. C1.

Vogl, A. J. "People, Dollars, and Ideas." *Across the Board*, September 1993, pp. 23–27.

Wallis, Joe L. "Integrating the Ideas of Dissenting Economists into a Theory of Transformational Leadership." *Review of Social Economy*, Spring 1993, pp. 14–39.

Want, Jerome H. "Managing Radical Change." *Journal of Business Strategy*, May-June 1993, pp. 21–27.

Webber, Alan M. "What's So New About the New Economy?" *Harvard Business Review*, January-February 1993, pp. 24–42.

Weisbord, Marvin. *Discovering Common Ground: How Future Search Conferences Bring People Together to Achieve Breakthrough Innovation, Empowerment, Shared Vision, and Collaborative Action* (San Francisco: Berrett-Koehler, 1992).

————. "When the Wall Comes Down." *Training & Development*, August 1992, pp. 33–35.

Wheatley, Margaret. *Leadership and the New Science: Learning About Organizations from an Orderly Universe* (San Francisco: Berrett-Koehler, 1992).

Willey, David. "Only the Strong Survive." *Journal of Business Strategy*, May-June 1993, pp. 30–33.

Zaleznik, Abraham. "Managers and Leaders: Are They Different?" *Harvard Business Review*, March-April 1992, pp. 126–135.

Zimmerman, John H. "The Demand of the Future: The Complete Executive." *Human Resource Management*, Summer-Fall 1993, pp. 385–397.

Index

· A NOTE ON THE TYPE ·

The typeface used in this book is a version of Century (Expanded), originally designed by Theodore L. De Vinne (1828–1914) and Linn Boyd Benton (1844–1932) for De Vinne's *Century* magazine; it was probably the first type developed for such a specific purpose. De Vinne, an innovative though practical printer and a scholar of typography, thought the type then used in periodicals feeble and proposed that the thin strokes of the "modern" typefaces be thickened while keeping the economical narrow letter forms so characteristic of late-nineteenth-century fonts (one of the "ungenerous" aspects of contemporary type that made William Morris look to the past). Century was later developed for wider use by Benton's son, Morris Fuller Benton (1872–1948), who devised the concept of a type "family"—several "weights" of a typeface with uniform design.